HOLY SMOKE

THE
BIG BOOK OF
NORTH CAROLINA
BARBECUE

JOHN SHELTON REED
& DALE VOLBERG REED
WITH WILLIAM MCKINNEY

THE UNIVERSITY OF NORTH CAROLINA PRESS
CHAPEL HILL

HOLY SMOKE

This book was published with the assistance of the Blythe Family Fund of
the University of North Carolina Press.

Title page illustration: Jess Swicegood, in hat and apron, cooking in Lexington,
ca. 1929.

Pig ornament: © iStockphoto.com/Kathy Konkle.

The paper in this book meets the guidelines for permanence and durability
of the Committee on Production Guidelines for Book Longevity of the
Council on Library Resources.

The University of North Carolina Press has been a member of the Green Press
Initiative since 2003.

A list of credits appears before the index.

Library of Congress Cataloging-in-Publication Data
Reed, John Shelton.
Holy smoke : the big book of North Carolina barbecue / John Shelton Reed and
Dale Volberg Reed ; with William McKinney. — 1st ed.
    p. cm.
Includes bibliographical references and index.
ISBN 978-0-8078-3243-1 (cloth : alk. paper)
    1. Barbecue cookery—North Carolina. I. Reed, Dale Volberg. II. McKinney,
William. III. Title.
TX840.B3R445 2008
641.7′609756—dc22   2008017084

12 11 10 09 08   5 4 3 2 1

University of North Carolina Press books may be purchased at a discount for
educational, business, or sales promotional use. For information, please visit
www.uncpress.unc.edu or write to UNC Press, attention: Sales Department,
116 South Boundary Street, Chapel Hill, NC 27514-3808.

HOLY SMOKE

Holy Smoke! What smells so good?
Is someone burnin' hickory wood?
What's that cookin' on those coals?
Why it's a pig! Lord bless my soul!
We're gonna have some barbecue.
Boiled potatoes, Brunswick stew,
Slaw that's white or maybe red,
Hushpuppies or fried cornbread,
And sauce from an old recipe,
Known only to the family.
A great big glass of sweet ice tea.
Holy smoke! That's heav'n to me.
—Tommy Edwards

Tommy Edwards is the lead singer and guitarist
for the Bluegrass Experience, from Chatham County.
He's also a songwriter, and when we told him the title
of our book, he dashed this off. Watch for the CD.

CONTENTS

HOLY SMOKE

oes the world really need another barbecue book? Well, maybe not, but we needed to write one. And if you're holding this book in your hands, you can see that it's at least a little different from the (literally) hundreds of others on the virtual shelf. For starters, we're focusing on *North Carolina* barbecue. You can count the good books on that subject on the fingers of one hand—not as many as you'd expect, given the subject's importance. We're obviously in the debt of the folks who've already written about it, but our book is meant to supplement theirs, not replace them.

We want to say up front what this book is *not*. It isn't a guidebook (although it will become clear what some of our favorite places are). For that, look at the section called "To Learn More . . ." and check those other books or one of the several websites devoted to Tar Heel 'cue—where, by the way, you'll discover that even experts' opinions differ widely. Nor, alas, is this a compilation of secret recipes from great North Carolina barbecue places. Although a few folks were gracious enough to share their recipes with us and we've passed those on, for the most part secrets remain secrets. We tried.

What you have here is an exploration of the Tar Heel barbecue tradition. It comes in three parts. First, we'll look at where North Carolina barbecue came from, how it has changed (not much), and the part it has played in the life of the Old North State. We'll look at the emergence of the Eastern-Piedmont split and how that gave birth to a rivalry that's right up there with the one between UNC and Duke. We'll examine barbecue's evolution from a food cooked mostly for special occasions to something served at stands, in joints, and eventually in proper barbecue restaurants. Then we'll tell you how to cook it yourself, and, while we're at it, we'll examine the history and nature of the limited array of side dishes traditionally served in North Carolina barbecue restaurants and give you some recipes for those. We'll talk with some of the people who cook barbecue for a living, who have some interesting things to say about the past and future of North Carolina barbecue. Finally,

Can We Get a Witness?

Jane and Michael Stern: "Of the several states that claim to be America's barbecue capital, North Carolina is the most convincing."

Charles Kuralt: "I have spent a good part of my life looking for the perfect barbecue. There is no point in looking in places like Texas. . . . Barbecue is pork, which narrows the search to the South, and if it's really good pork barbecue you're looking for, to North Carolina."

Rick Bragg: "This barbecue is as different from the tomato, mustard or molasses-basted meat of the lower South as white whisky is from hot chocolate. It has a zing, a whang and a fo-dee-doe-doe."

Craig Claiborne: "The flavor that lengthy smoking over hickory and oak coals gives the pork is delicious. The tender texture of the chopped pork is another plus and the sauce, with its acid taste, provides an ideal complement."

Steve Stephens: "The 'cue I found [in North Carolina] was like the crack cocaine of pork: succulent, tender, savory and almost impossible to leave unconsumed."

we'll discuss why North Carolina barbecue may be an endangered cuisine, why that matters, and what to do about it.

While we're introducing things, let's introduce ourselves. John and Dale Reed grew up across the mountains in Tennessee but have lived in Chapel Hill since 1969 (and Dale went to Duke before that). John taught for thirty-one years at UNC, and Dale taught piano privately. Both are members of the Southern Foodways Alliance and the North Carolina Barbecue Society. John has been a judge at the Memphis-in-May World Championship Barbecue Cooking Contest and gave the 1995 Kemp Plummer Battle Lecture to UNC's Dialectic and Philanthropic Societies on the subject "Science Lies When It Says Hogmeat's Got Little Bugs in It" (honest). He's not a pitmaster, but he *was* the Pitt Professor at Cambridge University in 1996–97.

William McKinney was raised in South Carolina, where his mother fed him barbecue sandwiches for lunch. He came to Chapel Hill in 1999 as a callow seventeen-year-old freshman and soon thereafter founded UNC's Carolina Bar-B-Q Society (CBS), devoted to celebrating and eating you-know-what. (The first guest speaker at a CBS event was John Shelton Reed.) William now lives and works in northern Virginia, where ice tea and a mediocre barbecue plate will set you back ten bucks. This is his first book, but John and Dale's previous collaborations include writing 1001 *Things Everyone Should Know About the South* and editing *Cornbread Nation 4: The Best of Southern Food Writing*.

You might ask—you should—where two Tennesseans and a South Carolinian get the nerve to write a book about North Carolina barbecue. Well, North Carolinians grow up taking their great native dish for granted. We didn't. We're converts, and like many converts, we can be more Catholic than the Pope. As our title suggests, for example, we're fairly fundamentalist about cooking with wood—more so than many leading purveyors of "North Carolina barbecue" these days. The distinguished historian Robert Conquest once remarked that "everyone is a reactionary about subjects he understands," and the more we've learned about this subject, the more we insist on barbecue cooked the old way. We will allow that, if you're hungry enough and can't find the real thing, pork cooked with gas or electricity, if it's done well, might—just might—be worth eating. But it's not worth writing a book about.

We also hope our origins—and the fact that our time in North Carolina has been spent pretty much on the fault line—give us some perspective on the Eastern-Piedmont fight. It's sort of like being a University of Kentucky graduate during the ACC tournament: you can appreciate some very fine basketball without taking sides (except that not many UK fans acknowledge that ACC basketball is superior).

If that's not enough to establish our credibility, read on. If you finish our book and still don't think we know what we're talking about—well, that's the way conversations about North Carolina barbecue usually seem to end.

THE LORE

WHAT IS NORTH CAROLINA BARBECUE?

When we told people we were writing this book, they immediately started asking questions. Had we heard that ——'s was closing after fifty years? Had we figured out the secret ingredient in ——'s sauce? Did we have a good Brunswick stew recipe? Where did we stand on the tomato question? And, always, did we know the best barbecue place in the state (which just happened to be in their hometown)? Californian Miles Efron has observed that "when North Carolinians discuss barbecue, they are prone to swoon. Even the most urbane among them wax[es] ecstatic when given a forum for extolling smoked meat. People who have lived in New York [drawl] like Daughters of the Confederacy about sweet tea 'n slaw." When the food writer for the *Milwaukee Journal Sentinel* attended a conference in Charlotte, she told her readers, "People here are passionate about their barbecue, not unlike Wisconsinites debating the best way to cook a brat." We wouldn't put it quite that way, but the point is that Tar Heels *care* about 'cue.

One friend from down east has gone so far as to claim that "barbecue is the great sacrament of our people. No transubstantiation required. It are what it are." His religious language is apt, and not unusual. In this matter the Tar Heel State just offers a double-distilled version of a more general Southern trait. As William Schmidt explained it for readers of the *New York Times*, in the South barbecue is not just a food, "it is a cultural ritual, practiced with a kind of religious fervor among various barbecue sects, each of whom believes their particular concoction of smoke and sauce and spices is the only true way to culinary salvation." Food writer John Egerton reached for the same analogy: "There are more barbecue factions and smoked-meat sects around here, each with its own hair-splitting distinctions, than there are denominations in the far-flung Judeo-Christian establishment."

Perhaps especially in North Carolina, barbecue is not a subject for the conflict-averse. *Raleigh News and Observer* sage Dennis Rogers

NASCAR *driver David Pearson used to stop by for a plate at Alston Bridges Barbecue in Shelby. He parked his helicopter in a lot nearby.*

"Barbecue is a taste of the South. It's a noun, a verb, and an entire religion served on a bun. . . . Roll up your sleeves, grab a pile of paper napkins, and wait for manna from Heaven." (Michael Lee West)

observes that "barbecue is a subject of intense interest and loyalties in North Carolina[,] a subject about which everyone thinks they're right and that everyone else wouldn't know a decent plate of 'cue from a cue ball." Food writer James Villas says that growing up in Charlotte he "learned never to air a preference on the complex and heated topic for fear of alienating family and losing friends."

Tar Heels are entitled to strong opinions. Georgian Jim Auchmutey, co-author of *The Ultimate Barbecue Sauce Cookbook*, notes that "the family tree of barbecue has spread all over the country, [but] its deepest tap root is in North Carolina." The Old North State is to American barbecue something like what New Orleans is to jazz. True, like jazz, barbecue has spread far and wide; by the mid-twentieth century, it could be found even in places like Kansas City, and now it's popping up from Boston to San Francisco. Also like jazz, it has changed as it moved, and not always for the better—in the case of barbecue, not even usually, if you ask us: in the immortal words of Dobie Gray, "Other guys imitate us, but the original is still the greatest."

So what *is* North Carolina barbecue? It's not just whatever is served in North Carolina and called barbecue. Let's start with a definition, keeping in mind that there is perhaps a little room for argument here and there and that there are exceptions to any rule. (This is the South, after all.) The definition comes in three parts. We are talking about meat

1. that has been *barbecued*—that is, cooked for a long time at a low temperature with heat and smoke from a fire of hardwood and/or hardwood coals;
2. that meat being *pork*—whole hog, shoulder, or (occasionally) ham—
3. sometimes basted and always served with a thin *sauce or "dip"* that is at most only a slight variation on a traditional recipe including vinegar, red pepper, and maybe (or maybe not) tomato.

Yes, there's more to be said about each of these, but let's not start arguing just yet. Got it? Pork, wood-cooked in a leisurely way, served with a traditional, vinegar-based sauce.

In most places outside North Carolina, either these components never came together, or the combination has fallen apart. Some

I Saw the Light: A Texan Goes to Stamey's

Cookbook writer and chef Gwen Ashley Walters testifies in the *North Carolina Literary Review*:

> I ordered the chopped barbecue plate. When it arrived, I gasped, "What happened to my food? Did somebody already chew this for me?" It was the most anemic tint of pale gray I had ever seen. And the coleslaw was . . . sitting in a pool of red vinegar sugar water. My husband quickly doused my chopped pork with . . . a dark orange-red sauce, very thin and fuming with vinegar, too. I was beginning to wonder if the cherry cobbler would emit vinegar as well.
>
> My first bite was almost as shocking as the pork-only menu. The vinegar-based sauce was first tangy, sending chills through my bones, followed by slightly sweet with a spicy hot finish. There was a taste convention going on in my mouth, and the exhibitors were fighting for tongue-space. I didn't know what to think. All my life, barbecue had one connotation. Now I was faced with a revelation. I ate what someone else called barbecue, and I liked it—no, I loved it! How was I ever going to rationalize what I thought of as an inalienable truth: only Texas does barbecue? Simple. What I ate that day and many, many days that followed wasn't really barbecue. It was NorthCarolinaBarbecue, one word. One really good word.

Stamey's plate

Cooking barbecue in Ayden in the 1930s

From "Barbecue Service"

I have sought the elusive aroma
Around outlying cornfields, turned corners
Near the site of a Civil War surrender.
The transformation may take place
At a pit no wider than a grave,
Behind a single family's barn.
These weathered ministers
Preside with the simplest of elements:
Vinegar and pepper, split pig and fire.
Underneath a glistening mountain in air,
Something is converted to a savor: the pig
Flesh purified by far atmosphere.

. . . .

We barbecue pigs.
The tin-roofed sheds with embers
Are smoking their blue sacrifice
Across Carolina.
—James Applewhite

Jim Applewhite is professor of English at Duke and a native of Wilson County.

When Luciano Pavarotti sang in Raleigh in 2002, he was served barbecue prepared by Lillington caterer Paul Long. The rotund tenor, who loved barbecue, ate from a silver bowl.

The band Southern Culture on the Skids, founded in Chapel Hill by UNC grad Rick Miller in 1985, sings a number entitled "Too Much Pork for Just One Fork."

South Carolinians hold a version of the true faith, but others have fallen into the mustard heresy. Mayonnaise cultists can be found in Alabama. Beef-eating Texans and mutton-fed Kentuckians have likewise gone astray. As for cooking techniques—well, outside the South, folks notoriously confuse barbecuing with grilling, and even speak of "stove-top barbecue." That way lies the Sloppy Joe.

In the unlikely event that someone from out of state has read this far in a book with this title, we say: Hold your fire. We actually like most of these dishes—even Sloppy Joes, once in a while. And it's a free country. We won't say that nobody else cooks "real barbecue." It's just that they don't cook *North Carolina* barbecue. That is, their barbecue isn't perfect.

Let's look at that perfection and how it was attained.

THE PREHISTORY OF TAR HEEL 'CUE

Soon after the expulsion from the Garden of Eden, probably after a prehistoric forest fire, someone discovered that meat was easier to eat and tasted better when it was not eaten raw. In time, folks figured out how to roast meat *on purpose*, and eventually people noticed that slow cooking at relatively low temperatures is an especially good way to cook the tough, muscular parts of animals. Maybe they also had the discernment to notice that the smoke from an open fire or coals nicely flavors meat. In any case, these cavemen had figured out how barbecuing differs from grilling: it cooks with a cooler fire. It takes longer, of course, but (as a joke that's probably prehistoric itself asks) what's time to a hog?

"I believe that when you combine wood, smoke, meat, salt, and fire, you are appealing to an appetite so deeply rooted in the human genome that it is instinctual."
(Peter Kaminsky)

By the time we start to get written records, most of the technology was in place, and it would remain unchanged until almost within living memory. Some folks cooked their meat beside the fire, over a pan to catch the drippings for basting and gravy; others cooked directly over the fire, letting the drippings hit the coals and hiss and produce fragrant smoke. If practitioners of these two methods had been North Carolinians, they would have formed separate schools and argued about it, but, as the latter-day barbecue cliché puts it, they were all cooking "low and slow."

Primitive barbecuing described in the Old Testament involved lambs, bullocks, and kids, but not pigs—not surprising, given what the Lord had to say about swine in Leviticus 11:7. But the ancient Greeks didn't have the Hebrews' pipeline to divine opinion; like Texans, they were indiscriminate in their choice of meats. As Homer reports in the *Iliad*, "Many a goodly ox, with many a sheep and bleating goat did they butcher and cut up; many a tusked boar moreover, fat and well-fed, did they singe and set to roast in the flames of Vulcan." Homer goes on about butchering ("They flayed the carcass, made it ready, and divided it into joints; these they cut carefully up into smaller pieces"), preparing the coals ("When the flame had died down, [Patroclus] spread the embers, laid the spits on top of them, lifting them up and setting them upon the spit-

Greek butchers on a Boeotian vase, fifth century B.C.

racks; and he sprinkled them with salt"), and who ate highest on the hog ("Agamemnon gave Ajax some slices cut lengthways down the loin, as a mark of special honour").

The Romans and the barbarians of northern Europe also ate hog-meat, along with mutton, goat, and beef, and the ritual slaughter and devouring of pigs had a special place in the culture of the Celts, whose Scotch-Irish and Rhinelander descendants would settle the North Carolina Piedmont. Their swine god, Moccus, had a name connected to the modern English word "muck."

But enough about that. The point is that the basic technique of barbecuing was understood very early and almost everywhere. Something the Kansas City Barbecue Society (if not some dogmatic Tar Heels) would recognize as barbecue has been served for centuries at British and German ox- and swine-roasts, at African animist feasts, and, for that matter, at Polynesian luaus—which, incidentally, makes it silly to argue about who "invented" barbecue. So we can pretty much ignore everything between the fall of Rome and the discovery of the New World. The Middle Ages gave us some great manuscript illustrations of pitmasters at work and identified St. Anthony of Egypt as the patron saint of swineherds, but the only real progress on the barbecue front was an early recipe for sauce (we'll get to that eventually).

There was still a long way to go. When Columbus sailed west, the questions of what kind of meat to cook and what kind of sauce to put on it were still open (in some circles, they still are). What's more, Europeans didn't even know what to *call* the stuff until they came across the North American version.

THERE'S A WORD FOR IT

In the first decades of the 1500s, Spanish explorers in the Caribbean found the locals using frameworks of sticks to support meat over fires. They didn't have pigs, but everything else went on the grill (one early drawing shows alligators, snakes, and some kind of wildcat). The Indians called their apparatus something that the Spanish heard as *barbacòa*, which soon became a Spanish word (one that is making its way into North Carolina these days, via Mexico— see page 286). A few years later, in 1585, Sir Walter Raleigh sent some folks to look things over on the coast of what would eventu-

Cooking and serving medieval pork barbecue (from the Luttrell Psalter, fourteenth century)

North Carolina barbecue,
ca. 1585

ally be North Carolina. One member of that party, John White, later
governor of the ill-fated Roanoke Island colony, made sketches of
what he saw, including Croatan Indians "broyling their fishe over
the flame—they took great heed that they bee not burntt." Unfor-
tunately, he didn't say what the indigenous Tar Heels called their
cooker, but whatever they called it, it was obviously a *barbacòa*, too.

Taking barbecue back to its roots:
The airport code for Barbuda, in the
West Indies, is BBQ.

The earliest use of the English word that barbecue historian
Robert Moss has found dates from 1661, when Edmund Hickerin-
gill's *Jamaica Viewed* reported that animals "are slain, And their flesh
forthwith Barbacu'd and eat," but by 1688 the word must have been
widely familiar because it was being used casually on the London
stage: In *The Widdow Ranter, Or, The History of Bacon in Virginia*, "the
rabble" fixing to lynch one Colonel Wellman cry, "Let's barbicu this
fat rogue." (The play was written by the remarkable Aphra Behn,
the first Englishwoman to be a professional writer, and "Bacon"
in the title refers to the leader of Bacon's Rebellion of 1676, not to
sidemeat.)

A few years later, John Lawson, surveyor-general of North Carolina, also used the word without explanation. In his *New Voyage to
Carolina* (1709), Lawson encountered "barbakued" venison, fish,
and even peaches. Some Santee Indians served him "fat barbacu'd
Venison," which "the Woman of the Cabin took and tore in Pieces
with her Teeth [note: pulled, not sliced], so put it into a Mortar,
beating it into Rags," then boiled. This meat had been smoked and
dried to preserve it, like jerky, but Lawson was also served "roasted

or barbakued Turkey, eaten with Bears Fat." A little later still, the physician and naturalist John Brickell's *Natural History of North Carolina* (1737) gave a very similar account (so similar, in fact, that it may have been plagiarized).

Most writers say that the English "barbecue" comes from the Spanish *barbacòa*, but Indians on the North American mainland had the same technology as their Caribbean cousins and may have had much the same word for it. In 1770 a French soldier named Jean Bernard Bossu reported that the "sauvages" of the Mississippi Valley cooked on some sort of grate that they called a *barboka*, designed "to roast and smoke at the same time" and originally used to cook captives taken in war. Sixty-five years earlier, Robert Beverly in his *History of the Present State of Virginia* had written that the Indians of Virginia and the Carolinas had "two ways of Broyling viz. one by laying the Meat itself upon the Coals, the other by laying it upon Sticks rais'd upon Forks at some distance above the live Coals, which heats more gently, and drys up the Gravy; this they, and we also from them, call Barbacueing." (They got the grilling versus barbecuing thing, too.)

The British may have copied the Indians' vocabulary, but they didn't feel constrained to copy their Stone Age gear. Anglo-Saxons and Celts had been roasting meat for a few thousand years themselves and had made a few improvements in the matter of cooking

frames. In 1732 Richard Bradley, in *The Country House-wife*, gave directions for "an Hog barbecued": "Take a large Grid-iron, with two or three Ribs in it, and set it upon a stand of iron, about three Foot and a half high, and upon that, lay your Hog, . . . Belly-side downwards." Still, the process of cooking or smoking meat on some sort of frame remained identified with the Indians. When Colonel George Washington, trying to get provisions for his troops during the French and Indian War, wrote his superior officer in 1758, "We have not an ounce of salt provision of any kind here; and it is impossible to preserve the fresh (especially as we have no Salt) by any other means than barbacuing it in the indian manner," he was evidently writing about smoking meat to cure it, not to cook it. Later, however, the future Father of His Country often wrote about going to "barbecues" where cooking was the object: "Went in to Alexandria to a Barbecue and stayed all Night" (1769); "Went to a Barbicue of my own giving at Accotinck" (1773); "Went to the Barbacue at Accatinck" (1774). (Notice that his spelling was as independent as his subsequent politics.)

Washington's use of "barbecue" to refer to a social event was not unusual (we'll come back to that institution): that use of the word dates at least from 1733, although among English-speakers it seems to have been an Americanism. (In an apparently independent development, Frenchmen in the Mississippi Valley had begun to

The French translator of a 1798 book about Virginia explained the word "barbacue": "This barbarous amusement consists of whipping hogs almost to death to make the flesh more delicate. I do not know that even cannibals practice it." (OK, Frenchie, let's talk about fois gras.)

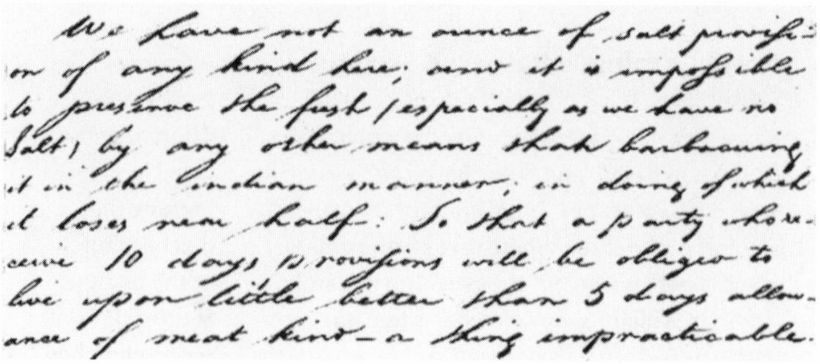

[Handwritten letter in cursive:]

We have not an ounce of salt provision of any kind here; and it is impossible
to preserve the fish (especially as we have no
Salt) by any other means that barbacuing
it in the Indian manner; in doing of which
it loses near half: So that a party who receive 10 days provisions will, be obliged to
live upon little better than 5 days allow-
ance of meat kind—a thing impracticable.

use the local Indians' *barboka* to cook whole wild pigs at *fêtes champê-
tres* they called *barbokas*.) When a young Virginian wrote to a London
friend in 1784 that he was "continually at Balls & Barbecues," he
added, "The latter I don't suppose you know what I mean," and
went on to explain: "It's a shoat & sometimes a Lamb or Mutton &
indeed sometimes a Beef splitt into & stuck on spitts, & then they
have a large Hole dugg in the ground where they have a number of
Coals made of the Bark [?] of Trees, put in this Hole. & then they
lay the Meat over that within about six inches of the Coals, & then
they Keep basting it with Butter & Salt & Water & turning it every
now and then, until it is done, we then dine under a large shady tree
or an harbour made of green bushes, under which we have benches
& seats to sit on when we dine sumptuously." This sounds pretty
pleasant, if you get to sit under the "harbour." Less so, of course, if
you're a slave on the digging and basting crew.

Most references at this time were to whole hogs or whole other
animals being cooked, the practice in the Caribbean and, now as
then, in eastern North Carolina. (We'll come back to those "other
animals.") When the poet Alexander Pope wrote in 1733 that a man
named Oldfield, who was famous for his appetite, cried, "Send
me, Gods! a whole Hog barbecu'd!" he added a note for his English readers explaining that "a whole Hog barbecu'd" was "a *West-
Indian* Term of Gluttony, a Hog roasted whole, stu'd with Spice, and
basted with *Madera* Wine."

Just so, Samuel Johnson's famous *Dictionary* (1755) defined the
verb "to barbecue" as "a term used in the West-Indies for dressing
a hog whole; which, being split to the backbone, is laid flat upon
a large gridiron, raised about two feet above a charcoal fire, with
which it is surrounded," and "barbecue," the noun, as "a hog drest

Still cooking the old way at Braswell Plantation, 1944

whole in the West Indian manner." Virtually identical definitions, probably cribbed from Johnson, can be found in many, many subsequent dictionaries. In 1828 Noah Webster's *Dictionary of the American Language* also defined the noun as, "in the West Indies, a hog roasted whole," but expanded the definition: "It is, with us [Americans], used for an ox or perhaps any other animal dressed in like manner."

Webster was from Connecticut, but an 1816 *Vocabulary, or, Collection of words and phrases, which have been supposed to be peculiar to the United States of America* had given the first indication that barbecue was becoming a Southern thing. Quoting an English source from 1798, it said that barbecue was "a porket . . . stuffed with spices and other rich ingredients, and basted with Madeira wine," then added, "*Used in the* Southern *states*" (although "not peculiar to the *United States; it is used in the West Indies* also").

So, by the mid-1700s, we had *barbecue* as an apparatus (Yankees and Australians still use the word this way) for a style of cooking called *barbecuing*, and we had *barbecue* as an event of the sort that George Washington went to, and we had *barbecue* as a word for the subject of the undertaking—pig, ox, shad, whatever (although this last use seems to have disappeared). But we apparently did not yet have *barbecue* as the point of all this: the dish prepared on a barbecue-device and served at a barbecue-event, what a barbecue-creature becomes after it is barbecue-processed. When did barbecued pork become *barbecue*?

Someone may trump us with an earlier example, but the earliest we've found comes from 1808. Oddly enough, it comes from a Massachusetts congressman—although he was disparaging Southern folkways at the time. In a speech on the floor of Congress, Representative Josiah Quincy of Boston denounced the kind of partisan stump speech commonly delivered "in this quarter of the country . . . while the gin circulated, while barbecue was roasting."

By the middle of the nineteenth century, this use of the word was increasingly common in print, especially in Southern newspapers. There are many examples from North Carolina, usually in the context of political rallies. In 1859, for instance, the *Raleigh Weekly Standard* wrote that one politician's "constituents had been bought up by whiskey and barbecue." In 1868 the *Petersburg Index* reported that

"Cue" as shorthand for "barbecue" is not a recent coinage. In occupied Georgia in 1865, Eliza Frances Andrews wrote in her diary, "The rebel 'cue' came off yesterday, in spite of [Union] Capt. Cooley's threats to stop it."

The Q Factor

In colonial America and the early days of the Republic, people spelled "barbecue" however they pleased. But the "-cue" spelling preferred by dictionary writers from Samuel Johnson (1755) to Noah Webster (1828) eventually became the standard. These days it is used roughly three times as often in the United States as a whole (and in Australia) as "barbeque," the next most frequent spelling.

But not in the South. Despite the shortcomings of "barbeque" (it looks as if it should be pronounced "bar-beck," and one dictionary huffily points out that no other word in English has "-que" as a stand-alone last syllable), Google shows it in a statistical dead heat with "barbecue" in the Carolinas, and over the mountains in Kentucky, Tennessee, Alabama, Mississippi, and Arkansas, it's about twice as common as the authorized spelling. Throw in "bar-b-que," "bar-b-q," "bbq," and so forth, and it's clear that Southerners really like that letter Q.

One of the few who have written about this is former Black Panther Bobby Seale, who argues that the "Q" spellings are more soulful; to him "-cue" represents "something drab, or even 'square,' as we used to say in the 1950s." It could also be that Southerners don't like Yankees telling us how to spell our national dish. But we suspect that folks just like the way the letter recapitulates the sound of that last syllable. And why not?

Consider the mystic Trigrammaton, "BBQ." It is not in itself a word. Nor is it an acronym. It is rarely sounded out, like TVA, NBC, or BBC. Usually it is pronounced "barbecue," just as "Xmas" is pronounced "Christmas." Which means that, linguistically speaking, it is an abbreviation.

But where did it come from? And why "BBQ"

rather than "BBC"? We haven't found an example of "BBQ" from before the twentieth century, and it's possible that it abbreviates the spelling "barbeque," which is older. It's more likely, however, that it abbreviates the *sound* of "barbecue" rather than its spelling—perhaps a predictable development in a culture where literacy has been a little shaky. It may be significant that it seems to have come into use only after there were barbecue stands whose owners needed signs to say what they were selling.

Some have asserted that "BBQ" comes from combination beer joints and pool halls that wanted to advertise "Bar, Beer, and Cues." We mention this ridiculous theory only for the sake of thoroughness.

the 3,000 Democrats at a Nash County rally "marched to the grove, near by, where a bountiful supply of barbecue, vegetables, etc., etc., refreshed the 'inner man,' and to which ample justice was done." True, as late as 1894, when the *Statesville Landmark* wrote of an occasion where "several hundred ladies were present, and the contents of their baskets, supplemented by 'barbecue' from the committee, composed the repast," the paper put the noun in quotation marks, suggesting that the usage remained colloquial. Still, by then everyone seems to have known that it meant something you could put on a plate or a sandwich.

Only after that was understood was the way open to argue about what barbecue *is*.

n 1766 North Carolinians were getting restive under high-handed British rule. As a gesture of goodwill, Royal Governor William Tryon laid on a barbecue in Wilmington for the New Hanover militia, but the local Sons of Liberty poured out the beer and threw the barbecued ox in the river. This was not an early expression of North Carolinians' preference for pork: the patriots were upset about the Stamp Act. (By the way, the Wilmington Barbecue took place a full seven years before the Boston Tea Party, which gets all the publicity.)

THE MEAT OF THE MATTER

In fact, beef seems to have been popular at community and political barbecues throughout the nineteenth century and into the twentieth. In 1815 a whole ox was cooked for a "grand barbecue and supper" in Wilmington to celebrate the Treaty of Ghent and victory at the Battle of New Orleans. Eighty-three years later, the *Statesville Landmark* interviewed "a disgusted Populist" who blamed the loss of Cabarrus County in a recent election on a barbecue the Democrats held at Concord. "The d—n beef was what done it," the man said.

Tar Heels have barbecued all sorts of meat—and until quite recently. An 1872 affair at Weldon featured "beeves and shoats roasted whole, whole sheep, and other refreshments," and as late as 1939 the WPA's *North Carolina: A Guide to the Old North State* reported that "whole pigs and often lambs, chickens, and cuts of beef are cooked over live coals [and] basted frequently with a special highly seasoned sauce, called barbecue sauce," at "barbecues, so popular and common throughout the State." Mutton is thought of these days as unique to Kentucky, but it was offered without comment by a 1927 ad in the *Gastonia Daily Gazette* for Goff's Olde Tyme Barbecue. And humbler creatures were sometimes barbecued at home. Emma Blalock recalled growing up as a slave on the Griffith plantation in Wake County: "In the winter we had a lot of possums to eat an' a lot of rabbits too. At Christmas time de men hunted and caught plenty

Fixing to barbecue a possum, from an 1883 sheet-music cover

Hungry pilots can pick up Eastern-style barbecue at Stanton's Bar-B-Que Fly-in Restaurant, located three miles across the South Carolina line from Laurinburg.

game. We barbecued it before de fire." In 1893 a letter-writer to the *Statesville Landmark* reported that a friend had grown a twelve-pound sweet potato and added, "Now if someone will present us with a possum . . . we will have a barbecue."

Notice, however, that, although an ox might be cooked at *a barbecue* and possums could be *barbecued*, no one was speaking of beef or possum *barbecue*. (The only North Carolina reference we've come across that even implies that barbecue could be something other than pigmeat comes from a single line in the *Statesville Landmark* in 1885: "According to an eminent Southern authority on Barbecue, it takes ten hours to roast a whole ox to perfection." This does seem to suggest that barbecued beef might be "barbecue," but we have our suspicions about that so-called expert: in our experience, ten hours isn't really enough for even a brisket.) It seems that as soon as North Carolinians had a word for the thing, they restricted it to pork. They might have allowed that beef and mutton and sausage and alligator and maybe even vegetables could be *barbecued*, but that didn't make them into *barbecue*. Many perfectly respectable North Carolina barbecue places serve barbecued chicken, but you never hear of chicken barbecue (and a good thing, too). In 1970 the Barbecue Barn in Wilson was advertising "barbecue beef"—but not "beef barbecue." Our, ah, beef with Texans isn't so much what they cook but what they call it. As Raleigh journalist Jonathan Daniels wrote in 1941, "Barbecue, which in North Carolina contends with the hamburger and the hot dog at roadside eating stands, is pig roasted, preferably over a pit full of coals, and basted with a peppery sauce while it roasts."

In this insistence, as we've seen, modern North Carolina fundamentalists have Samuel Johnson and most dictionary writers before Noah Webster on their side. But why this single-minded devotion to the swine? Ask a Tar Heel barbecue partisan, and you'll probably be told simply that it tastes better, maybe even that the Lord meant for it to be that way. (And never mind Leviticus: As Hillsborough writer Hal Crowther observes, "The Lord wouldn't have made the meat so sweet and the swine so fine if he hadn't wanted us to enjoy them.")

North Carolinians have had a thing for pigs since before there was a North Carolina. A pamphlet of 1666 designed to attract pork-

"Porcivorous people" in Johnston County

loving British immigrants claimed that hogs in the Carolinas "find so much Mast and other Food in the Woods, that they want no other care than a Swine-herd to keep them from running wild." This may have overstated things a bit (not unusual for a real-estate promoter), but it seems to have done the job. When the Virginia aristocrat William Byrd II of Westover visited our parts sixty years later, he found North Carolina populated by a "porcivorous" people whose "only business . . . is raising of hogs, which is managed with the least trouble, and affords the diet they are most fond of." Byrd went on at some length about "the foul and pernicious effects of eating swine's flesh in a hot country." Eating so much pork, he wrote, made North Carolinians "extremely hoggish in their Temper, & many of them seem to Grunt rather than Speak in their ordinary conversation." Mr. Byrd doesn't seem to have enjoyed his visit.

At any rate, with hogs cheap, plentiful, not hard to raise, self-basting, and easier than cattle to cook without dismembering, it's no wonder that pork became the preferred meat not just in North

Carolina but across the South, right up to where East Texas gives way to cowboy country. Not to say that folks didn't like beef when it was available, but day in, day out, pork—in many forms—was the table meat of the South. Each year between 1840 and 1860, two hogs were raised in the Southern states for every human being who lived there. For really special occasions like political rallies and community celebrations, with hundreds of people in attendance, an ox might be roasted. But for most barbecues, Southerners were content to take an ordinary porker (or part of one—we'll get to that) and do something extraordinary with it.

Duplin County is home to more than two million hogs, over forty for every human who lives there.

There are still more hogs than people in North Carolina: our state is second only to Iowa in hog production (and number one in hog waste problems, but that's another story). And the taste for pork persists—when it comes to barbecue, it's not just a taste but a dogma.

THE SECRET IS IN THE SAUCE

So North Carolina barbecue is pork, cooked slow over hardwood coals. But we pretty much share that with most of the South. What sets us apart is what we do to that pork while it's cooking and afterward.

People have been using marinades to tenderize roasted meat, mops and finishing sauces to moisten it, and all three to enhance its flavor since time immemorial. These concoctions have almost always begun with a mildly acidic base of wine, vinegar, or lemon or other fruit juice, then added something salty—salt, soy sauce, fermented fish sauce (the Romans' favorite)—and something spicy like red or black pepper, ginger, cinnamon, or cloves. Optional ingredients have included sweeteners, garlic or something in the onion line, and maybe some butter, lard, or oil to replace fat lost in cooking and to help the sauce adhere. The tomato was a relatively late addition, and of course it's still controversial in North Carolina, but put all this stuff in, and you've got something like the commercial sauces that line supermarket shelves today (or, better, like the Ridgewood sauce on pages 117–18).

That medieval table sauce mentioned earlier is found in a manuscript from around 1430, now in the British Library. It says to take the cooked meat, "pour thereon Vinegar & a little verjuice [the sour juice of unripe grapes], & powdered Pepper thereon enough, & Ginger, & Cinnamon, & a few yolks of hard Eggs crumbled thereon, & serve forth." These folks were at least on the right track. (At about the same time, the Aztecs in Mexico were roasting little hairless dogs — they didn't have pigs — and serving them with a tomato and chili sauce, which may have something to do with what goes on in Texas these days.) Some of the ingredients in that medieval sauce are seldom found nowadays — at least not east of Raleigh — but the vinegar and pepper have survived.

By the 1700s, sauce-makers were getting really warm, with what was called at the time "catsup" or "ketchup" (which didn't mean what it does these days: the early versions included no tomatoes at all). The first printed ketchup recipe, in Elizabeth Smith's *Compleat Housewife* (1727), calls for vinegar, white wine, lemon peel, pepper, cloves, ginger, mace, nutmeg, anchovies, and shallots — one or more entries from each of the major food groups mentioned earlier. That combination might make a good finishing sauce for slow-roasted meat (although we haven't tried it), and in fact that seems to have been one of the things it was used for.

Five years later, one of the earliest printed recipes for a sauce specifically designed for barbecuing appeared, in Richard Bradley's *Country House-wife*. To prepare "an Hog barbecued, or broil'd whole," Bradley says, season the hog with salt and pepper and cook it on a gridiron, skin-side up. After turning it, fill the cavity with water, white wine, lemon peels, sage, and cloves. Later, serve this liquid as a table sauce.

A number of English cookbooks from the 1780s and 1790s give variations on a basic recipe "to barbecue a leg of Pork" (not a whole hog — these are recipes for urban kitchens). They all call for the joint to be roasted beside the fire and the drippings collected, and for it to be basted with red wine (port, Madeira, or a mixture) while cooking. The finishing sauces take the wine and juices from the dripping pan and add lemon, "sweet herbs," and anchovies. Some call for some butter or touches of other ingredients (lemon-pickle, fresh tarragon or tarragon vinegar, "catchup"). All the sauces are to be boiled, strained, and served hot. (This anchovy business may

strike us as strange, until we recall that the fish are salty, and a major ingredient in Worcestershire sauce.)

Meanwhile, as we heard from the young ball- and barbecue-goer sitting under the "harbour," in the 1700s Virginians and Carolinians were cooking whole hogs outside and basting them alternately with salt water and butter, presumably what George Washington encountered at the barbecues he attended. Virginians are famously conservative: As late as 1860 at a Virginia barbecue, there were still iron pots beside the pit, "some filled with salt, and water; others with melted butter, lard, etc. into which the attendants dipped

"Lots of people say they're using an old family recipe that's 150 years old, but 150 years ago, all they used was vinegar, butter and pepper." (John Thomas Walker)

linen cloths affixed to the ends of long, flexible wands, and delicately applied them with a certain air of dainty precision to different portions on the roasting meat." (This process is reenacted each Labor Day at Colonial Williamsburg.)

These folks were groping, feeling their way toward the answer, some more successfully than others. In 1824 Mary Randolph, author of *The Virginia Housewife*, was still serving "barbecued" pork (roasted over a dripping pan) with something more like gravy than sauce: water, red wine, garlic, salt, pepper, mushroom ketchup, and butter—thickened with flour. Mrs. Randolph apparently hadn't noticed that by then some of her fellow Americans had found the solution: vinegar, peppers, salt, and not much more.

Food historian Karen Hess believes that vinegar-and-pepper sauces originated, like the peppers they require, in the West Indies. She points to the testimony of a Dominican missionary, Jean Baptiste Labat, who wrote in 1698 about a feast he attended, put on by islanders who were by then cooking pigs that had been brought from Europe and gone native. Père Labat observed that they used a mop of lemon juice, salt, and chile peppers, and served a similar table sauce in two strengths, hot or mild. (Incidentally, Labat's hosts called their cooker a *boucan*—a word that has entered English as "buccaneer," referring to the antisocial Caribbean elements who cooked the same way. It's really too bad that East Carolina University chose to be the Pirates rather than the Buccaneers.) A taste for this taste may well have been brought to mainland North America by pepper-bearing slaves or Creoles from the islands. Since lemon juice in quantity was hard to find in the Carolinas and Virginia, it was often replaced by vinegar, and—voilà!

Thomas Jefferson's Garden Book shows that he was growing cayenne peppers at Monticello in 1767, and in 1782 he recorded that he made "40 gallons of vinegar of the first running" from seventeen bushels of grapes. By 1812 he was also growing two other kinds of capsicum ("major" and "bull nose"), and in 1813 his correspondence finally mentions steeping peppers in vinegar to use as a seasoning—an early version, as Hess observes, of Eastern-style sauce. And, of course, he was raising hogs (although his overseer at Monticello said of him, "He never eat much hog meat").

Ode to Pork

Crisply braised,
A paragon of fat and lean
Drips juicily upon the pit.
Sustainer of the South,
The Pig doth yearn to
   sacrifice and serve.
I eat it lustily,
Sauce-stained and
   smiling.
—Anonymous

True 'Cue

Pig split,
fire lit,
slaw fixed,
sauce mixed.
Coals glow.
Roast slow.
Now eat:
pick meat,
hush pup,
drink up.
Gut big.
Good pig.
—Bruce Tindall

Bruce Tindall lives and writes in San Diego now but hasn't forgotten his North Carolina childhood (in Chapel Hill).

In 1831 a letter in the Tarborough Free Press *warned that "secret agents" planned to circulate copies of the abolitionist paper* The Liberator *among Edgecombe County slaves. "If you catch them," it advised, "by all that is sacred, you ought to barbecue them."*

After New York Times *food writer Craig Claiborne visited Goldsboro, he was inspired to cook "Eastern-style barbecue" for his friends. North Carolinian James Villas reports that the oven-roasted pork loin was served with a "credible" sauce, and champagne, but it wasn't barbecue.*

The basic combination of peppers, lemon juice or vinegar, and butter or lard (especially for meats less fatty than pork) caught on quickly. By 1829 the *Richmond Enquirer* was writing that a gourmand's "favorite *barbacue* . . . is a fine fat pig called 'shoat,' cooked on the coals, and highly seasoned with cyane [cayenne]."

Of special interest are the recollections of Martha McCulloch-Williams, the daughter of a Granville County tobacco planter who had moved to middle Tennessee. In a unique food memoir, *Dishes and Beverages of the Old South* (1913), she gave instructions for roasting lamb and pork in the oven ("as near an approach to a real barbecue, which is cooked over live coals in the bottom of a trench, as a civilized kitchen can supply"). She also shared her memories of both "barbecue edible" and "barbecue, the occasion." When she was a young girl (she was born in 1848), whole lambs, pigs, and kids were cooked on open pits, basted with salt water, "and turned over once only," then served with her father's "dipney," or finishing sauce, which was simmered for half an hour, then mopped, hot, onto the cooked meat: "Daddy made it thus: Two pounds sweet lard, melted in a brass kettle, with one pound beaten, not ground, black pepper, a pint of small fiery red peppers, nubbed and stewed soft in water to barely cover, a spoonful of herbs in powder—he would never tell what they were [of course!],—and a quart and a pint of the strongest apple vinegar, with a little salt."

This sauce, or something very much like it, soon became the standard almost everywhere. Martha's daddy had evidently taken his Granville County tastes and techniques with him when he moved west (and to this day, thin, vinegar-based sauces can be found in places like Lexington, Tennessee, and Blytheville, Arkansas). In 1896 *Harper's Weekly* reported an almost identical sauce from Georgia, also called "dipney" (surely the origin of the word *dip*, used for sauce in the Piedmont—and Kentucky). Lettice Bryan's *Kentucky Housewife* (1839) has one that sticks with lemon juice instead of vinegar, and a traveler outside San Antonio in 1883 found a similar sauce even in Texas, except with cow butter instead of hog lard.

Meanwhile, back in East Carolina, Sarah Frances Hicks, a Yankee married to a North Carolinian, wrote home to New York from Greene County in 1853: "Red pepper is much used to flavor

Three North Carolina Barbecue Songs

Barbecue, both real and metaphorical, was central to the Durham blues scene. In the early 1940s, Bull City bluesman Brownie McGhee (singing as "Blind Boy Fuller #2," in tribute to the recently deceased Wadesboro native) recorded "Barbecue Any Old Time," lamenting that

> When I was young, in my prime,
> I got my barbecue any old time.
> Now I'm old, bones is cold,
> Can't get no barbecue to save my soul.

In 2001 a state historical marker was erected in Durham's Hayti district to honor Fuller, Blind Gary Davis, and the other musicians who played there in the 1930s at a barbecue stand across from the tobacco factory.

Jack Herrick and Bland Simpson of Chapel Hill's Red Clay Ramblers have written a number called simply "Barbeque." Included on the album *Rambler* (1992), it goes, in part

> Cook it slow, cook it well, that Carolina way
> When you ring the dinner bell, everybody's
>   gonna say
> Whoa, mama, whatever you do
> Don't get behind on your barbeque
> Forget about your chicken and your Brunswick
>   stew
> But don't get behind on your barbeque.

These guys know what they're doing: they go on to specify hickory coals and some old bedsprings.

Clyde Edgerton grew up in the rural community of Bethesda outside of Durham, and the first of his novels set in small-town North Carolina was *Raney*. It was about a marriage between a Baptist and an Episcopalian, and it cost him his job at Campbell University.

Edgerton doubles as a singer and songwriter, and his song "A Quiche Woman in a Barbeque Town" is about a mixed marriage of another sort:

> A social worker from Boston on a trip to
>   Caroline
> Stopped in Burgaw for Beaujolais wine.
> 'Twas a hasty decision, but she liked the little
>   town.
> She married the mayor, and settled down.
>   She's a quiche woman in a barbeque town.
>   There's trucks and ticks and tobacco all
>   around.
>   She was Vassar cum loudy several years ago.
>   The adjustment . . . will be slow.

The song has a happy ending, though. The odd couple's daughter goes north to college at Cornell, finds herself with "city slickers, and Yankees, and bankers all around," and realizes that she's "a barbeque woman in a quiche town."

Southern Barbecue, lithograph, ca. 1940, by WPA artist Raymond Steth. As a child, Steth worked on the farm his uncle sharecropped, near Rocky Mount.

meat with the famous 'barbecue' of the South & which I believe they esteem above all dishes is roasted pig dressed with red pepper & vinegar."

As far as Easterners were concerned, perfection had been pretty much attained Before the War, and (despite some major technological innovations) their barbecue now is more or less what barbecue was then.

T hroughout the nineteenth century, barbecue in the Piedmont didn't differ much from the Eastern variety, although it seems that it may have been on offer less often: When the editor of the *Statesville Landmark* went east to an editorial convention in Durham in 1890, he was looking forward to a barbecue at Bennett Place (where Johnston had surrendered to Sherman twenty-five years before) and was disappointed when the event was rained out. He wrote: "The people in [that] part of the State understand the barbecue business better than we of the west do; they have them frequently during the summer and they are great festival occasions. I had very much wanted to attend one, with its feature of Brunswick stew and other trimmings."

Still, there were barbecues west of Durham—his own paper had advertised or reported eight of them during the 1880s, including an 1888 Democratic rally and barbecue in Statesville, where the assembled citizens were served "1300 lbs of beef and 300 lbs of pork, to say nothing of bread, chickens, pies, cakes and all such." The *Landmark* reported that "the crowd was noisy at times and some whiskey was consumed as a matter of course. There were two or three breaches of the peace and three or four arrests, but the general behavior during the day was quite creditable to Iredell [County]."

This story is unusual in that it mentioned what was eaten. Newspapers and diaries had a lot to say about the speeches at barbecues, but what food was on the long tables usually went without saying, probably because everybody knew what you got. But it appears the politicians who wanted the votes of the yeoman farmers and mill-workers of the Piedmont tried to buy them with the same vinegar-and-pepper-sauced open-pit barbecued pork and (even quite late in the century) beef that they deployed in the East.

A rare nineteenth-century view from pit-side was provided in 1937 by Wesley Jones, then over ninety years old. Mr. Jones had grown up in South Carolina, not North, but the plantation in Union County where he was a slave was less than fifty miles due south of

Shelby, North Carolina, in the heart of the part of South Carolina that today cooks "Lexington-style." In the 1850s, Mr. Jones was the youthful pitmaster for big barbecues that were held regularly at Sardis Store, with fiddling and political speeches. He cooked "whole goats, whole hogs, sheep and de side of a cow." He mopped the meat all night with a "sass" of vinegar, black and red pepper, salt, butter, a little sage, coriander, basil, onion, and garlic—a process he called "anointing" it. "Some folks drop a little sugar in it," he said, implying that this was a common sauce recipe for that time and place.

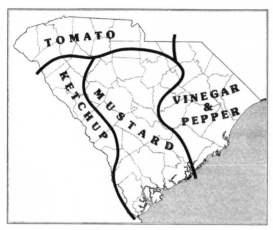

South Carolina
barbecue regions

This is basically an Eastern sauce, with a few spices that wouldn't be grounds for disqualification in Goldsboro or Wilson. Certainly it had no tomato in it. There's no reason to suppose that barbecue in nineteenth-century Shelby or Salisbury or Lexington was any different.

THE LEXINGTON HERESY AND THE GERMAN FACTOR

About the time of World War I, however, a new and competing version of barbecue emerged in the hills of the Piedmont. When early barbecue entrepreneurs in the East started selling barbecue by the sandwich or the plate, they were working in an established tradition, purveying the same peppery-vinegary whole-hog pulled pork that people had already been eating at community and family barbecues. But the first barbecue stands in Lexington and Salisbury were cooking just parts of the hog—loins, hams, and especially shoulders. And they served their barbecue in slices, as well as chopped or pulled. In an even more radical departure from tradition, they were lacing the classic vinegar-and-pepper sauce with tomato ketchup.

Although these innovations had precedents in domestic cookery, they were something new in the North Carolina barbecue world, and they were viewed by many Easterners with much the same enthusiasm that the medieval Catholic Church had for the Protestant Reformation. North Carolinians have been arguing about this ever since.

But why these particular innovations?

The humble creators of the Eastern tradition are known to God alone, but the pioneers of Piedmont-style have names: John Blackwelder of Salisbury; George Ridenhour, Jess Swicegood, and Sid Weaver of Lexington; and, a little later, Warner Stamey of Lexington, Shelby, and finally Greensboro. It's said that you are what you eat, but it's equally true that you eat what you are—and in one respect these men were all the same thing:

John Blackwelder's family had been in Mecklenburg,
    Cabarrus, and Rowan counties since soon after Gottlieb
    Schwartzwalder came from Germany to British North
    America before the Revolution.
George Ridenhour's people came to Salisbury in 1779 from
    Pennsylvania, where the Reitnaurs first settled after coming
    from German-speaking Alsace in 1719.
Jess Swicegood's family came to America from Germany in
    1724 and also passed through Pennsylvania before settling
    in Davidson County in 1775 and Americanizing their name
    from Schweissgouth.
Sid Weaver's antecedents are a little more elusive, although
    many North Carolina Weavers started as Webers, and his
    ancestor Andrew was listed as "Andras" in the 1860 census.
The North Carolina Stameys, Warner included, are all
    descended from a Peter Stemme who came from Germany in
    1734 and made his way down the valley of Virginia to what is
    now Lincoln County in 1767.

Can you spot the common element? Of course you can. When you add maternal lines, these family trees are as full of Germans

"We only use the shoulder. Someone else has a whole lot of hams."
(Tommy Monk, Lexington Barbecue)

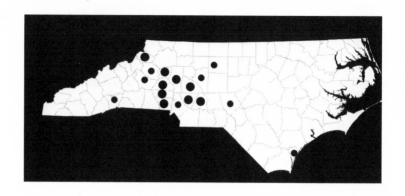

as a Munich beer hall at Oktoberfest. Compare those family names to the big names in Eastern barbecue, good British ones like King, Parker, Jones, Ellis, Shirley, and Melton, no matter whether they're affixed to white families or black ones. (Did we point out that Piedmont barbecue is a business conducted mostly by white folks?)

It's not exactly news that Piedmont North Carolina has had a substantial German presence since the "Dutch" started coming down the Great Wagon Road from Pennsylvania in the 1700s. This is still evident in the names found in telephone books and in the Lutheran and Reformed churches on the landscape. But until historian Gary Freeze (originally Friess?) at Catawba College got interested in it, Germans' role in shaping Tar Heel cuisine—liver mush aside— had been largely neglected. (Freeze notes that the early Lexington

Sid Weaver and George Ridenhour

barbecue men got their shoulders from Conrad and Hinkle—Conrath and Henckel?—old-style grocers still operating in downtown Lexington who raise the pigs themselves.)

The German influence in North Carolina has been more subtle than that of the German butchers in Texas who made sausage and beef brisket major parts of the Lone Star story, or that of South Carolina's upcountry Germans who introduced and sell to this day their state's peculiar mustard-based sauce. (Lake E. High Jr. of the South Carolina Barbeque Association points out the continuing importance of families with names like Bessinger, Shealy, Hite, Sweatman, Sikes, Price, Lever, Meyer, Kiser, Zeigler, and Dooley—originally Dula, as in Tom, of Wilkes County and the Kingston Trio song.) But in North Carolina, the German factor is obvious once you start looking for it.

In all of German-speaking Europe, pork was the meat of the peasant classes, and in the New World their descendants remained attached to it. When Germans and their hog-droving Scotch-Irish contemporaries arrived in the 1700s, they fit right in to porcivorous North Carolina. To this day, German cookery has a particular fondness for *smoked* pork, sometimes marinated in vinegar flavored with various spices; the Pennsylvania Dutch cousins of North Carolina Germans, for example, cook a dish called *saurer Seibrode*, basically a pork version of *Sauerbraten*. True, the smoked pork of German cuisine is salted or brined, smoked in a smokehouse, and soaked in water before being cooked, but the point is that vinegar-and-smoke-flavored pork was not an alien taste for German newcomers in North Carolina. All that was lacking were the cayenne peppers.

Here's the clincher. William Ways Weaver, who writes about the history of German and Pennsylvania Dutch cooking, points out that the shoulder of the hog was a particularly esteemed cut, indeed a "ritual consumption item" at hog-killing time, and *Schäufele* (smoked shoulder, served sliced) has something of a cult following in Germany today.

So what could be more natural than to smoke and cook pork at the same time by adopting the barbecue technique familiar from political and community events? And why barbecue the inferior

This Is *Southern Germany, After All*

In the Franconia region of Bavaria, where smoked pork shoulder or *Schäufele* is a specialty, some patriots have formed Freunde des fränkischen Schäufele (Friends of Franconian Schäufele), devoted to "caring for the Franconian lifestyle and promoting the consumption of Schäufele." The Freunde publish a guidebook to joints that serve their totemic dish, with ratings that range from 0 ("The pig died without good cause") to 10 ("Pig, pig, hooray!"). When a researcher at Erlangen University claimed that eating Schäufele reduces one's intelligence, they sprang to its defense.

A Minnesota German named Hormel took the pork shoulder in an entirely different direction. He chopped it, added preservatives, canned it, and sold it as Spam.

In 1997 students at Northern Davidson Middle School set up a cultural exchange program with Owensboro Middle School in Kentucky. They swapped ten pounds of Lexington's finest with barbecue slaw for ten pounds of Owensboro's mutton 'cue with potato salad.

parts of the hog when you could buy only the best part from your local butcher? Shoulders' fattiness meant that they didn't dry out and they absorbed even more of the delicious smoke flavor. That it was easier to transport them, to turn them, and to cook them evenly was a bonus. If you had a bad day at the stand, you had less left over. And if some folks wanted their meat sliced like pork roast instead of pulled or chopped like old-fashioned barbecue—well, why not? Germans have always had a reputation for practicality and thriftiness.

Moreover, by 1900 the whole Piedmont was coming into its own. From Raleigh west and south to Charlotte, mills and factories were springing up, towns were becoming small cities, and the sort of go-getting, can-do, New South attitudes that a son of the Piedmont named W. J. Cash mocked in *The Mind of the South* (1940) were increasingly widespread. By contrast, as the Piedmont saw it, the East remained predominantly agricultural, conservative, opposed to progress. Maybe that went for its barbecue, too.

Why change? Because Piedmont pitmasters thought it was an improvement and didn't see any reason not to make it.

LET'S TALK ABOUT TOMATOES

Then there's that tomato in Piedmont sauce, or dip, as it's called. Where did that come from? We suspect the story is similar.

Contrary to persistent legends, some Anglo-Americans were growing and eating "love apples" in the 1700s. Food historian "Hoppin' John" Taylor reports, for instance, that the Charleston planter and patriot Henry Laurens was raising them for his table by 1764 at the latest. The British had been doing it even longer, and the French and Italians longer still. But tomatoes' real acceptance dates from around 1820. In 1824 Jefferson's son-in-law, Thomas Mann Randolph, spoke to the Albemarle Agricultural Society about how everyone was eating tomatoes for their health, although almost nobody had eaten them ten years earlier. In that same year, Jefferson's cousin, Mary Randolph, put a recipe for "tomata catsup" in her *Virginia Housewife* (not the first cookbook to include such a recipe, although maybe the first Southern one).

Since the classic Eastern vinegar-and-pepper sauce wasn't really nailed down until about this time, its creators could have put tomatoes in it if they'd wanted to. But they didn't. And there's no evidence that much of anyone east of Texas fooled with tomatoes in barbecue sauce until after commercially bottled ketchup became widely available in the late 1800s. To the horror of East Carolina traditionalists, however, once store-bought ketchup was available, those Germanic barbarians in the Piedmont starting adding it to the classic vinegar-and-pepper sauce, adulterating God's intended condiment, turning their backs on a cherished tradition of the Old South.

Why did they do it?

A quick history of the product: In 1837 Jonas Yerkes started selling bottles of ketchup made from leftover tomato skins and cores from canning, tomatoes too green to can, vinegar, and sugar—recognizably the same stuff that Richard Nixon put on cottage cheese. But the breakthrough came when the H. J. Heinz pickle people showed their version (unchanged since, by the way) at the great 1876 Centennial Exposition in Philadelphia. (This is the same exposition that introduced kudzu to the United States—make of that what you will.) By 1900 there were over 100 ketchup-bottlers in the country.

You may have noticed that Yerkes and Heinz are German names, but our Piedmont Germans didn't bring this taste with them from Germany, or even Pennsylvania. They were in North Carolina before most people were eating tomatoes, and well before their compatriots started bottling this red goop. We suspect they thought barbecue tasted better with a *soupçon* of Heinz because the classic Eastern sauce had no sugar in it and adding ketchup brought it closer to the sweet-sour taste so common in German cookery.

Anyway, it's a thought.

THE SMOKE NEVER CLEARS

By the time of World War II, the distinctions between Eastern- and Piedmont-style barbecue were well established and widely understood within the state. The defenders of Eastern orthodoxy took pride in doing it the old way, Piedmont folks were equally proud of their new and improved product, and each region claimed its 'cue was better.

They still do. Many have learned the hard way that partisans can be fiercely loyal to their local traditions. "You ought to see what happens when we write about barbecue," says Kathleen Purvis of the *Charlotte Observer*. "That's when I want to crawl in a trench and pull sheet metal over my head." Rosemary Roberts, her journalistic sister at the *Greensboro News and Record*, agrees: "Write about the succulent glories of Tar Heel barbecue at one's peril. It's much safer to take on the National Rifle Association."

Fans of Eastern-style can be withering about the barbecue of their upstart upland cousins. Usually they attack Piedmont barbecue for its heretical sauce. As an Easterner who opened a "North Carolina Barbecue" establishment in Maryland put it on a warning sign: "WE DON'T HOLD WITH TOMATOES." "I've never eaten red barbecue," Andy Stephenson of Stephenson's Bar-B-Q in Willow Spring told *USA Today*. "I've seen it, but that's as far as I care to go." When the *Wilmington Star* devoted an editorial to sauce, it stated flatly that "Proper Barbecue [is] basted with God's Own Sauce, whose ingredients include cider vinegar, red and black pepper, salt and maybe another thing or two. But no tomatoes! That would make it the loathsome Lexington style." Dennis Rogers of the *Raleigh News and Observer* concurs, pointing out that "the Piedmont stuff is made with John Kerry's wife's ketchup vs. God's own apple cider vinegar, salt and pepper Down East," and adding that "somebody who would put ketchup on barbecue and give it to a child is capable of pretty much anything." Jack Betts of the *Charlotte Observer* sounded like a peacemaker when he remarked, "I like the eastern sauce myself, but don't regard the western style as blasphemy worthy of a fist fight"—but then he added, "A good western sauce can rescue a poorly-cooked pig."

As for those shoulders, Carroll Leggett dismisses what he sees as their dreary "textural sameness," deploring the absence of "ribs, tenderloin, and crispy skin"—"special parts to vie for" (even with the implication that there are . . . other parts). Ayden's Pete Jones always maintained, "We smoke the whole pig—if you don't use the whole pig, it's not barbecue." And Ed Mitchell of Wilson proudly proclaims himself "a whole hog cookin' man, from the rooter to the tooter." If you "cut 'em up," he asserts, "you've deviated from the real deal."

"Gristle and fat, hide, hair and goo: | East Carolina bar-b-que." (East Carolina University professor Meredith Neil Posey—a Texan)

The Skylight Inn goes whole hog.

Piedmont partisans respond in kind. Jerry Bledsoe writes, "In the East, you get all these little things in your mouth and wonder what the hell they are. They're ground up pork skin. That's the only way they have to give the meat any flavor." Peter Batke wonders about "people who would stuff a whole roast pig into a grinding machine snout first and douse the resulting detritus with pepper-speckled vinegar." Wayne Monk of Lexington Barbecue has observed, "As for 'whole hog,' there are some parts of the hog that I would just as soon not eat." And after Charles Kuralt criticized the shoulders at Statesville's Carolina Bar-B-Q as "too-refined, without the necessary grease and gristle" from whole-hog cooking, the management posted a notice next to the cash register that said "EXTRA FAT AND GRISTLE AVAILABLE ON REQUEST."

A BRIEF ASIDE ON MOUNTAIN BARBECUE

There's one more complication. When a North Carolina conversation turns to barbecue, the Appalachian counties tend to get ignored. Indeed, when people speak of "Western" barbecue, they usually mean the Piedmont variety. (We've tried to avoid that usage.) This is because the state's far West hasn't had much of a barbecue tradition until recently. In Jim Early's *Best Tar Heel Barbecue, Manteo to Murphy*, half of the fifteen establishments in the Mountain region whose founding dates are given were established after 1993; only

Burlington in the 1950s

Jerry Leath Mills recalls his boyhood: "Burlington was and is a kind of San Andreas Fault of barbecue styles, where the two collide and grind tectonically together, shaking the respective partisans up. Dewlon Thompson's Kilowatt Inn out close to the power company served the western variety—I still remember the mingling of sweet and acidic in the tomato sauce Thompson used—while several other places, including Woolworth's lunch counter, served it eastern. Both styles chopped it finer than is common today— no 'pulled' barbecue do I remember. If you wanted it unminced you ordered it sliced, which was like roast pork on a bun with either tomato sauce or hot vinegar, depending on the restaurant, and cost a nickel extra. Most barbecue buns were square in those days and more capacious than a regular hamburger bun."

two were in business before 1980, and none is older than the 1960s. Elsewhere in the state, half of the places Early discusses date from before 1970, and 40 percent were cooking barbecue when Ike was in the White House.

This doesn't mean there's not good barbecued meat to be found west of Hickory—there's more of it all the time—but it does mean that when people started opening barbecue places in the West, they weren't bound by tradition and often looked out of state for their models (especially since many cater to tourists whose idea of barbecue does not include North Carolina's thin vinegar-and-pepper sauces, or even necessarily pork). So what you'll find in barbecue restaurants in the mountains is often like what's cooked at the Blue Ridge BBQ Festival (see page 287): that is, something more closely akin to the 'cue of Tennessee, Alabama, Texas, or Kansas City than to anything served in Lexington or Goldsboro. Along with the pulled pork, you'll usually find ribs, not as one of the tastier results of whole-hog cooking but bought and cooked separately. (The Eastern and Piedmont attitude was summed up by one Piedmonter who told the *Washington Post*, "If you want ribs, go to a rib place.") You'll often find barbecued beef as well. And there'll probably be a choice of sauces, usually including a heavy, sweet, tomato-based sauce, similar to the bottled "barbecue sauce" introduced in the 1950s by Kraft Foods, since widely imitated (and improved), and now found on grocery store shelves and grilled burgers throughout the country.

Herb's Pit BBQ is a case in point. Fifteen miles beyond Murphy, nestled up against the Tennessee and Georgia borders, Herb's is undoubtedly the westernmost barbecue restaurant in the state. One of the oldest places in the mountains (founded in 1982), Herb's serves some good smoked meat, and they cook it with charcoal, which is rare everywhere these days. But their tasty pulled pork comes from loins and collars, not shoulders, and they serve ribs and beef as well. It's telling that the license plates on the wall are from Florida and New York.

In the hills, you're also likely to encounter strange, noncanonical side dishes, like the garlic bread that comes with the barbecue platter at Fat Buddies in Franklin. And you're more likely to find

As its name suggests, 12 Bones Smokehouse in Asheville specializes in ribs. They're served with a variety of sauces, including a blueberry-chipotle number that won the national Best Bites Award from ABC's Good Morning America Weekend.

Murphy to Manteo

Restaurants mentioned in Jim Early's *Best Tar Heel Barbecue, Manteo to Murphy* that were founded before 1960 are concentrated in the Piedmont and the eastern part of the state, and those founded in the 1960s and 1970s did not extend the range very much. But those founded after 1980 have taken barbecue (literally) from Murphy to Manteo.

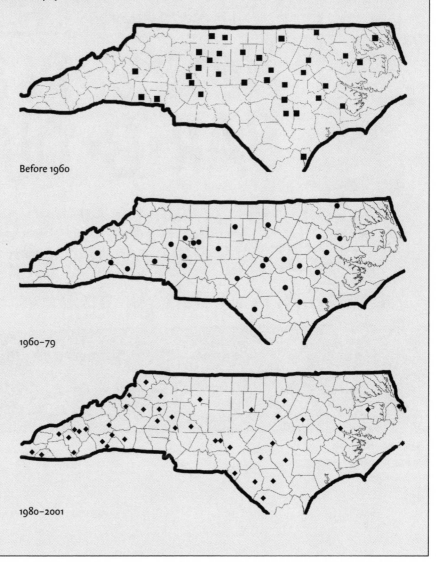

Before 1960

1960–79

1980–2001

US 64 west of Murphy:
last stop for barbecue in
North Carolina

names like "Fat Buddies"—most Piedmont and Eastern restaurants bear their owners' names.

Bob Garner writes disapprovingly in his classic *North Carolina Barbecue: Flavored by Time*, "You may find something *called* barbecue in some of the tourist destinations in the Smokies, but like the typical feathered, plains-Indian headdress worn and sold in Cherokee, it isn't authentic to this state, but is an import from the West." That's harsh, if accurate, and in time maybe all this innovation will settle down into a tradition in its own right, as Lexington-style did almost a century ago. Maybe a hundred years from now there will be three competing, mutually scornful barbecue regions in North Carolina.

Meanwhile, on the bright side, it does mean you can get pretty good Memphis, Texas, and Kansas City–style barbecue without having to leave the state.

THE CAROLINA CULTURE WARS

So, throw in those mountaineers with their thick, sweet sauces—not to mention South Carolinians with that scary mustard stuff—and you can see why food writers Jim Auchmutey and Susan Puckett once called the Carolinas "the Balkans of barbecue." In fact, after Dennis Rogers asked his readers a series of questions—"Hush puppies or corn sticks? Yellow slaw or red? Brunswick stew or not on the side? Will it be Wilber's mashed potato salad or the chunky kind? Boiled potatoes (with or without paprika) or—yecch!—French fries? The pungent, sinus-clearing tang of the East, the middling red of Lexington or the gooey stuff that comes out of the mountains?"—he concluded, "There is no such thing as North Carolina barbecue, you see."

These arguments sometimes baffle outsiders. Georgian Bobby "Bobby Q" Cresap marvels, "You're talking about a little tomato being the basic difference between the two [Eastern and Piedmont], and they act like it's the Civil War." When Craig Claiborne, longtime food editor of the *New York Times*, paid our state a visit, he found the differences between Eastern and Piedmont "slight and subtle, the main one being the sauce ingredients. And even there, the absence of a tomato tang in the down east sauce didn't make a whole lot of difference—vinegar is the key factor in both of them.

Shoulder vs. whole hog? Here again, not much to differentiate; in both cases the meat is cooked long enough to be fork tender."

Claiborne was a Mississippian and modest enough to allow that the differences might be "obvious and pronounced [to] an experienced North Carolina barbecue addict." But even Bob Garner, who fits that description, observes that Piedmont barbecue is more like the Eastern variety than either is like what's called barbecue in Memphis, Austin, Kansas City, or Columbia. And Garner asks a good question: How can we expect outsiders to understand that we have the best barbecue in the country when we can't even agree among ourselves what good barbecue is? This sounds like a classic example of what Sigmund Freud called "the narcissism of small differences."

When the UNC basketball program first tried to recruit Coach Roy Williams, athletic department employees drove an hour to get him some barbecue after they heard he liked it. He turned the Tar Heels down anyway (that time). Maybe they should have gone west instead of east, or vice versa.

Jim Early of the North Carolina Barbecue Society once proposed a truce. "We've been shooting ourselves in the foot with this eastern-western thing," he argued. "No other states fight within the state. Let's stop that. Let's fight somebody else if we have to fight. Let's unite as kin." But when the *Atlanta Journal-Constitution* asked Jerry Bledsoe about Early's proposal, Bledsoe declined to hold his fire. "If this guy's trying to end the feud, I'm totally opposed," he said. "The feud is as good as the food."

Why can't we all just get along?

One reason may be that the barbecue battle lines are old ones. Leave the mountains aside—everybody knows they've always been different—and focus on the main event: the rivalry between the East and the Piedmont. That low-level conflict has been going on since the 1700s. Over time the division has been cultural, economic, political, and demographic. The two regions were settled at different times by different peoples (two of them—English Episcopalians and Scotch-Irish Presbyterians—old adversaries). In antebellum times, different landscapes and resources meant that the fall line divided larger, wealthier, slaveholding farms in the East from smaller hardscrabble yeoman farms upcountry. The East had, and still has, a greater African American presence. And so forth. At the University of North Carolina, this division was reproduced in miniature almost as soon as the university was founded. UNC students formed the Philanthropic Society in 1795 and the Dialectic Society soon after, literary and social clubs that quickly became regional, the latter for students from west of Chapel Hill, the former for those from the East. (Their fierce competition lasted for over a century, and their colors, white and blue respectively, became the university's colors.)

This sort of intrastate division is not unusual: think of northern and southern California or Louisiana, or upstate New York and The City. Virginia's and South Carolina's divisions are quite similar to North Carolina's, having come about for many of the same reasons. But only in North Carolina, it seems, do different styles of barbecue correlate with these ancient fault lines. Only in North Carolina has barbecue come to symbolize the split and to serve as a badge of identity.

It is barely possible that folks in the Piedmont started cooking pork shoulders with a ketchup-inflected sauce just to be different.

TAR HEEL BARBECUES

"Barbecue in these parts is ever so much more than just the meat; it's also the preparation, the ritual, the social occasion, the fellowship, the anticipation, the realization, the memory." (John Egerton)

n the late 1700s, the barbecue heartland was found in Tidewater Virginia and adjoining parts of North Carolina, where "barbecue days" like those George Washington attended had become an institution. Strange as it may sound, community barbecues had been common in early New England, but the custom had waned there. South Carolina, on the other hand, had few public barbecues before the nineteenth century, according to Robert Moss (a South Carolinian himself). Subsequently, of course, Virginians were distracted by hams and Brunswick stew, leaving North Carolina in undisputed possession of the longest continuous barbecue tradition on the North American mainland.

At the time of the Revolution, however, whole communities from Maryland south to Wilmington got together now and then to eat, usually to dance, and often to gamble (Washington won eight shillings at cards at an Alexandria barbecue in 1769). Since these get-togethers lasted from morning until late at night and there was almost always serious drinking, they tended to be rowdy. In 1808 Virginia's Ketocton Baptist Association denounced local sinners for spending their days "in card playing, horse racing, cock fighting, fish frying, barbacueing, shooting matches, and other fashionable vices."

But barbecues have made North Carolina what it is. In *Tar Heels: A Portrait of North Carolina* (1941), Jonathan Daniels wrote, "When men gather at the plank tables under the big trees near the smell of the pigs roasting in the pits, North Carolina is probably present in the truest and most native fashion ever to be found in the State." Barbecue has never been "home cooking" (it's just too much trouble, and before refrigeration, it produced too many leftovers for even the largest family), so until stands and restaurants came along in the twentieth century, pit-cooked meat was usually served in the setting Daniels described—under the trees, on special occasions, to large gatherings. But North Carolinians have always managed to find a great many special occasions, and sometimes large gatherings assemble just to fire up a pit and be sociable.

"All differences are made as nothing by the benign influence of the barbecue.... At this great summer function in central North Carolina all men have become equal." (Forest and Stream, 1901)

Thanksgiving Day barbecue at Christian Hill Universalist Church, near Mount Olive, 1922

BARBECUE AND POLITICS

Independence Day was one excuse, and by 1800 Fourth of July barbecues had become annual events in towns throughout the South, North Carolina towns most definitely included. The first book of poetry published in the state, James Gay's *Collection of Various Pieces of Poetry, Chiefly Patriotic* (1810), contained poems written for Statesville's 1805 and 1806 celebrations and a third about the cancellation of the one in 1807.

Guion Johnson's *Ante-Bellum North Carolina* describes the typical proceedings at these affairs: eating barbecued meat, drinking toasts, discharging firearms, and listening to orations by politicians and local dignitaries. The former, like flies, have always been drawn to barbecue because early on they saw the vote-getting potential of giving it away. Reuben Davis recalled in 1890 that antebellum campaign seasons offered "the spectacle of whole communities given up to wild days of feasting, speech-making, music, dancing, and drinking, with, perhaps, rough words now and then, and an honest hand-to-hand fight when debate was angry and the blood hot." Davis concluded nostalgically that "only those who can remember the old South in its glory can have an adequate idea of a big barbecue in 1844," but well into the twentieth century, political barbecues remained so much an institution that Herbert O'Keefe was led to observe that "no man has ever been elected governor of North Carolina without eating more barbecue than was good for him."

North Carolina's Hickory-Smoked History

The story of North Carolina from the American Revolution through the Great War could almost be written in barbecue sauce. A few highlights:

The Revolution. In 1780 at a barbecue in western North Carolina (the part that's now East Tennessee), word arrived from British colonel Patrick Ferguson that if the backwoodsmen didn't swear loyalty to the Crown he would "lay their country waste with fire and sword." Annoyed, the "overmountain boys" marched to King's Mountain, killed Ferguson, killed or captured his entire force of British and Tories, and then went home.

The Treaty of Paris. When news of the treaty recognizing American independence reached New Bern, a visiting Spanish army officer reported, "There was a barbecue (a roast pig) and a barrel of rum, from which the leading officials and citizens of the region promiscuously ate and drank with the meanest and lowest kind of people, holding hands and drinking from the same cup. It is impossible to imagine, without seeing it, a more purely democratic gathering. . . . There were some drunks, some friendly fisticuffs, and one man was injured."

The Nat Turner rebellion. Planning for the largest slave revolt in U.S. history began at a plantation barbecue in 1831. (True, it was in Virginia, but just across the state line from Murfreesboro.)

The "log cabin" presidential campaign of 1840. Whig supporters of William Henry Harrison met regularly in cabins built especially for the purpose. The Tippecanoe Club of Raleigh held a three-hour "oratorical feast" at their place, "Harrison Hall," with barbecue and brandy served by society women dressed in down-home calico.

The sectional crisis. Citizens of northeastern North Carolina held a barbecue in Halifax County in 1860 to discuss their dissatisfaction with the federal union. After much strong drink, they passed a unanimous resolution asking Emperor Napoleon III to form a defensive alliance with North Carolina.

Preparation for war. When the Scotland Neck Mounted Riflemen were presented with a flag in 1860, the mistress of Looking Glass Plantation was there. When the knives and forks for the barbecue were forgotten, she wrote, the ladies "were some what puzzled to reconcile elegance with good appetites. Fancy a delicate lady tearing the limbs of a Barbecued Shoat apart!"

Going to fight the Yankees. Mr. Thomas Ruffin gave Company H of the 15th North Carolina Volunteers a barbecue when they left for Virginia. During and after his "vigorous speech," it was reported, "liquor was consumed freely."

Emancipation. The novelist Albion Tourgée, a carpetbag Republican in Greensboro, described a typical celebration: "The barbecue was roasting under the charge of an experienced cook; the tables were arranged, and the speakers' stand at the back of the school-house in the grove was in the hands of the decorators. All was mirth and happiness. The freedmen were about to offer oblations to liberty—a sacrifice of the first-fruits of freedom."

Reconstruction. Barbecues were at the heart of white resistance to Reconstruction. A big one was held in 1869 to celebrate the murder of Jones County's Republican sheriff by Klansmen from neighboring Lenoir County. The *Petersburg Index* reported one memorable Democratic rally in Lexington, however, when "the barbecue prepared for the assemblage was forcibly taken possession of by the negroes, and everything carried off."

The white-supremacy campaign. A crescendo of Democratic Party barbecues marked the 1880s and 1890s. One at Newton in 1888 fed 5,000 to 6,000 people (including 2,000 horsemen who arrived in procession) at 1,200 feet of table. 1898 was a bad year for race relations but a great one

Political parties and candidates used to throw barbecues *after* elections, too—at least when they won. Hillsboro Whigs offered one in 1836, for example, "in celebration of the triumph of Whig principles and constitutional liberty, so happily evidenced by the late elections in this state." (Less typical was one held fifty years later by the white prohibitionists of Concord "for the colored people who voted with them in the local option election.") These days, however, victorious politicians don't seem to be as grateful. Indeed, some have started getting free barbecue from voters—like

Bladen County barbecue for legislators, 1939

Bill Ellis Barbecue in Wilson runs one of the state's largest catering operations. It owns twenty-five eighteen-wheelers set up as mobile kitchens and its own hog farm.

a recent free lunch for state legislators provided by hog producers lobbying against environmental regulations. Other incumbents have stopped giving barbecue away and begun to charge for it, like Representative Charles Taylor of Brevard, who held a $1,000-a-plate "North Carolina Bar-B-Que" in Washington in 1997. (The congressman knew his pork, as his earmarking record showed.)

Now that North Carolina seems to be getting back to eighteenth-century attitudes toward wagering, our politicians have begun to gamble in public, and they've found a new use for barbecue in the process. We don't think George Washington ever paid off a barbecue bet with actual barbecue, but Governor Mike Easley had to send some to Massachusetts governor Mitt Romney when the Panthers lost the Super Bowl in 2004.

In North Carolina, barbecue has even figured as a campaign issue. Rufus Edmisten learned a painful lesson when he ran for governor in 1984. "I'd be eating barbecue three times a day for a solid year," he recalled, "and I got up one night and, in a very, very lax moment—the devil made me do it—I made a horrible statement. I said, 'I'm through with barbecue.' Well, you would have thought I had made a speech against my mother, against apple pie, cherry pie, the whole mess." (He lost.) More recently, in 2002, after Republican senatorial candidate Elizabeth Dole boldly announced her preference for Lexington-style barbecue, Democrat Erskine Bowles—who had criticized Dole for ducking tough issues—wouldn't say what he preferred. (He lost, too.)

BARBECUE AND LABOR RELATIONS

Politicians aren't the only folks who try to win friends with barbecue. Bosses have long used 'cue to butter up their labor force. On large plantations Before the War, Guion Johnson writes, "many masters habitually gave corn huskings for the neighborhood slaves as a reward to their own hands for work well done during the planting season, and they were careful to provide bountifully of barbecue, whisky, and brandy. After the corn had been shucked and the food cleared, dancing would begin to the music of the fiddle and banjo." In 1901 James Battle Avirett wrote a rose-colored description of an antebellum barbecue on his family's Onslow County plantation:

"Cooking meat, barbecue style, among the long leaf pines of North Carolina," ca. 1891 (box appears to say "Manly, NC")

Too Sad to Eat Barbecue

Sarah Debro, a former slave on the Cain Plantation in Orange County interviewed in 1937, recalled a feast "when de sojers mustered" in 1861:

I was 'bout wais' high. . . . I can see dey feets now when dey flung dem up an' down, sayin', hep, hep. When dey was all ready to go an' fight, de women folks fixed a big dinner. Aunt Charity an' Pete cooked two or three days for Mis' Polly. De table was piled wid chicken, ham, shoat, barbecue, young lam', an all sorts of pies, cakes an' things, but nobody eat nothin much. Mis' Polly an' de ladies got to cryin'. De vittles got cold. I was so sad dat I got over in de corner an' cried too. De men folks all had on dey new sojer clothes, an' dey didn' eat nothin neither.

Beef, mutton and pork are in that happy process of plantation cookery known as barbecue, and are in great abundance. Such quantities of bread, wheat and corn, with bushels of sweet potatoes and great baskets of pies and cakes as to require a full staff of these natural born cooks. The carpenters are erecting the simple but substantial tables, and Aunt Daphne is unrolling yard after yard of homemade white cloth to serve as table covers. . . . My sakes! How busy was old Uncle Shadrac in barbecuing five or six whole hogs and halves of young bullocks, taking care to baste them well with a long handled mop that had been dipped into a pan of vinegar, salt and homegrown red pepper, so that there should be no lack of highly flavored seasoning.

Textile mills were at least as important in the economy of postwar North Carolina as plantations had been earlier, and among the similarities between the two institutions was the practice of rewarding workers from time to time with pit-cooked meat. In 1920

"Colored" serving and dining area, Braswell Plantation barbecue for tenant farmers, 1944

"No one who has had the good fortune to attend a barbecue will ever forget it. The smell of it all, the meat slowly roasting to a delicious brown over smoking fires, the hungry and happy crowds...." (Strand Magazine, London, 1898)

the *Mill News* ("The Great Southern Weekly for Textile Workers") wrote about the annual fish fry and barbecue at Kinston's Caswell Mill, asserting that "if you have never eaten barbecue cooked down in eastern Carolina you don't know what barbecue is" and that "readers who do not know these things must only be pitied for what they have missed." As on the old plantation, the barbecue may have been a partial substitute for wages. In any case, former governor O. Max Gardner, owner of the Cleveland Cloth Mill, held a "barbecue, dance and general love feast" in 1933 in an effort to head off unionization.

BARBECUE AND RELIGION

As the estimable Nathaniel Macon lay dying in Warren County, Manly Wade Wellman tells us, the word went out, "Let the Buck Springs cooks barbecue carcasses of pork and lamb for those who would attend, and let there be broached a barrel of that corn whiskey which Macon so long had enjoyed at mealtime." Barbecue was a common feature of antebellum funerals, often accompanied by the consolation of spirits. In *Sketches of North Carolina* (1846), the Reverend Henry Foote wrote that "to preserve the appearance of religion, someone [asked] a blessing on the refreshments prepared," but "the solemnity of the occasion was sometimes lost in the excitement, and scenes of drinking invaded the house of mourning." Alas, this practice seems to have died out almost completely, except among Episcopalians.

But barbecue still appears in various religious settings. Writing in 1851, George Higby Throop reported that North Carolina churchgoers often brought food from home for a "dinner on the ground" after services. The typical offerings included "bread, fowls, barbecue (roast shoat), bacon, vegetables, and, very commonly, a dessert; which are placed upon the rude tables." The custom of cooking barbecue at home and taking it to church is less common today than it was when folks faced a long wagon-ride home before Sunday dinner, but special occasions like homecomings and anniversaries are still excuses for covered-dish dinners and even full-fledged, on-site pit-cooking. (On one *really* special occasion in 1996, more than 130 people were treated for food poisoning after they went to view a collection of deer heads and eat barbecue at Greensboro's Calvary Baptist Church.)

Many churches have used barbecues as fund-raisers. Poplar Tent Presbyterian Church near Concord held one in 1946, starting with "a ditch in the ground [and] five hogs"; when "we cleared $80 from them five hogs," a spokesman reported, the event became annual. It continues to this day. But the biggest and best-known church barbecue in the state is put on each October by the Mallard Creek Presbyterian Church near Charlotte. First held in 1929 to pay for a Sunday school addition, the Mallard Creek gathering began with two hogs and a goat; now it serves some 15,000 pounds of pork, 2,500 gallons of Brunswick stew, and 2 tons of coleslaw to over 20,000 hungry visitors. A plate that once cost 50 cents will set you back $9.00 now, but the proceeds go to a variety of good causes. The late October date and the presence of so many potential voters have, naturally, made Mallard Creek an obligatory stop for campaigning politicians. James Villas describes his childhood memories of this

"*Barbecue is good for a lot of these communities. These Fire Department boys get together and will do barbecue and slaw, and churches have done it. People have fun doing it. It's a long span of time in there. You can get really drunk trying to do it.*" (Keith Allen, Allen & Son, Chapel Hill)

Politicians meet and greet at Mallard Creek.

"lavish spectacle": "The hog pits stretched thirty or more yards, and communal tables under a massive tent groaned with platters of chopped hickory-smoked pork barbecue, Brunswick stew, tangy coleslaw, and oozing pies and cakes, and politicians up for election from all over the state circulated, handing out fountain pens, calendars, and crazy little hats."

BARBECUE FOR OTHER GOOD CAUSES

But it's not just churches that use barbecue to raise money. Villas reports that when he was growing up in Charlotte, "we were constantly attending one benefit pork barbecue or pig pickin' after another at churches, schools, country clubs, and private homes." We looked at well over a thousand stories in North Carolina newspapers since 1985 that had the word "barbecue" in their headlines, and we found a wonderful panoply of fund-raising events. They ranged from high-toned affairs like the Greensboro Opera Company's "Barbecue of Seville" and Charlotte's Artists-in-the-Schools pig-picking and karaoke party to down-home gatherings like the Fairview Volunteer Fire Department's annual barbecue, which began

"Yard Sale and Barbecue Fight World Hunger." (Charlotte Observer headline)

A volunteer fire department lures travelers on Highway 52 near Pilot Mountain.

McDowell Technical Community College, Marion

It's not every institution of higher learning that has an official barbecue caterer, but Elon University engaged Huey's in Burlington to cater its events.

in the early 1970s (no one really remembers when) and serves up nearly two tons of pork each year. (The West Mecklenburg High School PTSA barbecue, which celebrated its sixtieth anniversary in 2008, now cooks about *five* tons.) Our favorite, though, has got to be the fund-raising barbecue put on by the Hemby Bridge Board of Aldermen in lieu of a tax increase.

The truth is that in North Carolina almost anything can be—and probably has been—accompanied by a barbecue. In 1852 20,000 people ate, danced, and watched fireworks on the grounds of the Female Academy to celebrate the arrival of the first passenger train in Charlotte. The *Franklin Observer* told of a barbecue held in 1860 to

A high point of the Wilmington Azalea Festival is a barbecue for patrons, sponsors, volunteers, The Citadel's Summerall Guards, the Queen's and Princess's Court, and the horde of Azalea Belles.

That noted barbecue-lover George Washington was the first president-general of the Society of the Cincinnati, now an organization for direct male descendants of Revolutionary War officers. When the society held its national meeting in Asheville in 1917, members were treated to a barbecue lunch and given corncob pipes and leaf tobacco. When the Cincinnati returned to North Carolina in 1971, President-General Armistead Jones Maupin provided a classier barbecue lunch, this one at Orton Plantation. Mrs. Maupin wrote this description:

> White-coated colored folks everywhere. And then the repast: Oh, that outdoor Low Country eating! And on china plates—with silver—and huge linen napkins! Great bowls of marinated creek shrimp, lean pig barbecue, sliced tomatoes and Bermuda onions, cole slaw, hush puppies, corn sticks, pecan cookies, Spanish moss—Oh, no! That was on the trees!

watch the odd spectacle of Indian ball play "by twenty-four Cherokee Indians in Turkish costume." In 1905 a Davidson County man who killed his brother-in-law and escaped the gallows, then narrowly escaped assassination, celebrated with a barbecue for 150 friends. After a 1921 community rabbit hunt in Oak Ridge, according to the *Greensboro Daily News*, there was "a splendid barbecue and Brunswick stew." More recently, Delton Burnett fixed 200 pounds of barbecue, 200 pounds of ribs, 350 pounds of chicken, and 350 pounds of fish for a family reunion of more than a thousand people in Fayetteville, and every year Special Forces vets hold a barbecue somewhere in the state to reminisce with their former comrades, the Montagnards—appropriate, since North Carolina has both Fort Bragg and the largest "Yard" community outside Vietnam.

BARBECUE FOR BARBECUE'S SAKE

Finally—it had to happen eventually—North Carolinians who've always celebrated with barbecue started holding barbecues to celebrate barbecue. The granddaddy of these events began in 1984, when some 30,000 people consumed a ton and a half of barbecue at the first Lexington Barbecue Festival. These days at the late-October event, 5 times as many people eat 12 times as much 'cue, while being entertained from 5 stages and perusing the offerings of over 400 sellers of everything from crafts to candy. In 2002 roughly 1,150 pigs gave their all—anyway, 2 shoulders each—to produce the necessary pork. (Five thousand hot dogs were also sold that year. But why?)

A landmark episode in barbecue history occurred in 1995 when the annual (Eastern-style) North Carolina Championship Pork Cook-Off was held in conjunction with the Lexington festival. Although everyone agreed that this fraternal gathering was a success, it has not been repeated—and when a bill was introduced in 2005 to make the Lexington event North Carolina's "official barbecue festival," sharp-eyed Easterners squelched the proposal. (They let Lexington be the state's "official food festival" instead.)

These days dozens of festivals, competitions, and cook-offs take place in North Carolina each year—there were at least thirteen in October and November 2007 alone, from Kitty Hawk to Morganton. Some are more faithful to tradition than others (see page 287),

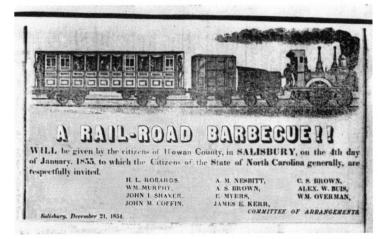

A RAIL-ROAD BARBECUE!!

WILL be given by the citizens of Rowan County, in **SALISBURY**, on the 4th day of January, 1855, to which the Citizens of the State of **North Carolina** generally, are respectfully invited.

H. L. ROBARDS,	A. M. NESBITT,	C. S. BROWN,
WM. MURPHY,	A. S. BROWN,	ALEX. W. BUIS,
JOHN I. SHAVER,	E. MYERS,	WM. OVERMAN,
JOHN M. COFFIN,	JAMES E. KERR,	
		COMMITTEE OF ARRANGEMENTS.

Salisbury, December 21, 1854.

Twelve thousand people at a Good Roads Barbecue, Yanceyville, 1920

but there's no denying that some pretty good barbecue and much good fun is regularly on offer. At Hillsborough's annual Hog Day, for instance, upwards of 35,000 folks cook pork shoulders, eat pickled pig's feet, throw hams, and carve Spam. Perhaps the most focused of these events was held in Elizabeth City in 2003, when Grizz Rader of Weeksville won the first ever World Championship of BBQ Eating by scarfing four large sandwiches in the allotted three minutes. ("I don't feel hungry anymore," he said afterward.)

EXPORTING THE PIG-PICKING

Now and then, expatriate Tar Heels have tried to introduce their new neighbors to the splendors of a North Carolina–style barbecue. Hillsborough restaurateur Sam Hobgood once trucked 4,000 servings of barbecue to Ottawa, for instance, for a Fourth of July party held by the U.S. ambassador and his wife (both Duke alums), and Corbette Capps from Warren County has cooked for homesick former North Carolinians on the Mall in Washington and the campus of St. John's College in Santa Fe. Some even work the mission field more or less full-time, like Mike Page from Winston-Salem, whose catering business brings the gospel to the heathens of Charleston, South Carolina. Alas, sometimes these efforts are wasted. When King's of Kinston served its barbecue at the Republican National Convention in 1992, Texan Rick Perry (later governor) observed, "I've had road kill that tasted better than that." We'd say "pearls before swine," but we like swine. Nevertheless, it is here in the Old North State that our barbecue is truly appreciated. Where else but North Carolina would you find a story like this one from the *Charlotte Observer*? The items attracting the highest bids at a 1988 Charlotte charity auction were a weekend in Paris and a pig-picking at Sheriff C. W. Kidd's ranch.

25TH ANNUAL
HILLSBOROUGH
HOG DAY
2

23RD ANNUAL
NC CHAMPIONSHIP BBQ COOKOFF

Blue Ridge
BBQ
FESTIVAL

FEAST
in the East
A Celebration of Eastern NC Bar-B-Que
Goldsboro
NC

Hog Happnin'
BIKES
CARS
BARBECUE

ROCKABILLY BBQ

HICKORY
SMOKE
3rd SmoKin'
MAY 26·27, 2006
BARBEQUE FESTIVAL

The North Carolina Museum of History's online "History Highlights" has two entries for 1924: the founding of Duke University and the opening of Bob Melton's Barbecue in Rocky Mount. It's not clear why Duke gets equal billing. North Carolina already had a university, after all, while Melton's, on the banks of the Tar River in Rocky Mount, seems to have been the state's very first sit-down barbecue restaurant. (It closed in 2003 after an unsuccessful relocation when the original place was destroyed by Hurricane Floyd.)

Until the twentieth century, barbecue was usually served at big gatherings on special occasions and cooked by specialist pitmasters, either enslaved or volunteer. Some made the rounds of such events and were paid for their expertise, but the costs were borne by the civic organizations, politicians, or prominent citizens who sponsored the barbecues. By the turn of the century, though, some of these barbecue men had begun to sell their product off the backs of wagons or from temporary stands or tents at places like courthouse squares, or tobacco warehouses at auction time. Soon the automobile made it possible to open more permanent businesses. Instead of going to where their customers were celebrating, attending court, or selling their tobacco, barbecue men could let their customers come to them.

Some just put up buildings downtown, more or less where their stands had been. The early joints on Greensboro Alley in Lexington show why this made sense. They replaced temporary stands that had sold barbecue to folks from downtown businesses and the courthouse across the street, and they still got that walk-in business. They were just behind the Conrad and Hinkle grocery and butcher shop, so they didn't need big refrigerators. And they could offer curb service—literally. In his memoir *Barbecue, Lexington Style*, Johnny Stogner wrote about "catching curb" in the early days: Curb boys from the restaurants on opposite sides of the alley competed to catch customers as they drove up or parked in the nearby municipal lot. (Many places in Lexington and elsewhere in the Piedmont

"*Sampson Anderson and Dick Hinton, of Wake County, and Arnold Sasser, of Wayne, all sons of old slaves belonging to aristocratic North Carolina families, were famous barbecuers in their day and served their communities for many years.*"
(*Jane McKimmon, writing in 1931*)

An 1893 ordinance in Kinston charged "barbecue dealers" an annual tax of five dollars for each "stand or table" and prohibited the sale of barbecue on Queen Street.

Bob Melton's after Hurricane Floyd, 1999: the waters have receded, but the damage was fatal.

John "Jack" Lynch at his barbecue stand, Wayne County, date unknown

still offer curb service, although these days you often have to honk to get it.)

Similar restaurants were emerging all over the South, but they really took off in North Carolina. By mid-century, scores of unpretentious eating places offered their communities' versions of barbecue when desired, or at least on weekends. As with so much else, however, things in the East and in the Piedmont were slightly different.

When a new parkway doomed Merritt's House of Bar-B-Que, a fixture on Wilmington's Fourth Street for twenty-eight years, the Cape Fear Museum retrieved a red Formica booth for its permanent collection.

Stamey's old pits, still behind the restaurant on Greensboro Alley

EASTERN-STYLE

In the East, the emergence of barbecue restaurants was largely a matter of individual entrepreneurs deciding more or less independently to give the business a try. There was a rough division of labor along racial lines. Although a few respected black pitmasters opened their own places, most of these restaurateurs were white. On the other hand, most of the cooks were black (although some were white men with family barbecuing traditions, like Pete Jones of Ayden). Whatever the races of owner and cook, however, the appetite for good barbecue transcended the color line.

Almost every Eastern-style place has its own idiosyncratic story. In Goldsboro, for example, the Reverend Adam Scott, a black Holiness preacher, started selling barbecue to customers of both races out his back door about 1917. Soon they started eating it on his porch, so he closed the porch in and called it a restaurant—probably the second one in the East, after Bob Melton's. Adam Scott's barbecue became so famous that he was invited to the White House to cook for Franklin Roosevelt. The restaurant is still in business, now run by Reverend Scott's grandson.

Another Eastern-style place that "just growed" was one of the most westerly. Josh Turnage, a white boy from Farmville who worked as a cotton buyer for Erwin Mills in Durham, started cook-

Separate but Equal

Ironically, black-owned Scott's in Goldsboro offered seating for white customers only, until a separate "black" dining room was built in the 1940s. Before the 1960s barbecue restaurants—like other public accommodations in North Carolina—were segregated by law. Like Scott's, the largest often had separate seating for blacks and whites. The place Warner Stamey built in Lexington about 1940 did, after he or his successor added a room next door for black customers. Others had tables only for whites but offered takeout service at a side window or back door for blacks—or vice versa. A few scoff-laws seated friends of the "wrong" race more or less surreptitiously: as early as the 1940s, for example, Pete Simos let blacks from his Winston-Salem neighborhood eat inside at Simos Barbecue Inn (now closed).

The Civil Rights Act of 1964 put an end to "whites-only" (and, for that matter, "blacks-only") restaurants. Some North Carolina places complied cheerfully, even anticipating the legislation—Turnage's Barbecue Place was the first white-owned restaurant in Durham to desegregate, for instance, in May 1963. Others were more grudging (although none was as reluctant as

Times have changed at Bum's, Ayden.

Ollie's Barbecue in Birmingham or Maurice Bessinger's Piggy Park in Columbia, which provided test cases for the Civil Rights Act that reached the Supreme Court).

These days there are still "mostly white" and "mostly black" establishments, but this results from individual customers' choices, not law or restaurant policy. One white Lexington barbecue man told us that most of his black customers still get takeout, which he finds puzzling. But many barbecue places these days are happily and unselfconsciously salt-and-pepper, a good deal more integrated than most other places of worship.

ing Pitt County–style whole-hog barbecue for his friends at home. Soon he was doing it most Thursdays ("maids' night out" for Durham's white community). When friends of friends and complete strangers started turning up, he started selling it: all you cared to eat was 75 cents for men, 50 cents for ladies. Eventually he built a place to sell it—still just on Thursdays. After the Second World War, he sold Turnage's Barbecue Place to Jim Warren, a young veteran who had worked for him before the war. Soon Warren built a new, larger place up the road. Until it closed in 1970, its family-style service was popular with students and faculty from Duke's medical school and with musicians from Durham and Chapel Hill.

Duke medical school trustees eat family-style at Turnage's in the 1960s

PIEDMONT-STYLE

The emergence of Piedmont-style barbecue restaurants was more organized (and better documented). For the most part, it's a story of masters and apprentices, gurus and disciples, a sort of genealogical descent from a handful of founding fathers. Around the time of the First World War, a few men who had been cooking for special occasions gradually got into the business of running barbecue stands. Bob Garner points out that the recorded history of "Lexington-style" barbecue places actually begins in Salisbury, where records show that John Blackwelder added a barbecue pit to his taxi stand in 1918 and started selling barbecued pork loin. Garner writes that "the popularity of Blackwelder's barbecue . . . is said to have quickly spread far and wide due to word-of-mouth reports from the railway workers who became customers as they traveled up and down the line. But of course the same line runs through Lexington."

Maybe earlier, maybe not, Sid Weaver and George Ridenhour set up their tent near the Lexington courthouse (see page 34) and started selling barbecued shoulders when court was in session. Soon Jess Swicegood set up a competing tent, and soon after that, both establishments were relocated to the more permanent sheds that later evolved into those Greensboro Alley restaurants. In the

Sid Weaver (left) in his cement
block restaurant

"The Original Lexington
Barbecue" is now Hill's.

late 1920s, a high-school student named Warner Stamey came to work for Swicegood, learned the craft, and went on to start his own place in Shelby in 1930. Stamey came back to Lexington for a while before opening his landmark place, which is still smoking in Greensboro. Along the way, Stamey trained, among others, Alston Bridges (his brother-in-law) and Red Bridges (no relation) of Shelby and Wayne Monk of Lexington, who trained still others and opened their own famous barbecue places, still cooking.

In fact, it's hard to find a Piedmont-style barbecue restaurateur who has not received the laying-on of hands in this apostolic succession. In 2006 at least eighteen of twenty-two places in Lexington and vicinity were, or had been, run by someone who had worked for someone who had worked for someone . . . who had worked for one of the founding fathers. The same was true for at least another dozen restaurants in at least seven other Piedmont towns, from Shelby in the south to Reidsville in the north. In Winston-Salem, for example, after Joe Allen Hill read in the newspaper that folks were driving to Lexington for lunch, he hired four men who had been working at barbecue restaurants in Lexington to cook for him and in 1950 opened Lexington Bar-B-Q (now Hill's Lexington Barbecue) on Highway 52 north of town. Soon T. H. "Fuzzy" Nelson showed up at Mr. Hill's place to learn the craft, then opened his eponymous place in Madison in 1954. (We're not about to write the definitive history of Lexington-style barbecue joints, but if you want to do it, we've made a start on the next page.)

IS "B" FOR BARBECUE?

As early as 1920, the Christmas Day menu at Gastonia's New York Café offered a choice of turkey or "roast barbecue pig," with applesauce, and you can still find barbecue on the menus of restaurants ranging from down-home meat-and-threes like the Mecca in Raleigh to country buffets like Fuller's in Lumberton to upscale New Southern cuisineries like Crook's Corner in Chapel Hill. You can even find it in the food court at Charlotte Douglas International Airport. But these are places that either cook it off-site or buy it in bulk from suppliers who cook it. We're talking here about *barbecue restaurants*, where the barbecue is what it's all (or mostly) about, places that cook their own, usually out back. Some aren't too nice to be called "joints," but most are, and that's interesting.

Barbecue fans from other states are likely to wax rhapsodic about the meat from places with sagging screen doors, smoke-blackened walls, toothless proprietors, and flies—the more the better. One of Vince Staten's rules for a good barbecue place is the presence of those flies: If there aren't any, you should ask what the flies know that you don't.

It's certainly true that a sanitation grade of A *can* be a bad sign. B ratings should be worn with pride if cooking with wood is the reason, and sometimes it is. County "environmental health" inspectors don't exactly forbid wood cooking, but according to Bob Garner, it's an almost automatic three- or four-point deduction,

"The typical barbecue restaurant is full of cigarette smoke. Look at the patrons. Is this where you are headed if you continue to eat barbecue?"
(Cam Hill in the Chapel Hill Herald)

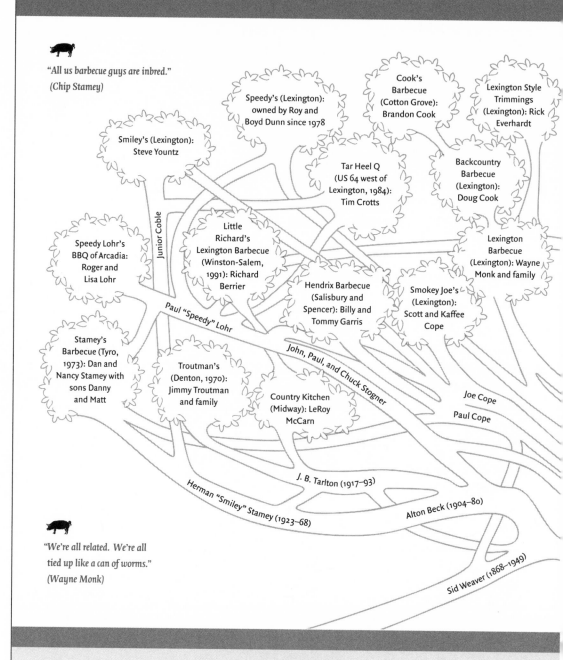

"All us barbecue guys are inbred."
(Chip Stamey)

Speedy's (Lexington): owned by Roy and Boyd Dunn since 1978

Cook's Barbecue (Cotton Grove): Brandon Cook

Lexington Style Trimmings (Lexington): Rick Everhardt

Smiley's (Lexington): Steve Yountz

Tar Heel Q (US 64 west of Lexington, 1984): Tim Crotts

Backcountry Barbecue (Lexington): Doug Cook

Junior Coble

Speedy Lohr's BBQ of Arcadia: Roger and Lisa Lohr

Little Richard's Lexington Barbecue (Winston-Salem, 1991): Richard Berrier

Hendrix Barbecue (Salisbury and Spencer): Billy and Tommy Garris

Lexington Barbecue (Lexington): Wayne Monk and family

Smokey Joe's (Lexington): Scott and Kaffee Cope

Paul "Speedy" Lohr

Stamey's Barbecue (Tyro, 1973): Dan and Nancy Stamey with sons Danny and Matt

Troutman's (Denton, 1970): Jimmy Troutman and family

John, Paul, and Chuck Stogner

Country Kitchen (Midway): LeRoy McCarn

Joe Cope

Paul Cope

Herman "Smiley" Stamey (1923–68)

J. B. Tarlton (1917–93)

Alton Beck (1904–80)

Sid Weaver (1868–1949)

"We're all related. We're all tied up like a can of worms."
(Wayne Monk)

LEXINGTON BARBECUE

Briarpatch

This briarpatch has been severely pruned to include mostly owner-pitmasters, and not even all of those. The definitive history—including every building with pits, every change in ownership, and every change of restaurant name—has yet to be written, and this information is

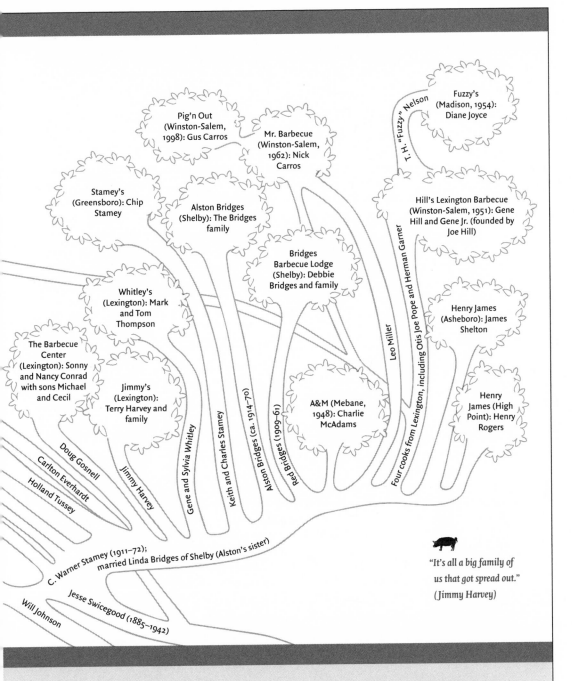

Pig'n Out (Winston-Salem, 1998): Gus Carros

Mr. Barbecue (Winston-Salem, 1962): Nick Carros

Fuzzy's (Madison, 1954): Diane Joyce

T. H. "Fuzzy" Nelson

Stamey's (Greensboro): Chip Stamey

Alston Bridges (Shelby): The Bridges family

Bridges Barbecue Lodge (Shelby): Debbie Bridges and family

Hill's Lexington Barbecue (Winston-Salem, 1951): Gene Hill and Gene Jr. (founded by Joe Hill)

Whitley's (Lexington): Mark and Tom Thompson

Henry James (Asheboro): James Shelton

The Barbecue Center (Lexington): Sonny and Nancy Conrad with sons Michael and Cecil

Jimmy's (Lexington): Terry Harvey and family

A&M (Mebane, 1948): Charlie McAdams

Henry James (High Point): Henry Rogers

Leo Miller

Four cooks from Lexington, including Otis Joe Pope and Herman Garner

Doug Gosnell

Carlton Everhardt

Holland Tussey

Jimmy Harvey

Gene and Sylvia Whitley

Keith and Charles Stamey

Alston Bridges (ca. 1914–70)

Red Bridges (1909–61)

C. Warner Stamey (1911–72); married Linda Bridges of Shelby (Alston's sister)

Jesse Swicegood (1885–1942)

Will Johnson

"It's all a big family of us that got spread out."
(Jimmy Harvey)

probably already out of date. The most common story is that people began by "catching curb," gradually learned the business, and started their own businesses or bought out their mentors. It should be understood that this is usually a family business, with wives and children part of the team.

Disclaimer: The inclusion of a restaurant in this tree does not necessarily mean that it still cooks with wood.

Fuller's steam table. This is just a start—salads and desserts get their own tables.

The Greek Connection

A great many seafood restaurants and meat-and-threes in twentieth-century North Carolina were operated by Greek Americans, although often there was no way to tell from the menu except maybe for the presence of a Greek salad. Given their experience in running small restaurants, it's not surprising to find a good many Hellenes operating barbecue establishments as well. In Concord, for instance, the Red Pig Café offered "BBQ, Greek and American cuisine" from 1945 until it closed recently. In Charlotte you'll find pictures of Greece on the walls and baklava on the menu at the Ole Smokehouse #1; Art's Barbecue and Deli has been in business since Art Katopodis opened it in 1976; and the Bar-B-Q King, with its classic drive-in architecture, has been run by Pete Gianniks since 1972. In Winston-Salem Pericles Apostolos "Pete" Simos opened Simos Barbecue Inn near Reynolds Tobacco in 1939 (his son Paul

ran this favorite hangout for Wake Forest students until it closed in 2003); Nick Karagiorgis was a partner in Little Richard's Barbecue on Stratford Road until he moved on to the Country Kitchen in Midway; and at one point recently Nick Carros ran Mr. Barbecue (founded by Tom Gallos in 1952), son Jimmy operated Pig Pickin's, and brother Gus owned Pig'n Out. In Wilmington, Mike Kyriakoudes ran Mike's BBQ until he retired in 1999, and Greek-owned, despite its name, Skinner and Daniels was on Market Street until a Wal-Mart was built on the site.

so if anything else is wrong, you wind up losing your A. The late Murray's Bar-B-Q in Raleigh, probably the last log-burner in Wake County, used to average a B, and we never heard of anyone getting sick there. Retired Chapel Hill English professor Jerry Leath Mills recalls his teenage years catching curb at Burlington's Oak Grove Café: "Everything was as clean as you please . . . , but we never got an A rating because the hand-washing sink was outside the toilets, rather than conveniently enclosed with the other facilities. The boss once pointed out to the inspector that this arrangement kept people from peeing in the sink, but to no avail."

The Red Pig in Concord used to sport its C rating as a badge of honor. That may be overdoing it, but don't worry too much about a B. On the other hand, let's not get carried away here. The correlation between funk and flavor seems to be weaker in North Carolina than elsewhere in the South. Most of our favorite North Carolina barbecue places—wood-burners all—manage to maintain an A rating, and in all but a couple of the hundred or so places we've visited, the after-church crowd would feel right at home (that is, if they were open after church: more than two-thirds of the places in *Bob Garner's Guide to North Carolina Barbecue* close on Sundays). Many good places are on the rustic side and a handful might qualify as funky, but they're almost all clean and tidy, as are the folks who serve you.

Wilber "Pete" Caldwell is the author of a celebration of down-home barbecue called *Searching for the Dixie Barbecue*, and we asked him why North Carolina developed differently from, say, Georgia. Caldwell speculates that you find fewer of "the old rundown places" because North Carolina barbecue places are longer-lived, and "as they grow older and more successful, they seem to expand and re-model with a great deal more savoir faire" than do places in the Deep South. He notes that many "Friday–Saturday-only places (the purer mom-and-pop tradition)" can still be found in other states, while North Carolina places that began that way have either evolved into more stable (and more presentable) restaurants or gone out of business.

B's in Greenville might seem to be an exception. "A throwback [to] what North Carolina was before modernity caught up with it,"

When the Hard Rock Café's lawyers got on Stamey's Bar-B-Que in Tyro about its "Hog Rock Café" T-shirts, a sympathizer observed, "No one is going to go into Hog Rock Café and be disappointed if Jimi Hendrix's jockstrap isn't hanging from the ceiling."

The Barbecue Lodge in Raleigh used to have a customer who came in, alone, every Saturday night near closing time and ordered four dinners, which he ate, one after the other. No one ever knew why.

as Peter Batke describes it, B's is about as down-home as North Carolina barbecue places get. It's small and simple, has no telephone, and closes when the barbecue runs out (so get there early). There are no waitresses, just a line at the counter. From the outside, it looks like a classic Southern barbecue joint. But you don't have to reconcile yourself to sacrificing a little hygiene for the sake of great smoke-cooked pork: After you stand in a line out the door for a while, you go inside and see that it's spotless. The last time we were there, we ate with a couple of lawyer-types in ties, some ladies who lunch, some working folks, and the sheriff—just a whole lot of hungry people from all walks of life.

In other states, grubby places in dodgy neighborhoods with

When the IRS investigated B's Barbecue because its expenditure on meat looked high for its reported sales, B's was able to prove that it discarded 45 percent more scrap than the average barbecue restaurant.

Keaton's sells beer, but you only get two.

scary customers can have great barbecue, but in North Carolina most barbecue restaurants aren't like that, and none of the great ones are. They're places to take the kids, and they offer an indoor continuation of the community-barbecue tradition, serving all sorts and conditions of men and women. What Wilber Shirley says of his Goldsboro establishment is true of nearly all of them: "It's nice enough and clean enough that anyone would feel welcome to come, but not so nice a working person or family wouldn't be comfortable." It may also help that only a handful of true North Carolina barbecue places serve beer.

Sign outside Bland's Barbecue: "Serving lunch, dinner, Gaston County, and Jesus Christ."

WHAT MAKES A GREAT PLACE

If you're looking for a first-rate barbecue place and don't have a reliable guide, here are some tips.

It's almost a cliché among barbecue writers that a mix of pickup trucks and expensive imports in the parking lot is a good sign. If everyone in town eats there, why shouldn't you? If the sheriff's car is there, hit your brakes immediately.

"Go about a half-mile and on the right-hand side you'll see all the cars and the most damn smoke you ever seen in your life." (Rodney "Country Boy" Cannon, giving directions to Murray's, Raleigh)

The outside can be—in fact, should be—unprepossessing. The absence of a visible woodpile isn't necessarily fatal (it may be in a shed or otherwise under cover to keep it dry, and some pretty good places have gone over to charcoal briquettes), but if there's a woodpile and it's not just for show (check for cobwebs), you may

---

US 70: Carolina's Corridor of 'Cue

The North Carolina Barbecue Society has designated a number of establishments as stops on a "historic barbecue trail." To be included—and to remain—on the trail, an establishment must (1) pit-cook with wood or charcoal, (2) use its own sauce, (3) have been in business for at least fifteen years, (4) offer a "sit down dining experience," and (5) be held in "high esteem [by] its community, the barbecue industry and barbecue aficionados." Those aficionados may quibble with a few selections and omissions, some may not like the fact that gas or electric assistance seems to be acceptable, and selections were limited to a maximum of two per town (which is a little hard on Lexington), but this list is a great place to start a barbecue pilgrimage. For driving directions and more information on each of the places, go to the society's website: www.ncbbqsociety.com/trail.html.

Should you undertake that pilgrimage, it will be made easier by the odd fact that of the twenty-five original places on the trail, in twenty-one towns, only Herb's in Murphy is more than thirty-five miles as the crow flies from old US 70.

Little Richard's in Winston-Salem smells wonderful.

When filmmaker Oliver Stone spoke at Duke, he was taken to Bullock's in Durham for barbecue. At last report, his photo had not gone on the wall with those of Dolly Parton, Catfish Hunter, Garth Brooks, and Burt Reynolds.

be in the presence of greatness. Obviously billowing smoke rates a stop.

Inside, the décor should be on the utilitarian side. Gumball machines by the entrance are a good sign: As Alan Richman observes, they mean the owner is a good citizen who is willing to help local civic clubs with their projects. Some decoration is all right. Pictures and figurines of pigs are fine, as are products of the taxidermist's art. Old advertising signs are acceptable if they've always been there (but not if they came from the antique mall). Photographs of obscure celebrities like the local TV weatherman are okay, too. There's nothing wrong with paper plates and napkins, or even plastic forks and knives.

Basically, you're looking for a place where the focus is on the food, not the setting. As Jim Auchmutey describes the classic, it's "a decidedly downscale affair with red checkered tablecloths, knotty pine paneling darkened by smoke and grease, and a sign out front

North Carolina Barbecue Out of State

Scores of places around the country serve something called "North Carolina barbecue," sometimes in unlikely settings and often with weird side dishes. Blue-Ribbon Bar-B-Q in Boston, for instance, serves "North Carolina pulled pork" with sides that include "black-eyed corn [sic]" and garlic mashed potatoes. In general, traveling Tar Heels would be well advised to sample local cuisines on the road and eat their barbecue back home.

A few places run by expatriate North Carolinians are worth a look-in, though. The barbecue might be at least OK, and the side dishes and accents could be right. Two New York institutions illustrate the range of possibilities, and offer quite different versions of what the Old North State is about.

Brother Jimmy's was founded by Duke and UNC alumni in 1988 on the Upper East Side of Manhattan as a home-away-from-home for graduates of the old ACC schools, offering barbecue, televised basketball, and a 25 percent discount to customers with a valid Southern ID on Wednesdays ("Southern Appreciation Night"). It has evolved into what was recently rated by Zagat's as the seventh most popular New York nightspot and now has five locations in the city,

including a fast-food operation at Grand Central Station. BJ's has been described as "New York's unofficial North Carolina consulate" and "a cross between Hooters and a frat party." These days the food seems to be less important than the bar scene (loud, crowded, with inebriated dancing on the bar—you get the picture), but the place still pays verbal homage to the "legendary Carolina slow-smokin' BBQ joints" that inspired it, and the owners do claim to slow-cook with hickory pellets in commercial smokers.

Over on the edge of Brooklyn's Bedford Stuyvesant, meanwhile, the Carolina Country Kitchen has been a bright spot in a bad neighborhood since 1988, and the North Carolina Country Store across the street has been there even longer. Both had their origins in 1970 when owner Patricia Lee's father, George, began weekly trips from his Duplin County farm to Brooklyn, hauling Southern vegetables to sell off the back of his truck. This business gradually developed into the present store and a cafeteria that serves downhome delicacies like fried chicken, braised oxtails, macaroni and cheese, potato salad, collard greens, cornbread, sweet potato pie, and (of course) barbecue. The vegetables are still brought in regularly from North Carolina—and so is the barbecue. "To get the Southern taste here is kind of hard," Ms. Lee observes.

showing a smiling pig that seems to be inexplicably happy about its contribution to the menu." Actually, as far as we're concerned, you can forget the tablecloths. We agree with Tony Moore of Clyde Cooper's in Raleigh: "A true barbecue place is supposed to look like a barbecue place—nothing fancy, just four walls and a roof. Get some tables and some booths, and that's all you need to run a barbecue business."

The same goes for the menu. As a general rule, the fewer items a place offers, the better the barbecue is likely to be. You want a *barbecue place*, not just a place that serves barbecue. Greensboro's

B's keeps its menu simple.

BBQ		CHICKEN	
PLATE	5.35	DINNER	6.95
DINNER	6.15	HALF OF	
SANDWICH	2.95	CHICKEN	4.80
POUND	6.40		
		WHOLE	8.50
COMBINATION-BBQ &			
CHICKEN		DRINKS & TEA	1.25
DARK	8.50	PINT	
WHITE	8.50	SLAW	2.00
LARGE	10.00	POT	
		GREEN BEANS	

When Dom DeLuise was on the rice diet at Duke University, he fell off the wagon long enough to visit Clyde Cooper's.

"With scores of side dish imposters suddenly mucking up the elegant brevity of traditional barbecue menus, many Southerners have become a bit disoriented." (Wilber W. Caldwell)

Chip Stamey observes that "if you do fewer things, you can do them better." Most places that serve Brunswick stew and chicken *with* barbecue will let you order the stew or the fowl as a main dish, if you really want to. Much beyond that, though, and we get suspicious. In truth, we agree with Jason Sheehan's observation that "any place with a menu longer than can fit on a single page—or better yet, just a chalkboard—is coming dangerously close to putting on airs." Again, we like the attitude at Clyde Cooper's, where Tony Moore said once, "Many trendy restaurants have menus so large it takes you fifteen minutes to read them. Here, you can read the menu and be done eating in fifteen minutes. Some days I catch myself fussing with the menu and then ask, 'Why?'" It's an especially bad sign when the menu aspires to "gourmet" status. Good country cooking just *may* be acceptable, but if you encounter goat cheese or spinach salad, watch out.

You should bear in mind that some of the best places in the state break some of these rules, and one or two break all of them. But if all these indicators are in place, you're likely to be in for a great barbecultural experience.

North Carolina Barbecue in Fiction

"He'd cook what people felt homesick for—[like] that wonderful vinegary North Carolina barbecue that Todd Ducken had to have brought by his mother several times a year in cardboard cups."
—Anne Tyler, Dinner at the Homesick Restaurant

You can't spit in North Carolina without hitting a novelist. Heck, you can't spit without hitting a prize-winning novelist. And barbecue's as ubiquitous in North Carolina fiction as it is in real life. Asked what kind of food he wants, a character in Clyde Edgerton's *Killer Diller* replies, "A barbecue with slaw, a bag of nachos, and a Mello Yello." The "Hot Hats" barbecue chain pops up repeatedly in the works of Hillsborough writer Michael Malone: all the roofs have red neon pigs tipping top hats, and we learn in *First Lady* that "the damn phone number spelled out HOT PIGS." A character in Lee Smith's *Last Girls* issues the invitation, "Why don't you come on down, too, and pick up some barbecue on the way, will you? And some hushpuppies, you know, the works?"

The surprisingly many mysteries set in North Carolina nearly all bring in barbecue for local odor. In Lillian Jackson Braun's *Cat Who Smelled a Rat*, a shop called the Pet Plaza "occupied the former premises of Chet's Barbecue"; its owner "assumed that lingering aromas of roasting meat might add to its success." Sarah Shaber puts 'cue in nearly all her novels; a character in *The Bug Funeral*, for instance, announces that while his wife is out of town, he's "going to watch ESPN, and drink bourbon and ginger ale, and eat barbecue and banana puddin' all day long." The narrator of Margaret Maron's *Storm Track* has a "cousin Steve [who] runs a barbecue house down Highway 48, a little ways past the farm, and it's the best barbecue in Colleton County." In Toni L. P. Kelner's *Wed and Buried*, characters go to "Pigwick's Barbecue for Eastern North Carolina–style pulled pork." The Red Pig in Concord figures, thinly disguised, in Jewel Deane Love Suddath's *Murder in Harmony* as "the closest thing to a pub we have. . . . Not that you can get a beer there. You go to Hub's on the outskirts of town for that. What Mabel serves you is a 10-ounce glass of ice tea and a plate of the best barbecue in North Carolina." In *St. Dale*, Sharyn McCrumb writes about "a shrine to Dale Earnhardt" that had "the usual barbecue restaurant ornaments: cartoon pig statues on shelves, and signed publicity stills of celebrity patrons, mostly of Nashville singers passing through on the way to gigs in Charlotte, but besides this standard fare, the pine-paneled walls were dedicated to the Intimidator."

We don't have nearly as many science-fiction as mystery writers, but in *The Folk of the Fringe*, Orson Scott Card has two characters wandering through a post–nuclear war North Carolina; "they could hear, not that far off, the crackling of a fire and folks laughing and talking. 'Mobbers?' whispered Pete. 'Barbecue,' said Teague."

Our favorite barbecue reference in all of North Carolina literature, though, is in *Farewell, I'm Bound to Leave You*, by Greensboro's illustrious man of letters, Fred Chappell. The narrator's father, telling of a dream of Judgment Day, concludes, "Well, if it's Saint Peter and the Archangel Michael and God Himself and Judge Lynch thrown in, I've got a slim chance, but if it is your mother and grandmother sitting on the bench, my ass is hickory-smoked Carolina barbecue."

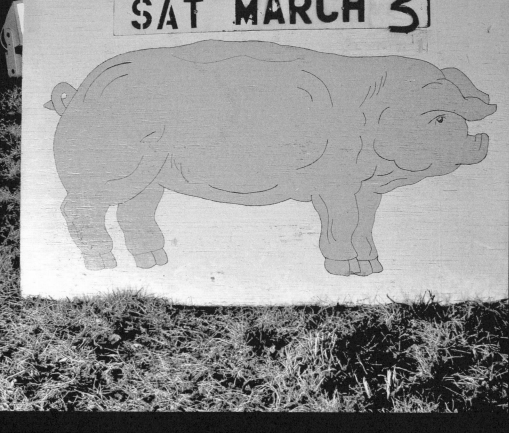

n *The Physiology of Taste* (1825), Jean Anthelme Brillat-Savarin wrote the discouraging words, "On devient cuisinier mais on naît rôtisseur"—roughly, "One becomes a cook, but one is born a pitmaster." Maybe so, but still, anyone can cook pretty good barbecue at home. And the way commercial barbecue operations are closing down or starting to cut corners, to get real North Carolina barbecue you may soon have to do just that. Even now, you ought to know how it's done the old-fashioned way, just so you'll appreciate the places that still take the trouble—and be willing to pay the higher prices that may be necessary to keep them in business.

We're going to assume that you've never cooked real barbecue before. If you have, and are happy with the results, you can skip this part. In fact, please do. If you know what you're doing, you may wind up throwing our book across the room in disgust, and we don't want that.

Although we're going to tell you how to do it, the problem is that there are reputable, sometimes renowned, pitmasters who would tell you something different at each and every step. Literally, each and every one. We know this, okay? But rather than give you all the alternatives and the arguments pro and con, we'll usually just tell you how *we* do it. After you've got that down, there are plenty of other books and innumerable websites that will tell you why our way's not the right way.

The upside of all this disagreement is that it's hard to go wrong. Don't serve it raw, and don't burn it up, but whatever else you do or fail to do, you're likely to wind up with something that tastes pretty good. Good barbecue is hard work, but it's not rocket science. *Great* barbecue may be another story, but you'll have to work up to that.

North Carolina barbecue comes in many forms. In the Piedmont it can be sliced, down east sometimes it's minced, anywhere it can be roughly chopped or "pulled" with forks or fingers, but that's all *after* it's been cooked. You start with pork shoulders or a whole hog. That's the Tar Heel Way: not ribs (by themselves), not brisket or

Brillat-Savarin

"I think about barbecue like some people think about wine. The good stuff? You know it when you taste it."
(Keith Allen, Allen & Son, Chapel Hill)

"Good barbecue won't keep you awake at night. Bad barbecue will."
(Wilber Shirley, Wilber's, Goldsboro)

North Carolina pit barbecue, 1930s

How to Fix a Pig
(As told by Dee Grimes)

Take a piece of tin that's
Blowed off a barn in a storm.
Pile little limbs and good chunks
Of hickory on top. Get the fire going
While you're finishing the pit.
Hickory burns orange, then blue.
Dig deep enough to hide a flat-bottomed
Creek boat. Put bars across the top
Closer together than the ones in a jail.
Flop the split pig skin side down
So his eyes won't watch you.
Take a little hit from the bottle in your pocket.
When you've got good coals,
Spread 'em out under him with
A flat-ended shovel. Pretty soon
The steam starts. Douse on the vinegar
And pepper. First time you sniff him,
You start to get hungry. But you can't rush a pig.

Eat that cold chunk of corn bread
You brought from the house in a greasy paper
    bag.
When that vinegar and wood ashes smoke starts
    rising,
And blowing in a blue wind over fields,
It seems like even the broom straw
Would get hungry. But you got to stand it
At first. It comes from down home,
When they cured tobacco with wood, and ears
    of corn
Roasted in ashes in the flue.
The pig was the last thing. The party
At the looping shelter, when the crop was all in.
The fall was in its smell,
Like red leaves and money.
So when you can't stand it, turn up the rib side.

If you didn't get started before light,
You may be finishing after dark.
The last sparks look at you red from underneath,
Like the pig's eyes turned into coals, but
    forgiving.
When the whole thing's finally so brown
And tender it near 'bout
Falls to pieces when you move it,
Slide it every bit into the pan.
They're waiting to chop it up at the house.
And they going to wonder one more time
Why a pig don't have no ribs when it's done.
—James Applewhite

sausage, and certainly not mahi-mahi. And why not do this right, or almost right, and cook with hardwood or at least with hardwood charcoal? Otherwise, what's the point? In the time it takes to do it wrong, you could probably drive to Goldsboro or Lexington and pick up a few pounds of first-rate 'cue to go.

THE MEAT (1): PORK SHOULDER

You may be from the heart of whole-hog country in eastern North Carolina, but start by cooking a shoulder. That doesn't make you

Miss White and Mr. Brown

Barbecue aficionados sometimes talk about the wedding of the rich "Mr. Brown" and the divine "Miss White." Other folks think that's just the sort of cuteness you'd expect from people who call themselves aficionados, and speak of "outside brown" and "inside meat" instead. In either case, they're talking about the dark, smoky "bark" of the meat, on the one hand, and the light, moist meat underneath, on the other. Like white and dark chicken meat, each has its partisans, and at a pig-picking you can stick to one or the other, if you really want to. (Hint: Miss White is tastiest right next to the bone.)

When pork is pulled or chopped, however, the two get all mixed up into something that combines the best features of each. Exactly what Mr. Brown brings to the party depends on what

marinades, rubs, and mops have been applied in the cooking, but count on him for intense flavor and a double dose of what distinguishes barbecue from pork roast. The succulent juiciness of Miss White is the perfect complement, offsetting Mr. Brown's occasional dryness.

Apparently these labels have been around for a while. In 1922 Leonard Heuberger of Memphis started serving pulled pork and coleslaw on a bun (very much like a North Carolina sandwich, except for the sauce); his motto was "Mr. Brown Goes to Town."

a traitor; it just means you're a beginner. Shoulders are harder to mess up, and some people think they're tastier. In fact, many well-known Eastern places are cooking them these days. Bob Melton's in Rocky Mount was one of them, before Hurricane Floyd did it in. Bob Garner reports that even Wilber's, the Goldsboro gold standard, cooks some extra shoulders to chop into its whole-hog barbecue because they provide "extra amounts of moist dark meat and additional shreds of the smoky, chewy 'outside brown' that add visual appeal and rich flavor."

Even after you've got the hang of it, you should ask yourself if you're really, really sure you want to cook a whole hog. If you're into eating rather than historical reenactment, you might leave whole-hog cooking to the professionals. It can be done at home, but you need to think about it.

Anyway, for Pete's sake, don't *start* with a whole hog. Warm up with a shoulder. As a matter of fact, why don't you start with a Boston butt? That's *part* of a shoulder. When people say "shoulder," they're actually referring to the hog's front leg and . . . the part above. The bonier lower portion is the picnic, or picnic ham, and

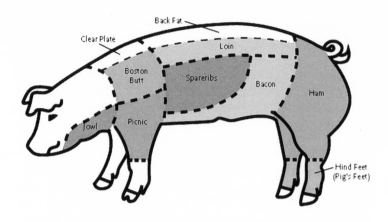

the Boston butt is the meatier upper part. (In other words, a Boston butt comes from the porcine equivalent of an arm. Evidently, when it comes to hogmeat, Bostonians don't know their ass from their elbow.) Picnics have a more hamlike taste than Boston butts (a few barbecue restaurants actually cook hams instead of picnics, but let's keep it simple), so you want both for 100 percent authenticity. But many establishments cook only butts, and one we know cooks at a ratio of two butts for one picnic. In other words, you can suit yourself. Since a bone-in Boston butt usually weighs six to eight pounds and a picnic about the same, your cooker may be too small to handle a whole shoulder anyway.

If you want to cook a whole shoulder, by the way, you may have a hard time finding one intact, but it doesn't matter— just buy the components, a Boston butt and a picnic. It'll all be mixed up at the end. Any butcher and most supermarkets will have these cuts available.

Do buy and cook your meat *bone-in*; it really does improve the flavor. When Benjamin Franklin observed in 1778 that "the nearer the bone the sweeter the meat," he was paraphrasing a proverb that goes back at least to the thirteenth century. The bone also conducts heat through the meat while you're cooking and gives you something to hold on to when you're chopping or pulling.

The night before you're going to cook, trim any loose skin and fat, season the meat with a generous application of salt, rubbed in all over, and let it sit in the refrigerator overnight. (There are fancy rubs that include stuff like black pepper, cayenne, and cumin, but plain salt is traditional and used by some of the best cookers in

In 1970 there were more than 70,000 independent hog farmers in North Carolina. By 2004 there were only 2,400, most of them working under contract with Smithfield Foods.

Pasture Pork

"Here is the miraculous thing about barbecue: Given that the pork from which it is made is almost always the nearly taste-less, nearly fatless product of a confinement operation, how is it that pit masters are able to create a cooked product that is, to my palate, almost always perfect, a culinary silk purse from a factory-farmed sow's ear? . . . I just keep asking myself, 'How much better would it be if the pigs were good, old-fashioned, outdoor-raised fatties?'"
—Peter Kaminsky

Is any other dish made with less attention to its basic ingredient than barbecue? The many barbecue books on the market hardly mention where the meat comes from, and nearly all barbecue restaurants cook basically the same pork you can buy at Food Lion or Harris Teeter, most of which comes from Smithfield Foods or one of the other corporate giants that account for more than two-thirds of the pork produced in the United States.

Some people have a problem with that. Farmer and food writer Tom Philpott of Valle Crucis, for instance, rants about "farmer-destroying, flavor-killing, environment-befouling, labor-exploiting profit machine[s]," whose hogs are "raised in filthy crowded pens and pumped full of hormones, antibiotics, and genetically modified, mass-produced, and highly subsidized corn."

Even if you're not that exercised about it, at least you could ask whether hogs raised some other way might be tastier. Philpott points out that fifty years ago most hogs eaten in North Carolina came from small farms and were fed on "forage, garden culls, and kitchen slop." When pitmaster Ed Mitchell of Wilson cooked one raised that way in 2003, he told *Gourmet*

Pasture pork, as seen by North Carolina photographer Bayard Wootten

magazine, "It tasted like the barbecue I knew from the tobacco days: juicy and full of flavor. I knew that was the pork my grandfather ate all his life. I knew that was the old-fashioned pork we lost when near about everybody went industrial."

You can still find this kind of meat if you're willing to pay for it. California's Niman Ranch sells bone-in shoulders from "pasture-raised" hogs online and through some local hippy-dippy groceries in North Carolina. Trouble is, it costs about three times as much as what the Smith-field product goes for at Food Lion (four times as much when Food Lion has it on sale), without even taking into account the shipping charges if you order online. That's one reason a sandwich at Lexington Barbecue costs only about a quarter as much as one at Manhattan's fancy Blue Smoke restaurant, which cooks only Niman Ranch pork.

It gives you pause, doesn't it? Gives us pause, anyway. To tell the truth, the taste differences between the high-end product and the factory-farmed stuff are pretty subtle. Some folks, like Glen White (see page 273), even prefer corn-fed hogs. Gene Hill of Hill's Barbecue in Winston-Salem says they're sweeter, brown faster, and have less shrinkage. And isn't the whole point of barbecue turning a cheap cut of meat into something transcendent? When it costs as much as steak to start with, some of the fun goes out of it.

Fortunately, the price of boutique hogmeat is coming down. The Ag School at North Carolina A&T, under a program funded by the Golden Leaf Foundation, has been working with small farmers in North Carolina to help them raise and market high-margin "pasture pork," and the results are starting to show up in places like Whole Foods in Chapel Hill, where a local, pasture-raised shoulder is only about twice as much as one from Smithfield at Food Lion. The industrial product will always be cheaper, of course, but supporting your local farmer and being kind to pigs is getting easier. And we think it really does taste marginally better.

the state.) Alternatively, if you're the type who turned in extended bibliographies with your middle-school papers, you might want to "brine" the cut by soaking it in salt water overnight, which some folks think keeps the meat juicier. (Again, there are brines that use stocks, herbs, juices, and so forth, but stick with salt and water, at least at first. A tablespoon of salt in a pint of water gives more than enough brine. If you're into kosher salt, read the box for the equivalent.)

When you're ready to cook, take the meat out of the refrigerator and let it warm up for a half hour at least. You *can* let it get to room temperature, but don't let it sit around in a warm place all day. Then follow the directions starting on page 96.

THE MEAT (2): WHOLE HOG

With a butt or two under your belt, you'll be ready to move on to a whole hog if you want to. You can do it — and when you're through, you'll really have a sense of accomplishment.

For that, you'll need a "dressed" hog. This doesn't mean one in a top hat and tails, like you sometimes see in the signs for barbecue joints. It means one with the feet and tail and innards removed and the bristles (blessedly) scraped off. Most people prefer to have the head cut off as well, although barbecue master Vince Staten prefers to leave it on (he says it gives him someone to talk to during the long hours of cooking).

Yes, that's right: "whole-hog" barbecue doesn't actually use the *whole* hog. If you happen to have the odd bits lying around, you can make western North Carolina liver mush, South Carolina–style "barbecue hash" (also with liver), head cheese, chitlins, brains and eggs, Hoppin' John with hog jowl, pickled pig's feet, pig tail perlow, hog lights (lung) stew, and stuffed hog maw (stomach). Oh, and you can inflate the bladder to give the young 'uns something to play with and feed the ears to your dog. But you'll need a different book for all that. And don't look for us to write it.

Killing and dressing a hog yourself would certainly be the manly way to do it, but you'll probably want to buy one. *Be sure to get it with the skin on,* and ask for it "butterflied" so you can spread it out open on the grill. Even with the piggy butterflied, to open the carcass all the way you may still need to crack its ribs. If you can't do it

When we asked Richard Monroe of Richard's Barbecue in Salisbury if he ever thought about retiring after cooking barbecue for thirty-odd years, he smiled and said, "Every day."

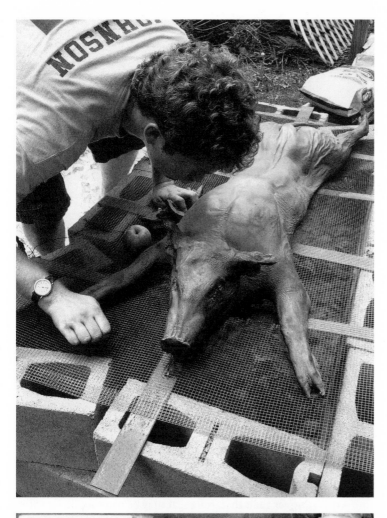

"Hello, big boy."

Leftovers for sale at Clyde Cooper's, Raleigh

Pig Ear
Dog treat
$1.00
Mike Tyson
Favorite

Hog-killing, ca. 1980

with your jokes, you'll just have to reach into the cavity and do the deed. (In fact, you might think about ordering the pig split down the backbone into halves. That's not traditional, but it does make it easier to turn over when the time comes.)

Any dressed weight up to 120 pounds (without the head) is fine—if it's bigger than that, the meat may be too tough. We think ninety pounds is about ideal. You'll get about 20 to 40 percent of the dressed weight as barbecue, depending on how scrupulous you are about removing gristle, veins, and burned meat. So do the math: The twenty or thirty pounds of pulled pork from a ninety-pound pig should serve upward of thirty of your closest friends. Remember: It's better to have too much than too little, and barbecue does freeze just fine.

Where do you buy a hog? Well, if you live in North Carolina, it's easy. Wayne County is home to "the largest all pork retail displayer in the eastern United States," the Nahunta Pork Center: they sell hogs there and also at the Raleigh farmers' market. We've also spotted specials on whole hogs at the Piggly Wiggly, appropriately enough. A good butcher can special-order one for you and, last we

heard, so could North Carolina branches of Sam's Club. If you have the misfortune to live out of state, you'll have to ask around. (Start with *your* good butcher.)

You can get your pig delivered the day before, salt it generously all over the meat side, and ice it in a cooler. Or if you want, you can put it in the bathtub overnight with ice and salt water to brine it. (At a tablespoon of salt per pint of water, you'll need a lot of tablespoons. Just throw in five or six generous handfuls. You'll need bags and bags of ice to keep the temperature near a refrigeratorlike 38°.) If you don't have a cooler big enough to hold a dead hog, and your spouse or roommate takes a dim view of the bathtub plan, arrange to pick the hog up or have it delivered a few hours (at most) before you're going to cook it. (Salt it when you get it.) A half hour or more before you're ready to cook, let the hog begin to warm up toward room temperature (but don't let it sit all day).

THE FUEL

You'll need hardwood coals. You may also want some water-soaked hardwood chunks to add to the burning coals for smoke, but we'll get to that.

The old, labor-intensive, and (many think) best way to get coals is to begin with logs and burn them down. The finest barbecue places in the state do exactly this, and we honor them for it. An acceptable compromise, at least for your early attempts, is to use hardwood charcoal. Some experts argue strongly for lump charcoal, others say it doesn't really matter and briquettes are easier, hotter, and more predictable; but everyone agrees that you should *not* use self-lighting charcoal. We know for a fact that several respected places, Eastern-style and Piedmont, cook excellent barbecue with Kingsford straight out of the bag.

The Tar Heel Division of Smithfield Foods in Bladen County is the largest hog-processing plant in the world. Its 5,500 workers "process" over 9 million hogs a year.

Storing Barbecue

Barbecue will keep a surprisingly long time in the refrigerator, especially when it's doused with a good vinegar-and-pepper sauce. For really long-term storage, it can be frozen quite satisfactorily. But the very best way to store it is with one of those vacuum-sealing deals. Put a pound or two in a plastic bag, seal it, and freeze it. When you get a barbecue craving flung on you, drop the bag in a pot of boiling water, and after a while it will be back up to 180° — just like it came out of the cooker. It will taste like it, too. Call this *sous vide* if you want (we don't).

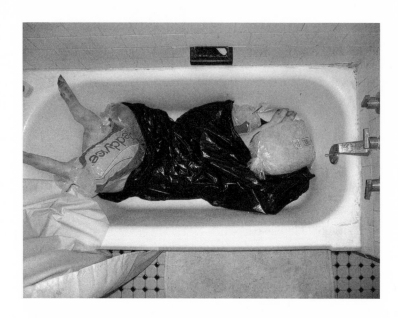

Another reason to avoid mesquite:
Three small colonies of scorpions
have been discovered in North
Carolina, all adjacent to Texas-style
barbecue places. It appears the critters
came with loads of the wood.

Even if your coals come from the grocery store and not the burn-barrel, though, you'll need some sort of separate fire pit or a smaller grill to prepare them for adding at a later stage of the process. Invest in one or two large chimney-type lighters. These ingenious inventions also mean you won't need chemical lighter fluid, which some delicate palates claim to detect in the finished product. (Another reason not to use charcoal lighter fluid: The *Greensboro News and Record*'s garden column advises against using the ashes on your garden if you do.)

Whether you're making your own charcoal or adding wood chunks to the store-bought kind, you'll want to use wood from trees that are native to North Carolina. (The heavy taste of mesquite is great for beef brisket—in other words, for Texans.) Stay away from softwoods like pine, unless you like the taste of resin. Oak is a common choice (especially white oak, although others work fine, too), but hickory is the classic, and there's a reason for that. You should use it if you can get it, or mix hickory and oak. Fruitwoods and nutwoods are good as well: We have a lifetime supply of aged apple wood, thanks to a major ice storm a few years ago, and we've had great results with that, mixed with hickory or on its own. Cherry's good, and maple—also pecan, walnut, and peach. Really, the differences among these hardwoods are for connoisseurs to savor and to fight about. The big difference is between smoke and no smoke.

THE RIG

So much for the raw material. What about the apparatus?

Open-pit barbecue has been done in pretty much the same way from time immemorial: The coals go in a pit, and the meat is put more or less directly above them, at some distance (to keep the cooking temperature low). The meat is kept moist by frequent mopping (basting), and most of the smoke comes from the meat drippings and basting sauce hitting the hot coals (coals produce very little smoke on their own). It's hard to improve on this technique for cooking whole hogs. In North Carolina, it's the traditional way

Since 1995 gas grills have outsold charcoal grills in the United States.

Sid Weaver cooking shoulders
in his backyard, Lexington

to cook shoulders, too, although modern technology has given us some alternatives that we think produce satisfactory results.

Let's talk about pits. You could dig a trench, the old-fashioned way, but if you don't feel like tearing up your backyard, you can make a (sort of) temporary substitute by stacking eight-inch concrete blocks in a rectangle (see page 94). Trench or concrete blocks—either way, you're making a big commitment. Why not start with a one-night stand?

If you're cooking a whole hog, you can borrow or rent a cooker—one of those roughly coffin-shaped jobs that you can tow behind your car. Be sure it's a charcoal cooker and not a propane one; after all, that's the point. One advantage of living in North Carolina is that most equipment-rental places have them. Cookers also have covers, so maybe you can forget about covering the meat with cardboard, as we suggest below. (Actually, we recommend the cardboard anyway: it keeps ash off, makes for a more uniform temperature, and slows down the browning of the skin, which makes it less shoe-leathery at the end. Besides, that's the way Wayne Monk does it at Lexington Barbecue, and if he does it, we're happy to do it, too.)

Weber pot: Somebody's been sampling.

For a Boston butt, you don't need a pig-sized rig—much less a humongous hole in your backyard. If you want to cook with direct heat—the way most great North Carolina barbecue restaurants do it—you can use either one, of course, but you can also use almost any covered apparatus large enough to separate the meat a foot or two from the coals, something like a large Weber pot or a Brinkmann water smoker with the water pan removed. It's really useful to have a hatch for adding more coals and it's great to have vents underneath that you can use to control the temperature, but the only thing that's absolutely essential is a cover you can close to keep in heat and smoke.

Brinkman smoker and chimney-type lighter

In fact, however, we're going to tell you how to cook a Boston butt with the method employed by most competition barbecuers these days: *indirect* heat, where the fire is not directly under the meat but off to one side or even in a separate firebox. You can use that Weber pot or Brinkmann water smoker for this, too. If you do, you'll want to add those hardwood chunks we mentioned, since the dripping fat and basting liquid won't hit the coals. Soak them in water for at least a half hour before adding them. You might also want to put a water pan under the meat to keep things moist.

Indirect-heat cooking is not completely traditional in North Carolina, but it works, and it may even have a few advantages, like less risk of grease fires. We're traditionalists, but we don't feel guilty about not using direct heat. The truth is that the distinction between these newfangled methods and the old-timey way isn't as clear as all that. Ayden's Skylight Inn is about as traditional as they

Cooker with side firebox

Build Your Own Pit

For about what it costs to rent a cooker, you can build a proper backyard pit, but you'll need a patch of ground roughly three by five feet that you don't mind sacrificing to this project. It will be pretty severely burned and have a greasy patina afterward. If you're comfortable with this, you've got your priorities in order, but your better half, landlord, neighbors, or roommates may not get it. You might want to lay in some potting soil or sod in case they don't appreciate your efforts.

These instructions are for a "temporary" structure—that is, if you want to get rid of it, you can—but it's sturdy enough to stick around for a while. You don't need an engineering degree, but it helps to have a friend with a truck. Take that truck to your hardware store and pick up

- 28 *cinder or concrete blocks*, 16" × 8" × 6" (16" × 8" × 8" works, too).
- 4 *unpainted metal slats* approximately 1 yard long and 1 *unpainted metal slat* approximately 6 feet long. Steel is strongest, aluminum is okay, but avoid galvanized metal—it might be poisonous. If you can find an unpainted metal trellis, bedsprings, or jail door, you've hit the jackpot and you can skip the slats.
- 2 *rolls of chicken wire* big enough to cover the surface area of the grill. You can substitute a piece of corrugated metal for one of the rolls.
- 2 *rolls of heavy-duty aluminum foil*.
- *Corrugated cardboard* to cover the pig. Get a big box and unfold it.

Stack the cinder blocks two deep. You want the meat at least a foot or two above the coals. You'll need to refresh the coals from time to time, so turn one of the corner blocks on the second level of each long side of the rectangle slightly askew so that when you remove the cinder block *next* to it (on each shorter side of the rectangle), there is a little extra wiggle room for adding coals. Make sure the remaining blocks connect so the heat will not escape.

You need some sort of grill to go on top. That's what the slats are for, if you can't find one of the more picturesque alternatives. Lay the long one down and put the others alternately over and under it. As an insurance measure, we like to lay one roll of the chicken wire over these slats. You can put a few bags of charcoal on the ends of the chicken wire to keep it from curling back up.

You will also want something to cover the meat with while it cooks, to hold in some of the heat and to give you a bit more smoke flavor to show for your efforts. You can use galvanized roofing, an old automobile hood, or that second piece of chicken wire covered with aluminum foil. We're not talking about building a homecoming float—just something simple to cover the cardboard, which will be covering the pig.

Keep in mind that when you're heating up the grill, you're heating a large area. The ground will have to warm up, so be patient. If you have to add extra coals to bring the grill up to the appropriate temperature, so be it, but don't overdo it: you don't want the pit to run too hot.

The genius of this method is heat control. If the grill is running hot, open a few concrete blocks until the temperature's where you want it. If it's too cool, it's easier to add coals than with a metal cooker: you don't have to open the top and let all the heat and smoke out. It's also easier to arrange the coals so you'll have more under the hams and shoulders. Finally, if you want to keep the pig warm on the grill afterward for picking, you can open up most of the cinder blocks and put some aluminum foil under the pig.

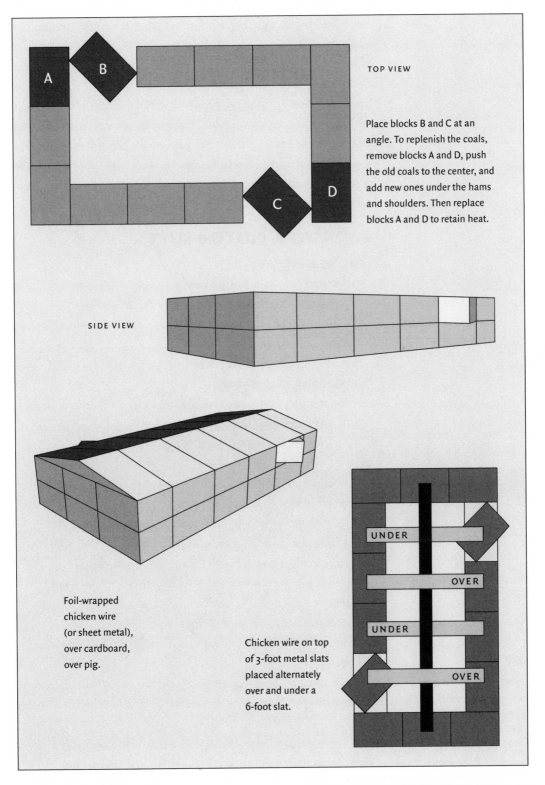

TOP VIEW

Place blocks B and C at an angle. To replenish the coals, remove blocks A and D, push the old coals to the center, and add new ones under the hams and shoulders. Then replace blocks A and D to retain heat.

SIDE VIEW

UNDER

OVER

UNDER

OVER

Foil-wrapped chicken wire (or sheet metal), over cardboard, over pig.

Chicken wire on top of 3-foot metal slats placed alternately over and under a 6-foot slat.

come, but owner Pete Jones once told an interviewer, "We put our coals around the pig, never under it—that is if you want to do it right." Wilson pitmaster Ed Mitchell uses a "banking" technique (see page 224) that also puts the coals to the side (and he uses wood chunks soaked in a vinegar, pepper, and salt mixture so they bring a bit more than wood smoke to the proceedings, but that's the kind of refinement you might want to pass up for now). Just don't burn logs in your firebox the way Texans do; stick with coals and maybe a few wood chunks for flavor, and you'll still be in the Tar Heel tradition.

COOKING A BOSTON BUTT

You'll need:

- A salted or brined Boston butt
- A cooker of some kind
- One or two large chimney-type charcoal starters (optional but *highly* recommended)
- A couple of bags of charcoal
- Some soaked hardwood chunks
- A water pan (water cookers have them built in; otherwise a disposable aluminum cake pan works fine)
- An oven thermometer (remote-read is great but not required [see below])
- A meat thermometer
- Heavy gloves
- A small shovel, scoop, or tongs for adding charcoal
- A squirt bottle of water to control flare-ups
- Thin, vinegar-based North Carolina barbecue sauce (Piedmont- or Eastern-style—your call: see "Sauces and Dips")
- Heavy-duty aluminum foil (for wrapping the shoulder at the end; also, if you line your cooker with it, cleanup's a lot easier)

How you go about cooking depends on what sort of cooker you're using, but start with the meat "face"-side (not "skin"-side) down.

If you have a fancy cooker with a firebox, you probably already know what you're doing and are just reading this so you can ar-

Raleigh's Clay Aiken was one of the most successful runners-up in the history of American Idol. "The Clay Train," a website for his fans, offers pretty good instructions for barbecuing a Boston butt.

gue with us. But for the record, you should start the coals and put them in the firebox (or start them in the firebox if you want), let the temperature get up to 200° or so, add a few soaked hardwood chunks, and put the shoulder in the cooking chamber over a drip pan filled with water. Or, alternatively, forget about the firebox and put your coals in the cooking chamber itself, on the side away from the chimney, with the meat over a drip pan at the other end; you won't need as much charcoal to keep the temperature in the ideal range.

If you're using a pot cooker, you'll want to put the water-filled drip pan on one side and start some coals on the other. Put the cover on until the coals are gray all over and the temperature is up around 200°, then add some soaked (not dripping) hardwood chunks to the coals, put the grill in place, put the meat over the drip pan, and put the cover back on with the vents in the lid above the meat.

With a water cooker, put the coals in the bottom pan and start them (or vice versa if you have a chimney starter), fill the water pan and put it in place, and let the temperature get up there. Then add some hardwood through the side door, put the meat on the grill, and close everything up.

However you do it, you want *a temperature between 200 and 235° (215–220 is ideal) for the first three or four hours.* Then you can let it creep up to 250 or 260 if you want to move things along. If you have a cooker with an external thermometer, you can use it as a general guide, but it won't necessarily be measuring the temperature at meat level, so put an oven thermometer next to the meat. (Gadget-philes might think about buying a remote-read electronic thermometer. It not only keeps you updated on the grill temperature without having to open the cooker but also liberates you to mill around the house, make barbecue sauce, put out plates, and so forth.)

When a headline warned that "barbecue" might be linked to cancer, a Wilmington Star editorial pointed out that the story was about meat grilled at 400° or more, not real barbecue cooked at 225° or less.

You'll want to *cook the meat at least six hours on the covered pit or in the smoky cooker.* After that, less smoke is absorbed, and you can wrap the meat in foil and move it to the oven without losing much flavor. You really shouldn't, but we did once, when it was snowing and miserable.

Finally, you want *an internal temperature at the end of at least 170°.* We think 180 is even better (especially if you're planning to pull the meat, because it shreds a little easier), but don't go much over

190. Use that meat thermometer (don't touch the bone). Old-timers know it's done by the look and feel of the meat, but you're not an old-timer, are you?

In a pot cooker or water smoker, start with maybe twenty briquettes and three or four hardwood chunks. Store-bought chunks usually come with some strands of wood—these should go in your gerbil's cage, not in the cooker. Big hunks of soaked wood bedevil the fire and produce that luscious smoke, but shreds and splinters just catch fire and add heat, which is what you have coals for. Speaking of flare-ups, they're a blight worse than uninvited guests who follow the smoke to the party, but they come with the territory, so have a squirt bottle around to knock them down. Besides, this gives you something to do after you've read the newspaper twice.

After a while, start another batch of charcoal, so you'll have more coals to add. If your temperature gets too high, you can lower it instantly by raising the cover or slowly by closing the vents (if your cooker has them). To raise the temperature, open any vents or add three or four lit pieces of charcoal from your reserve. Might as well put in another soaked hardwood chunk, too.

Try not to check the temperature more than every half hour *at most* since it cools things off when you do. There's really no reason to open the cooker for the first couple of hours unless you think things are going too fast. As the saying goes, if you're looking, it ain't cooking. After that, every hour or so you can mop the meat with your sauce and check the temperature while you're at it. Many good barbecue places don't bother with the mopping, but we like the results.

This temperature thing causes a lot of needless anxiety. Don't get hysterical if your temperature gets out of the ideal range. Lower temperatures are no problem—it just takes longer—and spikes up to higher temperatures are not a calamity. There are even a few reputable cooks who'll tell you to cook at 275–300°, but we prefer lower and slower.

After about six hours, you'll want to turn the butt over. The easiest way is to use your hands (wear heavy gloves). Once is probably enough, but if you want to do it at hourly or two-hour intervals after that, it's okay with us.

How long it will take depends on all sorts of things—the size of

Charlotte journalist and barbecue writer Dan Huntley has developed a barbecue-scented perfume. It smells just like hickory smoke, he says, "but the gals aren't too fond of the brown stain it leaves on their necks and we're fine tuning our alchemy."

Dr. Alan R. Hirsch of Chicago's Smell and Taste Treatment and Research Foundation claims that his research shows that the odor of barbecue inhibits sexual desire in women. Damn Yankee.

Chopping a shoulder at Bridges Barbecue Lodge, Shelby

the cut, the weather, how tightly sealed your cooker is, the kind of coals you use—but figure maybe 1 1/2 to 2 hours per pound of meat. That's just for planning purposes, though. You're not finished until the meat thermometer says so. When it does, take the butt off the grill, wrap it in aluminum foil, and let it "rest" for a half hour. (You may be ready for a rest yourself.) Then you can slice it, if you like it

I Saw the Light: A New Yorker Discovers Outside Brown

Food critic Jim Leff, cofounder of Chowhound .com, tells of his conversion:

I found God. And God is Brown. Or, at least, He orders Brown.

Brown is crunchy and succulent. Brown is salty and smoky and deep. It is the yang to the yin; the prosciutto to the melon; the hot ironing and lemon juice that expose the invisible writing and make the paper convey A MESSAGE!

NC barbecue ordered with Brown is like your first taste of fresh-filled cannoli. No, it's so much more than that. It's like having a really great burger after a lifetime of Wendy's. No, it's like your first lasagna after the taste bud transplant. I'm struggling here, but stay with me. In one bite I went from appreciating Carolina barbecue in an intellectual

Bridges Barbecue Lodge outside-brown tray

food-writerish sort of way to appreciating it in an I'm-selling-all-my-belongings-and-moving-down-here sort of way. Genre utterly redefined, attention riveted, appointments dropped, cholesterol swelled, lapels stained, political party switched, Jesus Christ adopted as personal savior. Finally, I got it!

"My uncle said if I put a cleaver in each hand, I wouldn't cut my fingers off." (Pete Jones, Skylight Inn, Ayden)

that way, or pull it with a couple of sturdy forks or your hands, or chop it with a cleaver on a block. Remove the bone, any remaining fat, and anything else that's not tasty. If you're chopping or pulling, mix the "outside brown" throughout. You can add your sauce (lightly) to the meat in the kitchen or just set it out as a table sauce for people to add for themselves.

Bone appétit, as some cute folks say.

COOKING A WHOLE HOG

If you decide to take the plunge, here's how it's done. These instructions are no substitute for getting someone to show you—in a pinch, there are some good videos on the internet—but if you want it spelled out, read on. Actually, first, go back and reread the previous section because a lot of that applies to cooking whole hogs, too.

Ordinarily we subscribe to the "too many cooks" rule, but ordinarily you're not cooking enormous hunks of meat over an open fire. Get some friends to help you, if you can. You might as well make an occasion of it, anyway, because you'll have a lot of meat when you're done. Besides, whole-hog cooking at home is as much show business as it is cookery. As Don McCullough of the National Barbecue Association observes, "Doing a whole hog lends a festive atmosphere to things. Everybody wants to see it. It's like watching a wreck."

"Even the police who came to shut down the party complimented us on how nice the pig looked." (William McKinney)

But remember that this is supposed to be fun. There may be moments when it doesn't feel that way—say, early in the morning when there's nobody awake to help you waltz a pig through the backyard or late in the afternoon when your nosy neighbors want you to open the cooker so they can see what's cooking. But just remember, this is fun. You are having fun. You *will* have a great time eating, and you should have a great time cooking, too. For the most part, cooking your own barbecue is peaceful and relaxing. You don't move too much, and people come to you. Your only task for the day is to cook this pig—in fact, it will probably be the week's major focus as well.

You should develop a game plan for the day, even for the week. Know when you want to serve the barbecue and work backward. Give yourself plenty of margin—at least twelve hours start to finish, and fourteen is better. You don't want a bunch of hungry friends hanging around asking how much longer it's going to be, and it's not a problem if you finish early. Budget time (and drinks) accordingly.

We know that some of these directions will seem vague, almost nebulous. You know why? Because you're cooking a 100-pound animal. The instructions for making four servings of gumbo can be exact, but this is barbecue—whole-hog barbecue. Yes, there's some guesswork involved, some adjusting as you go along, but this is the Masters, the Final Four, the Super Bowl. This is the A-team. If you're not up to the challenge, send out.

You'll need:

- A salted or brined dressed hog, ideally 90–100 pounds
- A pit or cooker
- One or two large chimney-type charcoal starters (optional but highly recommended)
- Approximately 70 pounds of charcoal (or a third to a half of a "face" cord of hardwood logs, but we'll assume you're using charcoal)
- Lots of soaked hardwood chunks
- Two pieces of wire-mesh fence or chicken wire big enough to go under the pig or some other aid for turning it over (optional)
- A sheet of cardboard large enough to cover the pig (optional but recommended)
- An oven thermometer (remote-read is great but not required: see above)
- A meat thermometer
- Heavy gloves
- A small shovel, scoop, or tongs for adding charcoal
- A squirt bottle of water to control flare-ups
- Thin vinegar-based Eastern-style barbecue sauce (see "Sauces and Dips")
- Heavy-duty aluminum foil (optional, but if you're using a cooker, use this to line it and cleanup will be a lot easier)

Light about a third of your charcoal. When the coals are uniformly gray, spread them under where the hog will go, with more under the thick, slow-cooking hams and shoulders (at each end)

Hank Hill *of television's King of the Hill has observed that barbecue is "the only cooking that should be done by a man." The program's animator Mike Judge and writer John Altschuler met as freshmen at* UNC *in Chapel Hill.*

and fewer under the faster-cooking ribs and tenderloin (the rope of meat running down the backbone). Let the temperature at grill level reach 215–225° (old-timers can tell by putting their hands over it, but you should use an oven thermometer—or that remote-reading electronic gizmo we mentioned earlier).

Put a half-dozen soaked wood chunks where they'll smolder, but not directly under the pig. Put the pig on the grill *skin-side up.* (Yes, like everything else, this is a matter for debate, but do it our way for now.) You might want to put a piece of that wire-mesh fence or chicken wire under it, for reasons we'll get to, and as we said earlier, you might should put a sheet of cardboard over the pig. Close the cooker, or if you're using a pit, cover it.

After a while, start another batch of charcoal. Every hour or so, check the temperature. If it's dropping off, put some more charcoal (not a lot by any means) under the shoulders and hams and a couple of hardwood chunks off to the side. Use something like a shovel or an old tiki torch to push the dying embers into the middle of the pit where the ribs and loins are. (This arrangement cooks these parts with less heat than the shoulders and hams.) You can also mop the hog with some of your sauce—or not. If you're using a cooker, resign yourself to opening it to do this; just remember that each time you do you're adding serious cooking time on the back end.

"I always ask myself when I'm done, 'Did I waste my fat grams here?' I hate that more than anything—that or that a pig died in vain." (Lynda Harrill)

After six or seven or eight hours, the hams and shoulders should be looking nicely brown and wrinkled. Stick a meat thermometer in those thick parts—don't touch the bone—and see if the temperature has reached 165°. Keep cooking until it passes this test (it may be longer, even *much* longer, depending on conditions).

When it's right, put those heavy-duty gloves on and turn the meat over. (Some people don't even flip, but they're making a mistake: It's a good idea to expose the skin directly to the heat eventually.) You *will* need help for this. If you've put the carcass on that wire fencing, you can put another piece on top and you and a friend can just lift and flip. Alternatively, run a spatula under the pig to loosen it up, then—with a friend—gently lift it and roll it over. (If you're using a cooker, roll the pig toward the hinges; that way, if you drop it, it won't be on the ground.) Don't worry if the pig sort of comes apart while you're doing this. Once the skin-side is down, you'll be looking at the ribs. Fill the cavity with sauce. Be generous now (we use whiskey bottles for our sauce, and a fifth is about right). Be sure to sauce the shoulders and hams, too. Let the meat cook for another couple of hours, adding coals and wood as needed, until your meat thermometer reads at least 170°. (Again, we think 180° is better.)

You're almost done. Hoist the pig off the fire and let it sit until you can handle it without burning your bare hands—perhaps as much as an hour. While it sits, it will cook a bit more. Then it's pig-picking time in Carolina. By tradition, the cooks get first crack at the ribs and the tenderloin before the guests are informed that the pig is ready to eat.

If you and your friends don't feel like picking, or if anything's left

"The sounds I associate with barbecue are listening to [my brothers] chopping barbecue on the chopping block to whatever beat was going through their head at the time and sometimes making up words to fit. . . . You know, they were rapping before rapping was cool." (Johnny Stogner)

over, you'll need to do some chopping or pulling. Set any remaining ribs and tenderloin aside as special treats, remove any big pieces of fat, then break or cut the meat into big (5–10 pound) chunks. Chop or shred these, discard the bones, collect the meat in a pile, and mix it thoroughly, splashing it with the same sauce you used to baste. You want meat from all parts of the pig in each serving, if not each bite.

See why we suggested you start with a shoulder?

Some backyard cooks think that sauce is what makes barbecue, a fallacy encouraged by the makers of sauce. But folks who really know their business will tell you that the sauce is actually a secondary consideration. Even in North Carolina, despite all that Eastern-Piedmont cross fire about ketchup, pitmasters from one end of the state to the other agree that it's how you cook it, not what you put on it, that makes good barbecue. The late Pete Jones of Ayden's Eastern-style Mecca, the Skylight Inn, once observed that "it's the quality of the meat and the flavor cooked into it that makes for the best taste. If it's pure barbecue, it's barbecue before the sauce goes onto it." Greensboro's Chip Stamey, heir to an illustrious Piedmont tradition, agrees with that, at least: "If you've gotta use a lot of sauce, it's not good barbecue." The Legendary Smokey Pitts of the Society for the Preservation of Traditional Southern Barbecue sums it up: "You make some good barbecue, it don't really need no sauce at all. A little sauce goes a long ways. You don't want to cover up that smoky taste. Of course, if it wasn't for the dip, we wouldn't have much to argue about, would we?"

Nevertheless, thin vinegar-based sauces (with tomato or without) are at the heart of what makes North Carolina barbecue. Too sweet and too thick, and you have what *Raleigh News and Observer* columnist Dennis Rogers calls—"gag—that red stuff from Asheville" (and points west). Visible mustard, and you have what a *Wilmington Star* editorial once deplored as "the abominable South Carolina style." Most Tar Heels agree with Ron Smith's summation: "We like our tea sweet and our barbecue with a bit of bite. That's where the vinegar comes in. It's sort of a Southern sweet and sour sensation."

So if you're cooking your own, you'll need a recipe or two. There are a lot of them out there, because almost every barbecue cook has his (almost always "his") own. But don't think you can just find one you like and ask for the formula. "You would no more ask a

"I don't eat meat. At least not much, but the one meat I can't resist is barbecue. Barbecue doesn't look like an animal. It just sort of lies there all cut up on a plate, oozing with spicy sauce and not looking remotely like a pig." (Melissa Clement)

Mopping the meat at Braswell
Plantation, 1944

barbecue man for his sauce recipe than you would for the use of his
dog," says *Oxford Public Ledger* editor Al Carson. Most North Carolina
sauces are made with simple ingredients and not many of them,
but, as Peter Kaminsky writes, "the recipes are as closely guarded
as the formula for Coca-Cola." Kaminsky thinks "the secretiveness
must be a Southern guy thing—the same way you don't tell people
about your fishing holes or duck blinds."

Fortunately, most of these recipes are relatively minor variations on two basic themes, Eastern and Piedmont. We'll give you some that have been published or are in the public domain. Start with them. Later you can add your own secret ingredients so you'll have your own recipe that you can refuse to share.

Unless it says otherwise, these recipes will make three to five quarts, enough for most purposes, and if that's too much, it can be put in tightly capped bottles and kept indefinitely in the refrigerator. If the sauce isn't hot enough for you, you can always pass around the hot sauce (and make it hotter next time).

EASTERN SAUCES

Eastern-style sauce started out simple, and it still is. Here's a recipe from the North Carolina Pork Council that isn't much different from Thomas Jefferson's pepper sauce:

Old-Time Eastern North Carolina Barbecue Sauce

1 gallon cider vinegar

1 1/3 cups crushed red pepper

2 tablespoons black pepper

1/4 cup salt

Mix the ingredients and let stand for at least 4 hours. This one doesn't even need refrigeration.

(The Skylight Inn's sauce is even simpler, if that's possible: It uses Texas Pete instead of crushed pepper.)

The most common addition to this basic formula is just a touch of sweetness. Some traditionalists like to leave the pork tart and maybe eat it with sweetish coleslaw, but by now enough people have put sugar or molasses in the sauce itself that it's no longer what the Sons of Confederate Veterans would call a "heritage violation." If you want a sauce with a bit of that sweet-sour taste, here's a nice, mild one from Dennis Rogers:

Dennis Rogers's "Holy Grub" Sauce

1 gallon cider vinegar

1 cup firmly packed brown sugar (or 1/2 cup molasses)

"We North Carolinians, of course, know—we are not taught, we are born knowing—that barbecue consists of pork cooked over hickory coals and seasoned with vinegar and red pepper pods. No serious Tar Heel barbecue chef would disclose his or her preferred proportions of the latter ingredients: 'season to taste' is the proper commandment." (Tom Wicker)

We Have the Numbers

In the interests of science, we have analyzed the ingredients of twenty-one Eastern and twenty-three Piedmont sauces from recipes painstakingly collected in a couple of hours on the internet. The table below shows the results:

	Eastern	Piedmont
Vinegar (usually cider)	100%	100%
Salt	95	91
Crushed red pepper (usually), cayenne, and/or hot sauce	100	78
Black pepper	67	69
White or brown sugar (rarely, molasses)	67	90
Tomato (almost always ketchup)	—	100
Water	24	56
"Secret ingredients"	38*	70

*Eight of the twenty-one. However, two have only a bit of lemon juice, and one has only optional celery seeds.

The ingredients of Eastern sauces are fairly standard (although the proportions vary). All start with vinegar (usually cider vinegar), then add cayenne, hot sauce, and/or (most often) crushed red pepper. Almost all add salt. Two-thirds have black pepper. A quarter or so dilute the sauce a bit with water. The only thing that isn't utterly traditional is the sweetener of some sort that has snuck into two-thirds of these sauces. (Fewer than half—38 percent—include both sugar and black pepper.)

That's pretty much it. Thirteen of the twenty-one recipes don't have anything else, and the others almost never get much more adventurous than some paprika, a dash of Worcestershire sauce, a squeeze of lemon, a few celery seeds, a little onion, or garlic. Only two recipes had even three of these wild and crazy ingredients, and none had more than three.

West of Raleigh, things get more . . . complicated. Piedmont dips begin as basically the stock Eastern sauce: vinegar, almost always salt, plus red and/or black pepper. They're somewhat more likely than Eastern sauces to be sweet—nearly all have sugar and usually more of it—but there's nothing so far that would occasion comment in Goldsboro or Wilson.

Some Piedmont places stop right there, and serve their pork shoulder with what amounts to Eastern-style sauce. And this isn't just at places, like Chapel Hill's Allen & Son, in the Eastern-Piedmont borderlands: check out Wink's and Richard's in Salisbury, for instance, or Kyle Fletcher's in Gastonia.

But the presence of tomato, notoriously, defines Lexington-style dip. It's what partisans fight about. So all the Piedmont sauces in the table include ketchup (except for one sport that calls for canned tomato sauce)—in fact, we used ketchup to decide which column an otherwise unidentified

The sauce at Speedy Lohr's, Arcadia, sits on top of the barbecue.

"North Carolina barbecue sauce" belonged in. Since ketchup by itself would make a sauce thicker, about half of the Piedmont recipes call for water to thin the mix, producing a consistency more like Eastern sauce than like what you find in the mountains, Kansas City, or your grocery store.

But most Piedmont dips are a bit more than just a redder, sweeter version of the typical Eastern sauce, with the added taste of tomato. When it comes to "secret ingredients," the Piedmont imagination goes to town. The Piedmont recipes are twice as likely as the Eastern ones to include something beyond the basics: two-thirds do, and half of those have three or more of these additions (one has six). The extra ingredients include nearly all of the Eastern add-ons, plus such exotica as chili powder, nutmeg, cloves, soy sauce, ginger ale, and *nuoc mam* (Vietnamese fish sauce—see "Flavor Enhancers," page 115). This means that Piedmont dips differ not only from Eastern sauces but to a considerable extent from one another.

3 tablespoons crushed red pepper

2 tablespoons cayenne

1/4 cup salt

Mix the ingredients and let stand for at least 4 hours.

The late Jeanne Voltz, the prizewinning food writer who lived her last years in Fearrington Village outside Pittsboro, favored a hotter, saltier version with the same amounts of vinegar and sugar but 1/2 cup crushed red pepper, 1/3 cup cayenne, and 1 cup salt. Obviously, anything in between would work, too.

If for some reason you'd prefer to buy an Eastern-style sauce, try the one from Scott's in Goldsboro. Scott's stopped cooking with wood long ago, but the sauce is still the Reverend Adam Scott's original formula, tweaked by his son in the 1940s and sold ever since as "The Best Ye Ever Tasted." Scott's now sells over a million bottles of sauce a year, and the sauce was chosen by *Food & Wine* magazine as runner-up in a national competition. Adam Scott claimed that the secret recipe came to him in a dream, but it's a basic Eastern sauce: vinegar, red pepper in some form, black pepper, salt, and not much else (maybe some onion or garlic powder). Watch out, though: whatever's in it, the stuff is hot. In 1957 a burglar hid from the police in a drum of it until he couldn't stand it anymore. Scott's didn't press charges, observing that the man had suffered enough.

It's kind of hard to take Eastern-style sauce uptown. The Food Network once featured a garlicky "Eastern North Carolina" sauce from Chapel Hill's innovative Barbecue Joint that we thought about including here—until we tasted it. Eastern-style sauce has been pretty much frozen in time for going on 200 years, and it could be there's a reason for that. Anyway, if you mess with it, it becomes something else.

PIEDMONT SAUCES

Of course some people around Lexington did mess with it once, and liked the results. The original Piedmont "dip" was essentially just an Eastern-style sauce with a little ketchup added, cooked a bit to blend the ingredients. Several great Lexington-style places still use it.

Wayne Monk's Lexington Barbecue and Sonny Conrad's Barbecue Center are two of them. It used to be said that Wayne Monk only made his dip on Sundays when nobody else was around and kept the formula in a safe-deposit box, but these days an employee makes the dip and even told the world—the Travel Channel, anyway—

Blackwelder's Barbecue in Salisbury is long gone, but a modified version of its sauce has been served since 1948 at Kepley's in High Point, whose founder came from Salisbury. It is less sweet than most Lexington-style sauces.

what's in it. He was a little vague about the proportions, but Jim Auchmutey and Susan Puckett came up with the adaptation below for their *Ultimate Barbecue Sauce Cookbook*, and it tastes about right to us. Sonny Conrad has always taken a different approach to secrecy ("We don't have any secrets—it's real simple"), but a home-sized version of his recipe shows that he and Monk have pretty much the same approach to dip:

"Lexington Barbecue" Dip	Barbecue Center Dip
3 quarts white vinegar	1 quart cider vinegar
1 quart water	1 quart water
5 1/3 cups ketchup	1 1/2 to 2 quarts ketchup (according to desired thickness)
1/2 cup sugar	10 teaspoons sugar
1 tablespoon crushed red pepper	
4 teaspoons cayenne	3 teaspoons cayenne
4 teaspoons black pepper	5–7 teaspoons black pepper
3 tablespoons salt	10 teaspoons salt

Combine the ingredients in a saucepan and simmer for 15 minutes. Bring to a boil, then let cool.

Just as the Eastern traditionalists feared, though, once the ketchup was out of the bottle, other ingredients started creeping in. One common addition is Worcestershire sauce, in quantities ranging from a barely discernible dash to so much that it becomes almost the dominant flavor. Two examples aren't enough to define a microregion, but north of Greensboro, in Reidsville and Madison, the dips at Short Sugar's and Fuzzy's may have the strongest Worcestershire flavor in the state. A recipe our friend Mike Page got from Forsyth County fire chief Reece Bauguess, who supposedly got it from someone who worked for Warner Stamey, calls for a more modest four ounces of Worcestershire for about a gallon and a half of dip. That's about the same as in this recipe from the *Yadkin County Homemakers Extension Club Cookbook*—not as strong as Short Sugar's, but you can certainly tell it's there:

Before Davidson County sheriff Gerald Hege resigned amid a flurry of felony charges in 2004, he had become a Court TV celebrity, put prisoners in stripes, painted his jail cells pink with blue teddy bears, and started selling "Sheriff Hege's Lexington-Style BBQ Dip."

Yadkin County Dip

4 onions, chopped
6 cups cider vinegar
2 cups water
2 cups ketchup
1/2 cup brown sugar
1/4 cup Worcestershire sauce
1 teaspoon cayenne
4 teaspoons salt

Mix the ingredients in a saucepan and boil slowly for 15 minutes.

Most North Carolina barbecue cooks like to dump on South Carolina's mustard-based sauces ("If French's went out of business, there'd be no such thing as South Carolina barbecue," one told Charles Kuralt), but some put it in their sauces anyway. They usually

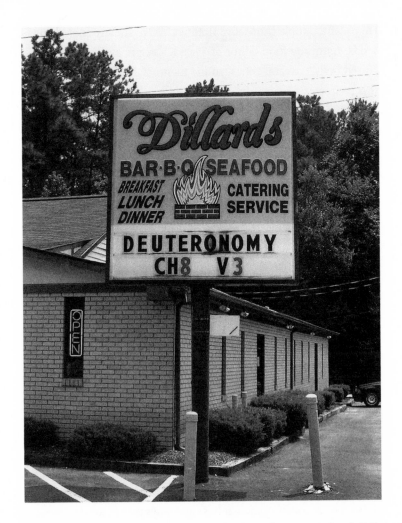

treat it as a "secret ingredient," but one shameless exception is Dillard's Bar-B-Que, in Durham since 1956, which couldn't make a secret of the mustard in its tasty sauce if it wanted to. Founder Sam Dillard was black (a proud graduate of Tuskegee Institute who liked to quote Booker T. Washington on the virtue of hard work), and his independent way of doing things illustrates Bob Garner's observation that "barbecue customs among North Carolina's African-Americans often cross or ignore the established boundaries."

But some white folks in the Piedmont furtively use some mustard, too, either dry or spooned right out of the bottle—not enough to turn the sauce a telltale Sandlapper-yellow, but once you realize it might be there, you can taste it. We can't prove it, but it seems to be more common as you get closer to the South Carolina line.

The sauce at Hobgood's Family BBQ in Hillsborough included ketchup, vinegar, mustard, and eleven other ingredients, four of them top secret. Sam Hobgood won the recipe in a horseshoe game in Virginia.

Here's an example from a Charlottean. We've already quoted James Villas, longtime food editor of *Town & Country* and self-described "hired belly," several times. In his memoir, *Between Bites*, he gives this recipe:

Southern Piedmont "Secret Ingredient" Dip

3 quarts cider vinegar

3 cups ketchup

1/2 cup plus 1 tablespoon light brown sugar

6 tablespoons French's mustard

3/4 cup Worcestershire sauce

3 tablespoons crushed red pepper

2 teaspoons black pepper

6 tablespoons salt

Combine the ingredients in a saucepan and simmer for 5 minutes. Remove from the heat and let stand for 2 hours.

Once you start adding things, it's a slippery slope, and if you're not careful, you wind up in Memphis or Kansas City or, God help us, California, where one writer celebrates "the endlessly creative cooks" who use stuff like "soy, teriyaki, oyster, fish, and hoisin sauces, as often as lime, orange, and pineapple juices, mixed up with ginger, cumin, garlic, and a variety of chiles." But as long as the sauce has a strong vinegar base and stays thin instead of gloopy, you're still in the Piedmont tradition. Al Carson shared this spicy, sweetish number with television's Food Network, so it's not such a secret anymore (but the cloves are a nice medieval touch):

Al Carson's Secret Sauce

1 gallon cider vinegar

28-ounce bottle ketchup

2 3/4 cups firmly packed brown sugar

1/4 cup hot sauce (optional—try it without this first)

1/4 cup garlic powder

1/2 teaspoon ground cloves

1/4 cup crushed red pepper

Flavor Enhancers

It's an ill-kept secret that many—maybe even most—competition barbecuers use monosodium glutamate (MSG) in their sauces or rubs. MSG's chem-lab name and reputation for giving some people headaches mean they don't want to admit it, but since MSG does for the taste of food roughly what steroids do for athletes, they don't want to give up their edge either. Few are willing to share their recipes, but when you hear the phrase "secret ingredients," just smile and nod knowingly.

Thanks to the FDA, the makers of grocery-store barbecue sauces are sometimes more candid, but even there MSG may sneak in as a "natural flavoring" because the truth is that it's made from fermented molasses or starch and there's really nothing unnatural about it. These folks, too, use MSG for a reason: they're not just trying to poison you. Like parmesan cheese, mushrooms, tomatoes, bacon, and the English nursery food Marmite, MSG is a potent source of glutamates. On their own, glutamates have the savory "fifth taste" that goes by the name *umami*. In small quantities, they mysteriously accentuate the taste of other foods—hence, the euphemism "flavor enhancer." It should be obvious that we take a generally dim view of innovation when it comes to barbecue, but there may be something to be said for this one. If, like us, you don't like

the idea of MSG, find an Asian food store—easier all the time in North Carolina—and buy a bottle of the Vietnamese fish sauce called *nuoc mam*. (A popular brand is called "Three Shrimp"—although it contains no shrimp.) Like Worcestershire sauce, *nuoc mam* is made by fermenting whole fish, usually anchovies. The result is mixed with water and salt as a preservative. That's it.

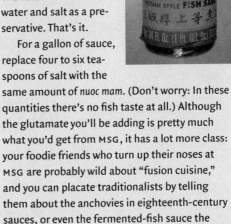

For a gallon of sauce, replace four to six teaspoons of salt with the same amount of *nuoc mam*. (Don't worry: In these quantities there's no fish taste at all.) Although the glutamate you'll be adding is pretty much what you'd get from MSG, it has a lot more class: your foodie friends who turn up their noses at MSG are probably wild about "fusion cuisine," and you can placate traditionalists by telling them about the anchovies in eighteenth-century sauces, or even the fermented-fish sauce the Romans used.

1 tablespoon black pepper

1/4 cup salt

Combine the ingredients in a saucepan and bring to a boil. Reduce the heat and simmer for approximately 15 minutes or until the crushed red pepper sinks. Remove from the heat.

The next recipe is about as complicated as Piedmont sauces get, and it comes with a story. In the 1970s, folks in Bingham Township

Big Bubba chows down.

Real Pit!

Real Pit! Real Pit! Real Pit!
Vinegar-based or 'mater.
You can taste it now,
And you can taste it later.
Real Pit! Real Pit! Real Pit!
—Singing commercial for
Dub's Real Pit Barbecue
Sauce, from *Kudzu: A
Southern Musical,* by Jack
Herrick, Doug Marlette,
and Bland Simpson

fought a plan by the Orange Water and Sewer Authority (OWASA) to dam Cane Creek to create a reservoir. They lost, but raised over $50,000 in legal fees by cooking barbecue. (Bland Simpson of the Red Clay Ramblers, one of the original Luddites, still has "Centurion," their cooker.) Here's the Lexington-style sauce that the embattled farmers used, from pitmaster Fred Summers:

Evelyn Teer's "Stop OWASA" Sauce

2 quarts cider vinegar

2 cups water

2 cups ketchup

1/2 cup molasses

1/2 cup brown sugar

1/4 cup Worcestershire sauce

1 tablespoon Tabasco sauce

1 tablespoon dry mustard

1/2 cup paprika

1/4 cup chili powder

2 tablespoons crushed red pepper

1/2 cup black pepper

1/2 cup salt

Put all ingredients in a good size pot and bring sauce to a boil. Let it cool, jug it, and use it.

THICK TOMATO-BASED SAUCES

Thick, sweet, tomato-based sauces without a marked vinegar taste are not indigenous to North Carolina, but, oddly enough, one of the best commercial ones in the world comes from Raleigh, where the Ford family (whose patriarch, Andrew, founded the first produce house at the old city market in Raleigh in the 1940s) introduced their original Bone Suckin' Sauce in 1992. The formula starts with vinegar and tomato paste, sweetens it with honey and molasses, adds some peppers and horseradish for kick, and goes on from there. The sauce is now sold worldwide in a range of heat and viscosity, even in a mustard-based version, and it has won all sorts of awards: the "Hot" version was named the country's best barbecue sauce two years in a row by *Food & Wine* magazine. It's certified kosher, even if your barbecue isn't.

As we said, sauces like these are non-native species, but you can find them at an increasing number of barbecue restaurants these days, especially those that cater to a non-native clientele in metropolitan areas, on the coast, and in the mountains. A sauce like what many far-western places serve (but better, if you ask us) is found maybe twenty-five miles into Tennessee in what *used* to be North Carolina (right where those ruffians who whipped the Brits at King's Mountain came from). Just outside the town of Bluff City is a joint known simply as "The Ridgewood," a modest-looking place praised by *People* magazine, by Jane and Michael Stern (the *Road Food* people), and even by North Carolinians like poet and publisher Jonathan Williams, who said that going to The Ridgewood put him in a "reverential mood, like a first visit to Chartres." Still more impressive, perhaps, The Ridgewood is the only out-of-state establishment mentioned in Bob Garner's *North Carolina Barbecue: Flavored by Time.*

The Ridgewood's sauce is marvelously complex. Yes, it has the color and consistency of ketchup, but this is what ketchup will taste like in heaven. As Mrs. Grace Profitt, who founded the place in 1948, used to say, "It's got a whang to it." Naturally the ingredients are a closely guarded secret, but a few years ago some ladies in Kingsport, Tennessee, came up with a reasonable facsimile— so good, in fact, that when something purporting to be the actual recipe surfaced, it was virtually identical, except that the ladies had used fresh garlic and onions instead of bottled salts and hadn't used liquid smoke. It's not the kind of sauce you make by the gallon unless you're in the restaurant business, so this recipe is for about a quart:

Saucy Tar Heels: The Ultimate Barbecue Sauce Cookbook reported in 1995 that North Carolina was number 1 in locally made sauces, with 51 promoted by the state Department of Agriculture. (Texas was number 2 with 28.) A decade later, the NCDOA was pushing 141 sauces.

When Taste of the South sampled "small-batch" Southern barbecue sauces in 2006, three of the eight winners were Honky Tonk Pig Original (from Lewisville), Oink Moo Cock-a-Doodle Doo (Yadkinville), and Bone Suckin' Sauce (Raleigh).

Mock Ridgewood Sauce

1 medium onion, finely chopped
1 large garlic clove, minced
1/4 cup cider vinegar
1/2 cup oil

24-ounce bottle ketchup

5 tablespoons sugar

3 tablespoons molasses

1 tablespoon Kitchen Bouquet

1 tablespoon good prepared mustard

1/4 cup Worcestershire sauce

1 tablespoon hot sauce

1/4 teaspoon black pepper

1/4 teaspoon salt

Mix the ingredients in a bowl, then blend the mix in a blender.
Put the stuff in a pot and heat it to the boiling point, then
simmer it for 15–20 minutes. This sauce freezes just fine, and if
you're not going to use it within a few days, you should do that.

This is a finishing or table sauce (it will turn black and ugly if you
baste with it). At the restaurant, it goes onto pulled pork, but it's
also good with ribs, hamburgers, or chicken.

AND, SPEAKING OF CHICKEN

Many barbecue restaurants in North Carolina serve chicken, either
fried or barbecued, as a sort of side dish. One of the most unusual versions is that served at Keaton's Barbecue, a black-owned
place near the Rowan-Iredell line since 1953 (the mailing address
is Cleveland), which Jane and Michael Stern have proclaimed "the
best chicken on earth." Keaton's fries the chicken nice and crisp,
then dunks it in a pot of boiling sauce. The sauce recipe is secret,
of course—all we can tell you is that it's thin, Piedmont-style,
with enough sugar to caramelize a bit, and the result is delicious.
Keaton's is also unusual in other ways: it sells beer, but customers
are limited to two, and signs in the dining room prohibit loud talking, profanity, changing seats after you're seated, and taking pictures of the staff without permission.

A more conventional barbecued chicken recipe comes from
Johnny Stogner, an old-time Lexington barbecue man whose 1996
memoir, *Barbecue, Lexington Style*, is essential reading for any serious student of the subject. His son, John, shared the formula for

Behave yourself at Keaton's.

his father's chicken mop with us, and it has become our personal favorite.

Johnny Stogner's Butter Dip for Chicken

Makes about 2 quarts

2 lemons, cut in half
1 quart White House cider vinegar
1 quart water
1/2 cup butter
1 tablespoon black pepper
Salt to taste

Bring to a boil in a pot with a lid. Use to mop chicken.

NASCAR-themed Lancaster's Barbecue in Mooresville serves a "Chic-a-que" sandwich: chopped pork barbecue on a fried chicken fillet.

"UNC Barbecues Chickens, 108-67." (Fayetteville Observer headline after Tar Heel–Gamecock basketball game, 1992)

SLAW, AND THE SANDWICH

East and west, coleslaw is now an almost universal side-kick to barbecue. As Joe Adams puts it, "Coleslaw and barbecue are like Moon Pies and RC Colas." Goldsboro's Wilber Shirley insists, "You gotta have coleslaw. I won't even sell somebody a barbecue unless they get coleslaw. If they want a barbecue and they don't want coleslaw, there's something wrong with that person. It all goes together." So you'll need a good slaw recipe or two. First, though, some history.

THE STORY OF SLAW

Coleslaw goes back a long way in the United States and even longer in Europe, where the Romans apparently ate it. The Dutch called it *koolsla* (cabbage salad) and brought it to Nieuw Amsterdam. North Carolina slaw-eaters can thank the Dutch and Germans (who called it *Krautsalat*) who came down the Shenandoah Valley from Pennsylvania on the Great Wagon Road and settled in the Piedmont. Their descendants put it on the menus of barbecue restaurants almost as soon as there were such establishments. According to Johnny Stogner (the family name was originally Stoegner), Sid and Vergie Weaver and Vergie's sister, Dell Yarborough, introduced what became Lexington-style slaw to barbecue, based on what the family did at home. (Stamey's in Greensboro serves the original recipe to this day.)

Slaw had been served with barbecue before. In fact, *The Kentucky Housewife* (1839), which contains the first printed slaw recipe we've found, recommends serving "cold slaugh" with barbecued shoat (basted with salt water and pepper and seasoned with lemon juice). Lettice Bryan, the author, wasn't a Tar Heel, but her grandfather lived in Virginia just north of Mount Airy, and if he'd taken a left rather than a right when he left Barren Springs, she would have been ours. Her spelling was not eccentric. In an understandable mishearing of the Dutch, slaw was called "cold" in most recipe books well into the twentieth century. (We wonder who managed to convince an entire country to correct it.)

Mrs. Bryan's slaw is simple—chopped cabbage, vinegar, white mustard seeds, pepper, and salt ("Never put butter on cabbage that is to be eaten cold, as it is by no means pleasant to the taste or sight")—and it is obviously related to the *Krautsalat* of her grandfather's German neighbors in Virginia and western North Carolina. An undated recipe for "Dutch slaw" in Elizabeth Hedgecock Sparks's *North Carolina and Old Salem Cookery* calls for dousing chopped or shredded cabbage with a solution of sugar in vinegar, with a few celery seeds added and possibly chopped green pepper and pimento. This dish, "better after a day or so," is served at Moravian church suppers in Winston-Salem. (Notice that the Moravians like their slaw sweet.)

There are many descendants of these Dutch/German/Moravian-style slaws, often called "seven-day slaw" or "nine-day slaw" or even "three-week slaw," loved partly because they are safer for outdoor events than mayonnaise-based slaws. Here's a recipe from Hendersonville:

Susan Metts's Marinated Coleslaw

Serves 9–12

1 (approximately 7 inches diameter) head cabbage
1 large onion, chopped or slivered
1 cup sugar
1 cup cider vinegar
3/4 cup vegetable oil
1 teaspoon dry mustard
1 teaspoon celery seed
1 teaspoon salt

In a large bowl, shred the cabbage and add the onion; mix in 1 cup sugar, minus 2 tablespoons. In a saucepan, combine the remaining 2 tablespoons sugar, vinegar, oil, mustard, celery seed, and salt. Bring to a boil, stirring constantly. Pour the hot mixture over the cabbage and mix. Cool. Cover and refrigerate for 24 hours before serving.

The sauce on a "small" tray at Whispering Pines in Albemarle is invisible, the notional "tray" is a luncheon plate, and the slaw is definitely red.

PIEDMONT-STYLE "BARBECUE SLAW"

The slaws served by most Piedmont-style barbecue restaurants are clearly in this vinegar-based tradition, although there has been some evolution, notably the addition of tomatoes, usually in the form of ketchup, either per se or as an ingredient of the Piedmont-style barbecue sauce used to flavor the slaw. (Yes, while slaw in eastern North Carolina is usually served as a cool contrast to the barbecue, Piedmont barbecue lovers like their dip so much that they can't get enough of it and often add it to their slaw as well as their pork.)

Lexington Barbecue's Wayne Monk has kindly listed the ingredients in his slaw—just not the amounts. We think this recipe is a reasonable approximation (notice that the vinegar, ketchup, hot sauce, and salt amount to dip):

Lexington Barbecue Slaw

Serves 8–10

1 medium head cabbage, chopped (you can use a food
   processor)
1 tablespoon cider vinegar
4 tablespoons ketchup

3 tablespoons sugar
Dash Texas Pete (a Tar Heel slaw deserves a Tar Heel hot sauce)
1/2 teaspoon black pepper
1/2 teaspoon salt

Mix the dressing ingredients and toss with the cabbage. Like all slaws, this one is better if refrigerated several hours.

The barbecue slaw at J. S. Pulliam's Barbecue in Winston-Salem is unique: It starts with homemade sauerkraut.

A high-toned version of this red slaw comes from chef Bill Neal, who grew up near Shelby, where his family's favorite restaurant was Bridges Barbecue Lodge. Neal served this adaptation of Red and Mama B's slaw at his own restaurant, the famous Crook's Corner in Chapel Hill:

Crook's Corner Uptown Piedmont Slaw

Serves 8–10

1 small head cabbage, finely chopped
14 1/2-ounce can tomatoes, diced
1/2 bell pepper, chopped
3-ounce jar pimientos, drained and chopped
1/2 cup cider vinegar
1/4 cup sugar

Making slaw at Bridges
Barbecue Lodge

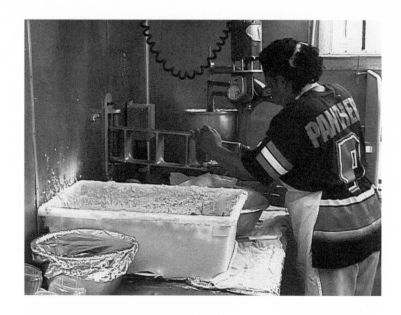

1/2 tablespoon hot sauce
1/8 teaspoon black pepper
3/4 teaspoon salt

Combine the tomatoes, bell pepper, and pimientos in a blender or food processor and process for a few seconds until chopped finely but not mushy. Mix all dressing ingredients, toss with the cabbage, and chill for at least 1/2 hour before serving.

MAYONNAISE IN SLAW

If you want a creamy slaw, these days you'll probably use mayonnaise, but during most of the nineteenth century, that wasn't an option for ordinary Southern cooks since it required expensive imported olive oil. (Commercial vegetable oils were not yet available.) To make a creamy slaw, Southerners made "boiled dressing" (which isn't really boiled, only heated). An early version from the manuscript recipe book of Elizabeth Labbé Cole, who lived in Virginia in about 1837, calls for beaten eggs, vinegar, water, butter, and dry mustard, heated and poured over the cabbage. Here's a similar recipe from Mrs. R. F. Anderson of Burlington, published in 1951 in *Marion Brown's Southern Cook Book*:

Burlington Boiled Dressing

Enough for 4 cups of shredded cabbage

1 large egg
3/4 cup vinegar
1/4 cup water
1 tablespoon butter
1/2 cup sugar
1 teaspoon dry mustard
1/16 teaspoon cayenne
1/2 cup milk
1 tablespoon flour

Beat the egg in the top of a double boiler; add the vinegar, water, butter, sugar, dry mustard, and cayenne; cook, stirring constantly, over boiling water until heated. Make a paste of the milk and flour and stir into the egg mixture. Cook, stirring constantly, until the dressing is as thick as heavy cream.

Once New Yorker Richard Hellmann began marketing his mayonnaise commercially in 1912, things got easier. Store-bought mayonnaise soon found its way into coleslaw, and Southerners still tend to prefer Hellmann's, or Duke's, which began in 1917 in Greenville, South Carolina. (Oddly, given Southerners' notorious sweet tooth, Duke's contains no sugar.)

Eugenia Duke, mayonnaise entrepreneur

Mayonnaise-based slaw is more common in the East than in the Piedmont, but it is sometimes found in ketchup country, where the combination gives a sort of Russian-dressing effect. Not surprisingly, this hybrid is often found at places on the Eastern-Piedmont frontier, like the A&M in Mebane. The resulting pink slaw looks a little alarming, but it can be very tasty: The mayo-and-ketchup slaw at R.O.'s in Gastonia, devised by Pearl (Mrs. R. O.) Black in 1947, made the *Saveur* magazine "100" for 2003. *Saveur* noted that it had "a nice pepper and ginger kick."

Southern Living once published the recipe for a "Barbecue Sundae": pulled pork, baked beans, and creamy slaw layered in a Mason jar, garnished with a dill pickle.

You'll need some Piedmont-style dip to make this slaw, adapted from a recipe provided by the North Carolina Pork Council:

Piedmont Slaw with Mayonnaise

Serves 8–10

1 head cabbage, chopped
2 cups mayonnaise or whipped salad dressing
2 tablespoons vinegar
2 teaspoons ketchup
2 tablespoons sugar
1 teaspoon salt
Lexington-style dip to taste (pages 110–16)

Mix the mayonnaise, vinegar, ketchup, sugar, salt, and dip. Toss lightly with the cabbage and refrigerate.

EASTERN SLAWS

East of Raleigh, slaw is less exotic. The ketchup disappears, and mayonnaise (or whipped salad dressing) is almost universal, as in this basic Eastern-style slaw from Wilber's of Goldsboro, shared with Rich Davis and Shifra Stein, authors of *The All-American Barbecue Book*:

Wilber's Green Slaw

Serves 8–10

1 head cabbage, shredded (bright green leaves only)
1 cup store-bought whipped salad dressing
1 tablespoon white vinegar
1 tablespoon sugar
1 tablespoon prepared mustard
Salt to taste

Mix the dressing ingredients and toss with the cabbage. Chill.

Occasionally there's even no vinegar. Pete Jones of Ayden's Sky-light Inn claimed to have turned down $10,000 for the secret of his great, pale yellow slaw. When we asked his grandson, he said he could tell us, but then he'd have to kill us (which became a predictable refrain in our conversations while preparing this book). But

The slaw at the Skylight Inn is the color of sunshine.

Pete Jones did say once that the ingredients were cored cabbage, Kraft mayonnaise, sugar, and salad dressing—no vinegar.

That "salad dressing" could explain the color, but when we tried Durkee's Famous Sauce (created in 1857, by the way), it wasn't quite right. Of course, the yellow of Durkee's and similar dressings comes from mustard, and it's a curious fact that many North Carolinians who look down on South Carolinians for putting mustard in their sauce don't hesitate to put it in their slaw—often in serious quantities, as in this recipe from the late, lamented Bob Melton's in Rocky Mount, which owner Pattie Smith disclosed to Rich Davis and Shifra Stein:

Bob Melton's Mustardy Slaw

Serves 8–10

1 head cabbage, shredded
1/2 cup white vinegar
1/2 cup mayonnaise
1 cup sugar
1 cup prepared mustard
Dash dry mustard
1/2 teaspoon celery seed

Mix the dressing ingredients and toss with the cabbage. Refrigerate.

Notice the amount of sugar, by the way. Many like their slaw sweet, and this one certainly is.

In fact Eastern slaws are something like Piedmont dips: they tend to be sweeter, and there's a lot more variation. It's almost as if Easterners, who can be rigidly fundamentalist about their vinegar-and-pepper sauces, let themselves go wild when it comes to slaw. Grady's in Dudley adds sweet pickle relish, with excellent results. (Truth is, we've been known to dice apples into ours.)

THE BARBECUE SANDWICH

All right. So you've got your barbecue and your slaw. Now you're ready to make what food writer Alan Richman has called "America's greatest regional dish": a North Carolina barbecue sandwich. Richman was writing specifically about Eastern-style barbecue, but the sandwich transcends even the Eastern-Piedmont divide.

It's simple: You take a bun, add a mound of chopped or pulled barbecue, a splash of sauce/dip, a topping of coleslaw, and that's it. There's not much to be said about the bread, except don't get fancy. You want a cheap, commercial white-bread bun: Wonder, Merita, Kern's, Bunny, Holsum, the Food Lion house brand—some taste-

A barbecue sandwich at Wilber's

less, absorbent vehicle like that. A couple of Eastern places offer sandwiches on cornbread, and that's pretty good, too, but don't fool with crusty French bread, or chewy sourdough, or brioche, or deli-style Kaiser rolls. The bread's role is mostly structural. It's just a medium; the barbecue is the message.

This is the dish that sent *New York Times* food columnist Craig Claiborne into rapture. "I will state unequivocally," Claiborne wrote, "that the chopped pork sandwich served in these two North Carolina areas [East and Piedmont] is by far my favorite kind of barbecue. . . . In a bun with a little cole slaw, it's as close to perfection as barbecue can be."

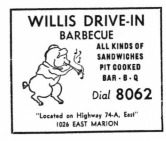

INorth Carolina barbecue restaurants almost always serve some sort of baked or fried cornmeal batter—most often hushpuppies but sometimes cornpone or cornsticks—with their barbecue and slaw. In most places, in fact, a barbecue "tray" means a cardboard boat full of barbecue and slaw, with hushpuppies. Some folks down east prefer old-fashioned cornpone—notably in Ayden, where the Skylight Inn and Bum's both serve thin, crispy rectangles of the stuff. Some serve cornsticks, either baked or deep-fried like hushpuppies—and possibly bought frozen. (Parker's in Wilson has been serving sticks a long time, B's in Greenville has switched to them from cornpone, and Bum's offers them as well as pone.) And Fuller's Barbecue in Lumberton serves tasty Indian fry-bread—not surprising, given that founder Fuller Locklear and his family are Lumbee Indians.

Fixing a tray at Scott's, 1944

Barbecue with cornbread and saltines at Braswell Plantation, 1944

But North Carolina barbecue almost always comes with a side of *some* cornmeal product, unless you're just having a sandwich, and even then you can get your sandwich on thin squares of cornbread at Bunn's in Windsor or on a large, split hushpuppy at King's in Kinston (a sandwich called—what else?—a Pig-in-a-Puppy).

Given all this, it may be hard to believe, but cornbread hasn't always been the bread of choice with barbecue in North Carolina, and in some other parts of the South it still isn't. Accounts of old-time community barbecues report both white bread and cornbread, and early barbecue restaurants were at least as likely to serve wheat rolls or loaf bread as corn products of any sort. At Braswell Plantation's barbecue for its tenant farmers in 1944, they had cornpone, light bread, and saltines.

As for hushpuppies, it wasn't that long ago that they went with fried fish and not much else. In fact, all the early hushpuppy recipes we've found say things like "fry in fish grease." So how did deep-fried cornmeal dough-balls come to be such a common accompaniment to Tar Heel barbecue? Everyone agrees that this innovation, like many others, goes back to the great entrepreneur Warner Stamey. Stamey was the first person—at least the first west of Raleigh—to combine the two, sometime in the 1950s. It isn't clear whether he got the idea from some eccentric down east who did it first or just had a eureka moment while eating at a fish camp, but once he'd hit on the idea, it proved to be a winner. Other Piedmont places followed suit, and soon the innovation trickled back east (where, in fact, it may have originated).

There are still old-timers who prefer their barbecue with wheat

"It's not that we don't like [cornbread]; rather, it's as if we somehow think we've risen above it. . . . I have not turned my back on corn dodgers and hoecake, nor will I. That would be a betrayal of my heritage and a denial of my roots—not to mention a punishment for my taste buds." (John Egerton)

The small tray at Richard's with a hushpuppy *and* a roll

Hursey's Barbeque
1 lb. BARBEQUE
Slaw & Rolls or Hushpuppies
$2.64
5 lb. BUCKET....$8.75
526 Rauhut St.
228-9255
For Take Out Order

"The South is steadfast in its loyalty to the native grain." (Bill Neal)

bread (Warner Stamey's son, Keith, was one of them), and Stamey's in Greensboro still offers a choice of rolls or hushpuppies, as does the Barbecue Center in Lexington. Richard's in Salisbury gives you both, in a unique presentation. But these days hushpuppies have become the default bread with North Carolina barbecue. Alas, many places—even some good ones—use frozen pups, bought by the box. Shame on them, we say. Don't you do it. We'll give you some recipes and some sources for good cornmeal, but first some background.

Corn is the Southerner's staple grain. In *Carolina, or a Description of the Present State of that Country* (1682), Thomas Ashe called it "a Grain of General use to Man and Beast." In Ebenezer Cook's satirical poem "The Sot-Weed Factor" (1707), pork, molasses, and corn in the form of pone ("pon"), mush, and hominy are the main ingredients of a planter's dinner, and there was an agricultural reason for that: when colonists arrived in the South, they saw the wheat seeds they had carefully brought from England sprout and die of rust in the hot, humid climate, while the corn the natives were growing flourished. In the antebellum South, corn was the main food crop, needed to feed man and beast. A cursory survey of Sarah Rutledge's *Carolina Housewife* (1847) reveals twenty-nine bread recipes using cornmeal, grits, or corn flour. Cornbread was the daily bread for

White Meal or Yellow?
Stoneground or Boring?

Glenn Roberts, owner of Anson Mills in Columbia, South Carolina, writes that "historically, white corn was popular in the urban port cultures of the South (Wilmington, Charleston, Savannah, New Orleans) that were settled by Europeans with a predilection for white mill goods. Moving inland, through the rural American South, yellow corn and grits predominated." He observes that "white corns of the antebellum era were less intensely bred away from their Native American antecedents than yellow corns[, which] may explain why white corns, to this day, possess heightened flavors of the earth, and carry

The Old Mill of Guilford is one of many Tar Heel sources of water-ground meal.

pronounced mineral and floral nuances." Yellow corns, on the other hand, "fall to robust corn flavor in the front palate; the best of them show fine citrus flavor in the back." (Is there a cornbread equivalent for the phrase "wine snob"?)

Edna Lewis, sometime North Carolinian, said white corn "has a clear, clean taste that's a little sweeter." For whatever reason, it has certainly taken over in cookbooks, and many seem to think it has more class. *The Picayune's Creole Cookbook*

(1901) says, "In the South the yellow meal is only used to feed chickens and cattle." Joe Dabney quotes William Riley Tallent of Sylva to the same effect ("White corn is for folks, yellow for critters"), and Bill Smith says that was true when he was growing up at the other end of the state ("We were never allowed to eat yellow corn; that was for cows").

We suspect, though, that a survey of Southern homes and restaurants would yield a surprisingly high percentage of yellow-corn users. We wish we'd kept a cornbread diary—we had sweet yellow cornbread just the other day at a famous South Carolina barbecue place.

By the way, if you're in North Carolina, you don't have to buy cornmeal from the Yankee in the funny hat who disguises the origin of his cornmeal by calling it Aunt Jemima (although his company is part of PepsiCo, which of course has North Carolina origins). If you have to go for an out-of-state product, Martha White or White Lily are old and honorable Tennessee brands, but the Tar Heel State is blessed with a number of old mills that still produce stoneground cornmeal or a reasonable facsimile of it. Most North Carolina grocery stores have meal from Atkinson Milling Company (1757) of Selma; House-Autry (1812) of Fair Oaks; Moss' of Kittrell; Moss' subsidiary Barton's of Roxboro; Tenda-Bake of Newton; Old Time of Como; Abbitt's Mill of Williamston; or the Old Mill of Guilford (1767) in Oak Ridge. Lakeside Mills (1736) on Highway 70 east of Kinston is now part of a huge business, distributing (from Spindale—go figure) its own brand as well as Yelton's, Blue Ribbon, Tube Rose, Joy Grand, and even South Carolina's Adluh (which makes wonderful grits). North Carolina even has a company that manufactures mills: Meadow Mills in North Wilkesboro.

all but the wealthiest Southerners, and wheat bread was uncommon enough to need a distinguishing adjective, "light" or "white" bread, just as "sweet" milk needed an adjective to distinguish it from buttermilk. In ordinary households, the biscuits that have become emblems of Southern cooking were reserved for Sunday dinner and other special occasions.

BAKED CORNPONE

The oldest cornbread was just cornmeal, flour, salt, and water. The name *pone* comes from the Virginia Algonquian *apan*, which means something baked. The amount of water depended on how it would be cooked—as small pones or "dodgers" cooked in the ashes or in a skillet or as a bigger pone baked in a Dutch oven or, later, in a skillet in a regular oven. Here's a description of making pone outdoors from 1890: "Corn meal is stirred up with water and a little salt, and the solid mass is put on to bake, or rather to dry, on a board by the fire. Sometimes to make it more palatable and digestible, it is baked in the fat after the bacon is cooked." (Don't you love the idea that bacon fat makes it more digestible?) North Carolina's Wilma Dykeman, in her historical novel *Tall Woman*, wrote, "So she had found meat and a pone of bread for him to carry as he went." She didn't have to bother to say cornbread. Today, we tend to think of pones as small, but it's clear that a skillet-sized piece was also called a pone: "Back in my day, you put a pone of bread on the table and passed it around for everybody to break 'em off a piece," one North Georgian told food writer Joe Dabney.

The Skylight Inn and Bum's in Ayden serve their barbecue with a thin, crispy rectangle of old-fashioned baked cornpone, the way folks down east seem always to have done. Since Bruce Jones and Bum Dennis are cousins, it's not a surprise that their cornbreads are also close kin. Shirley Dennis (Mrs. Bum) at Bum's kindly shared the recipe. It's classic: finely ground cornmeal, salt, water (warm or cold but not boiling), and lard. (There's a lot of lard in this chapter. Don't worry about it. Gastroenterologist John J. Dietschy of the University of Texas Southwestern Medical School points out that "lard's no big deal. The real danger in the human diet is in total calories consumed. All oils are extremely rich, about nine calories per gram.") The Skylight used to use fat from the pigs, but Samuel

From "When de Co'n Pone's Hot"

Tek away yo' sody biscuit,
   Tek away yo' cake and
   pie,
Fu' de glory time is comin',
   An' it's 'proachin'
   mighty nigh,
An' you want to jump an'
   hollah,
   Dough you know you'd
   bettah not,
When yo mammy says de
   blessin'
   An' de co'n pone's hot.
—Paul Laurence Dunbar,
1895

"Real cornbread is sunny tasting and golden crispy, thin with a high ratio of crust to center." (Ronni Lundy)

Jones says pigs now don't yield enough fat. He needs rectangular pans to make the pone for the Skylight's unique barbecue tray, a sort of tian of barbecue in three layers: a cardboard boat of barbecue on the bottom, a rectangle of cornbread, and a boat of slaw on top.

This is pretty close to what you get in Ayden:

Ayden Cornpone

4 cups finely ground white cornmeal

2 teaspoons salt

4 cups water (or more—you want a batter you have to spread
   a bit, like cake batter; if you prefer the texture of hot-water
   cornbread, boil the water)

1/4 cup lard

Preheat the oven to 500°. Melt the lard in a 9″ × 13″ pan in the preheating oven. Mix the dry ingredients, add the water, and stir well. When the oven reaches 500°, take out the pan and pour most of the hot lard into the batter. Stir well. Pour the batter into the hot pan. Lower the heat to 450° and bake for about 1 hour.

This bread is great without barbecue, too. Fry little pones for breakfast and serve them with sorghum, or sorghum foam—heat a quarter cup or so of sorghum in a pan and drop in a large pinch of baking soda. (Southerners were doing molecular gastronomy long before it had a name.) Better yet, let the kids do it—they'll love it. If you want to make your pone in an iron skillet, as most folks do, cut the proportions in half for a nine-inch skillet. In hot weather, you might want to do the entire process on top of the stove rather than in the oven. If so, heat the pan with the lard on top of the stove, pour the lard into the batter and stir, immediately spread the batter in the skillet, and cook over medium-low heat about fifteen minutes, until it's crisp on the bottom. Slide it out onto a plate and flip it gracefully back into the skillet, raw-side down. Cook another five or ten minutes.

EVERYDAY CORNBREAD

There's a whole book to be written on cornbread variations, but this isn't it. (Craig Claiborne said, "There are more recipes for cornbread than there are magnolia trees in the South.") The first refinement seems to have been to make it with buttermilk rather than water and add a bit of baking soda. As cornbreads developed, wheat flour, sugar, baking powder and/or baking soda, and eggs became common additions. *The Carolina Housewife* contains twenty-two recipes for cornbreads. Almost all have eggs and milk, but only two have wheat flour and two have sugar. Since that book was published in 1847, however, wheat flour and sugar have been sneaking into our cornbreads (perhaps more in the lowlands than in the mountain South), and we've seen a surprising amount of yellow cornbread, too.

Here are some cornbreads with some of those modern additions. (You can always leave out the sugar.) Dried buttermilk works adequately and keeps a long time, or you can use plain yogurt, thinning the batter with water as needed. You can also make sour milk by putting a tablespoon of vinegar in a cup of milk and letting it stand five minutes.

Basic Oven Cornbread

1 cup cornmeal
1 cup flour

"For mercy's sake, don't put any sugar in your corn bread. That's like trying to eat grits with sugar and cream. A Yankee strays down this way and tries it once in a while, but it's a pitiful thing to see." (Betsy Tice White)

Cornbread gussied up with eggs and baking powder and such

1 tablespoon sugar (optional)

4 teaspoons baking powder (plus 1/2 teaspoon baking soda if using buttermilk)

1/2 teaspoon salt

1 large egg, beaten

About 1 1/4 cups sweet milk or 1 1/2 cups buttermilk

4 tablespoons fat (butter, bacon grease, or lard)

Preheat the oven to 350°. Heat the fat in an 8″ × 8″ pan or a 9″ skillet. Mix the dry ingredients, add the egg and milk, and stir well. Pour most of the hot fat into the batter and stir quickly. Pour the batter into the hot pan and bake for about 30 minutes.

Cornbread with Self-Rising Meal and Flour

1 cup self-rising cornmeal

1/2 cup self-rising flour

1 tablespoon sugar (optional)

2 large eggs, lightly beaten

1 1/4 cups buttermilk or sweet milk

Preheat the oven to 350°. Mix the dry ingredients, then add the eggs and milk and stir well. Pour the batter into a greased 8″ × 8″ pan or 9″ skillet and bake for about 30 minutes.

Hot Water Cornbread

Some recipes call for scalding the cornmeal with boiling water before it's mixed with the other ingredients. Bill Neal says stoneground meals are irregular and slow to absorb liquid, so pouring boiling water on them softens them. We don't see much of a pattern behind which recipes call for boiling water and which don't; nearly all recipes for spoonbread do, though, probably because spoonbread has such a delicate texture.

Then there's cracklin' cornbread, just in case you want a little more fat with your modern lean pork. Cracklin's were a by-product of rendering pork fat to make lard at hog-killing time. Because few of us render our own lard any more, we've borrowed Bill Neal's directions for making cracklin's.

Cracklin's

2–3 ounces pork sidemeat (fatback)
1/4 cup cold water

Remove any rind from the sidemeat and dice the sidemeat finely. Combine the sidemeat with the water in the skillet over low heat. Cook, stirring occasionally, until the fat is rendered and the cracklin's are crisp and brown, approximately 40 minutes. Drain the cracklin's on a brown paper bag. The rendered fat may be used as the shortening in the cornbread, if desired.

You can put cracklin's in any cornbread recipe—try one part cracklin's to two parts meal.

CORNSTICKS

Cornsticks occupy a sort of middle ground—they're more refined than pones, but they keep the high ratio of crust to center that makes cornpone so satisfying. Parker's in Wilson has served deep-fried cornsticks for years, and we've noticed that some other folks down east have taken up the habit. We assume they've switched because they can buy frozen cornsticks and fry them to order, but they are clearly a popular item. Here's a recipe from *Marion Brown's Southern Cook Book* (1951) for making them yourself. After you've made them, you, too, can deep-fry them at the last minute.

Cornsticks

Makes 1 dozen

2 cups water-ground cornmeal
1 teaspoon sugar
2 teaspoons baking powder

B's in Greenville serves cornsticks.

1/2 teaspoon salt

1 large egg, beaten

1 cup milk

1 rounded tablespoon lard, melted

Preheat the oven to 450°. Grease a heavy iron cornstick pan. Mix the dry ingredients, then add the egg and milk. Stir well, then mix in the lard. Pour the batter into the cornstick pan. Bake for about 20 minutes or until brown and flaky when pricked with a fork.

HUSHPUPPIES

The Romans discovered the joys of deep-fried dough (theirs sounds like a sourdough funnel cake). Sweet or savory fritters abound throughout food history, so the hushpuppy is no surprise. *The Carolina Housewife* includes a recipe for "hommony" (grits) fritters made of cooked grits, wheat flour, eggs, milk, and butter. They sound pretty much like hushpuppies, as do the "Beignets de Farine de Maïs" in *The Picayune's Creole Cook Book* from 1901, which are dropped by spoonfuls into boiling lard, but the first use of the word "hushpuppy" in print found by the *Oxford English Dictionary* was in 1918.

Shaping Hushpuppies

The time-honored way is to scoop up some batter in a spoon and use another spoon to scrape the batter into the hot fat. Some restaurants make so many they have to use machinery, usually a pancake dispenser. Lots of ingenuity and quirkiness have been brought to bear on the problem. Country Junction in Carrboro uses a doughnut machine (and Sweet Betsy mix, so they might as well be corn doughnuts). We know places that squeeze them out of a pastry tube and lop off the desired length—at Fuzzy's in Madison they're so long they're almost funnel cake. The Barbecue Center in Lexington still does them by hand, piling the batter on a wide spatula, then using another spatula to scrape it off. It's labor-intensive but makes big, relatively uniform, hushpuppies.

Jesse Matthews, "The Hushpuppy Man" of Autryville, has invented something even better than a better mousetrap. "Uncle Jesse's Hushpuppy Dropper" drops just the right amount of hushpuppy dough into your fryer, and at $8.00 it's a steal. "I knew there had to be a better way than a spoon," he says.

Making hushpuppies at the Barbecue Center

Uncle Jesse's hushpuppy dropper in action

John Egerton says the name was probably invented around St. Marks, Florida.

Hushpuppies vary from crunchy nuggets of cornpone to airy, sweet creations that, with a little powdered sugar on top, could give New Orleans's beignets a run for their money. Some hushpuppies have onion. Some even have sugar and onion. Every time we think we can generalize about who does what where, we are confounded by so many exceptions that we give up. Here are a few North Carolina recipes to think about trying. Since humidity and fineness of grind make a difference in how much liquid the meal will absorb, these are proportions to start with. Fry them at 350° about three minutes. If they're not done in the middle, add a little more cornmeal to the batter, and if they're too heavy in the middle, add some liquid.

Years ago, a friend from Chicago would always stop by O.T.'s Barbecue in Apex as he headed for RDU and pick up a couple of pounds of barbecue to reconcile his wife to his absence. The first time he did this, he tried to get O.T. to sell him some hushpuppies. O.T. honorably said he wouldn't sell them because they don't travel but he'd give him the recipe. O.T.'s restaurant is gone, but his hushpuppies live on in Chicago and Chapel Hill at least. Here's our version:

OT's Hushpuppies

Serves 6

2 cups self-rising cornmeal
1 cup self-rising flour
2 tablespoons sugar
1 teaspoon salt

Milk or water (*not* buttermilk: it makes them too sour)
Mix the dry ingredients, add enough milk or water to make a thick batter, and stir well. Drop into hot fat.

"*He's married a woman that can't even cook corn bread.*"
(*Not attributed, Foxfire*)

Here are two hushpuppy recipes from the Sanitary Fish Market and Restaurant in Morehead City, the first from *Marion Brown's Southern Cook Book* and a smaller (and somewhat sweeter) version from the restaurant's website:

Sanitary Hushpuppies (Party Size)	Sanitary Hushpuppies (Household Size)
Serves 30 or so	*Serves 6*
5 pounds fine cornmeal	1 pound fine cornmeal (just under 4 cups)

1 tablespoon sugar	1 tablespoon sugar
1 teaspoon baking soda	Pinch baking soda
4 tablespoons salt	1 tablespoon salt
4 large eggs, beaten	1 large egg, beaten
1 quart buttermilk	1 cup buttermilk
Water	Water

Mix the dry ingredients, add the eggs and buttermilk, then add enough water to make a thick batter. Stir well. Drop into deep fat (they use peanut oil). Cook at 375° until golden brown.

You can modify this recipe by adding 1 medium chopped onion, sugar to taste, and/or 1 teaspoon sage or thyme.

Hushpuppies with Self-Rising Meal and Flour

Serves 4

1 cup self-rising cornmeal
1/2 cup self-rising flour
1 small onion, chopped
1 large egg, beaten
3/4 cup buttermilk
2 tablespoons vegetable oil

Mix the dry ingredients; add the onion, egg, buttermilk, and oil; and stir well. Drop into hot fat.

Food historian Damon Lee Fowler, who grew up in Clover, South Carolina, not far south of the state line, reports that his mother used to beat the egg whites and fold them into her hushpuppy batter, which made them deliciously light. We tried hers topped with a little powdered sugar and liked them better than funnel cake.

Hushpuppies are so easy that you don't really need a mix, but many restaurants use one, usually from North Carolina companies like Lakeside Mills. Hursey's, in Burlington, has its own recipe prepared by a local mill.

any North Carolina barbecue restaurants offer the choice of a barbecue tray or a barbecue plate, the difference being that a tray gives you barbecue, slaw, and some cornmeal product, while a plate gives you all that and something else, too. Often the added element is just french fries, but if you're lucky, it can be Brunswick stew.

The simplest description of Brunswick stew is from Roy Blount: "Brunswick Stew is what happens when small mammals carrying ears of corn fall into barbecue pits." Lacking a knack for training small mammals, most folks used to hunt them and then fill out the pot with bits of larger animals, poultry, and most anything ripe from the garden. Gradually, they have let other people do the butchering, and nearly everyone has given up on small mammals altogether, but it's clear that Brunswick stew was originally just a kind of hunter's stew, made with whatever was handy. As John Egerton explains it, "When people were living in the woods, this was kind of their Campbell soup. It was just a staple: You took a little bird, a little squirrel, a little rabbit, some vegetables, and you made something warm and hearty."

"Despite the fact that [Brunswick] stew and tender picked pork barbecue share many common flavors, most Southerners find the redundancy quite satisfying." (Wilber W. Caldwell)

"When you get away from a cast-iron pot and firing with wood, you've done got away from the Brunswick stew business." (Joe Dabney)

A barbecue plate at Chapel Hill's Allen & Son includes a bowl of Brunswick stew.

The Feds nixed the plans of King's Barbecue in Kinston to sell its Brunswick stew by mail order because it is made with only one meat (pork). "They said it can be possum and cats if you want," Wilbur King told the Charlotte Observer, *"but it has to have two."*

James Villas points out that although "some of the best Brunswick stew on earth is found at dozens of legendary barbecue joints in the eastern part of [North Carolina,] Georgians and Virginians hardly consider Tarheels real contenders: they don't have much impressive Brunswick stew history and they don't even *respect* it enough to serve it primarily as a main course." He's right about that last part. As Kathleen Purvis has put it, in North Carolina "Brunswick stew is the poor cousin in the barbecue world. Always hanging around in the background, hoping somebody will notice it. Tucked on to a plate of barbecue more to round out the meal than to actually be eaten." So we don't really care whether Georgians or Virginians prevail in their everlasting argument about where B.S. originated. Since the Indians had stews of squirrel and hominy and bear and deer and squash and corn, they're really only fighting over their right to claim the name anyway. If we had to take sides, we'd go with Virginians, who say they started it in 1828—we certainly haven't seen the name any earlier.

Mary Randolph's *Virginia Housewife* (1824) has an "Ochra Soup" containing chicken, okra, lima beans, squash, tomatoes, and bacon or pork and thickened with butter and flour. Omit the okra and squash, and you have standard Brunswick stew ingredients. What are those? We'll start with where we've ended up—government regulations. In its wisdom, the Department of Agriculture's Food Safety and Inspection Service (which has authority over all products containing more than 3 percent fresh meat or at least 2 percent cooked poultry meat) has decreed that anything labeled "Brunswick stew" must contain at least 25 percent meat, made up of at least two kinds of meat, including poultry meat, and must contain corn as one of the vegetables. Anything called "*poultry* Brunswick stew" has to have at least 12 percent poultry meat and must contain corn. Other than that—well, see the list on the opposite page.

We'll let Virginia and Georgia continue to fight over who invented Brunswick stew—y'all let us know when you've sorted that out. Since the honor of our ancestors is not at stake, Tar Heels do pretty much whatever we want with our stew. Thicken it with rice? Down at Mallard Creek, practically in South Carolina, that makes sense to us. Add mashed potatoes, like some Virginians, or puréed pork and beans, like Clyde Cooper's? Fine, too. We haven't heard of any North Carolinians grinding the meat from hogs' heads, but most other variations turn up somewhere or other. This laissez-faire attitude makes it hard for us to generalize about North Carolina stew. Barbecue places ten miles apart can have stews that seem like they came from different planets.

Brunswick stew is often served as a full meal, with bread and tea. *The Southern Literary Messenger* rhapsodized in 1863 that "there was no other dish but the Brunswick stew, and that was enough; for it contained all the meats and juices of the forest and garden magnificently conglomerated and sublimed by the potent essence of fiery Cayenne, pod upon pod, lavishly thrown in." Like barbecue, it is often cooked outdoors (in huge iron pots), is often served at community fund-raising events or church gatherings, and takes forever to make. In the nineteenth century, the stew seems to have been more common in the East than in the Piedmont, which would make sense if it came from Virginia.

You may have noticed that we haven't gotten to a recipe yet. That's a matter of some dispute, as you would expect. In fact, we can't tell you how many times we've run into assertions like, "Our stew is different because we use chicken *and* pork and most folks only use chicken"—which shows only that the speaker has no idea what's really in most folks' stew but wants to claim that his is better, which is the point, after all.

Here's an approximation of a nineteenth-century North Carolina–style Brunswick stew. North Carolina barbecue website proprietor H. Kent Craig got the original recipe years ago from his

The Barbecue Center in Lexington serves "barbecue soup": vegetable soup with a handful of chopped barbecue added.

"Brunswick stew, often cooked out-of-doors to serve community groups, is a thick stew usually made of chicken, butter beans, onion, corn, and tomatoes, and seasoned with salt pork." (North Carolina: A Guide to the Old North State, 1939)

then-101-year-old grandmother, Betty King, whose family's history in North Carolina goes back to a land grant from King Charles II. It called for squirrels, but Kent suggests that you can still get that traditional flavor by using chicken and rabbit instead. (If you really don't like that small-mammal idea, use three pounds of chicken and a pound of round steak.) If you've got some venison, go ahead and throw that in, too.

The Secret of Stew

"Everyone who claims to know the true secret of Brunswick stew disagrees about what the secret is. Indeed, it would appear that there is not just one secret, but rather thousands or even tens of thousands of secrets, at least one for every Southerner who makes the stuff. And given the true Southerner's impossibly stubborn nature, his unbending intransigence, his almost religious reverence for tradition, his outbursts of prideful braggadocio, and his irrational resistance to change of any kind, true sons (or daughters) of the Deep South will not forsake their granddaddy's secret, behind-the-barn Brunswick stew recipe. 'Now, this is real Brunswick stew,' they will loudly declare, 'not that limp-assed chick'n 'n' frozen vegetable crap you usually git.'"
—Wilber W. Caldwell

King Family Brunswick Stew

Serves 8–10

About 2 pounds chicken
About 2 pounds rabbit
1 tablespoon salt
6 ears corn, kernels cut off cob
2 cups fresh lima beans
6 potatoes, peeled and diced
1 onion, minced
3 drops pressed garlic or to taste
1/2 pound salt pork
1 teaspoon black pepper
1/4 teaspoon cayenne
2 teaspoons sugar
4 cups sliced tomatoes
1 cup butter
1/4 cup sifted flour

Cut the meat into serving pieces. In a large pot, add the salt to 4 quarts water and bring to a boil. Add the corn, lima beans, potatoes, onion, garlic, pork, black pepper, cayenne, and meat. Cover and simmer for 2 hours, then add the sugar and tomatoes and simmer for 1 hour more. Ten minutes before removing from the heat, add the butter cut into walnut-sized pieces and rolled in flour. Bring to a boil.

Notice the presence of salt pork. Very common in North Carolina stews, it has many names, including "sidemeat," "fatback," "white bacon," or even "white meat" (which gives new meaning to "the other white meat").

Here's another stew with a good pedigree, from Ben Averett, interviewed by David Cecelski for the University of North Carolina's Southern Oral History Program. Mr. Averett got the recipe from Mrs. Sterling Carrington, who "ran the stew at Hester Baptist Church."

Mrs. Carrington's Oxford Brunswick Stew

Serves a crowd — 80? 100? More?

2 squirrels

8 pounds beef

8 pounds pork

7 frying-size chickens (never use frozen)

2 pounds onions, sliced

2 cayenne peppers

1 gallon tiny butterbeans

10 pounds potatoes, peeled and quartered

8 quarts tomatoes, peeled and squeezed to remove seeds and
  watery pulp

120 ears of corn, kernels cut off the cob

1/2 cup vinegar

1 cup sugar

1 small bottle Heinz ketchup

1 cup butter

Salt and black pepper (add 3 tablespoons of each every time you
  add a new ingredient)

6:00 A.M.: To boiling water in a 25-gallon pot add the meat, onions, and cayenne peppers. Keep it boiling, adding water as needed. As the meat settles, pick out the bones.

10:00 A.M.: Add the butterbeans, salt, and pepper. Keep it boiling.

1:00 P.M.: Add the potatoes, salt, and pepper. Keep it boiling.

About 3:00 or 4:00 P.M.: The potatoes should be done, the butterbeans will have nearly disappeared, and you can no

longer identify the meats. Add the tomatoes. Cook for about 1 hour, until they've fallen to pieces.

30 minutes before serving: Add the corn.

15 minutes before serving: Add the remaining ingredients and taste for seasoning.

Between 5:30 and 6:00 P.M., you should be ready to eat. Serve with slaw, white bread or crackers, and iced tea.

Finally, here's an easy, family-sized recipe for a first-rate Virginia-style stew, adapted from one in James Villas's *Bacon Cookbook*.

James Villas's Brunswick Stew

Serves 8–10

3-pound chicken, cut up

1/4 pound thick-cut sliced bacon

1 pound potatoes, peeled and diced

1 pound potatoes, peeled and quartered

1 1/4 pounds onions, chopped

4 tablespoons butter, divided

5 teaspoons salt, divided

5 teaspoons sugar, divided

3/4 teaspoon freshly ground black pepper, divided

3/4 teaspoon cayenne, divided

28-ounce can crushed tomatoes, with juice

28-ounce package frozen baby lima beans

16-ounce package frozen corn kernels

Place the chicken and bacon in a heavy 12-quart pot and fill with water to cover by an inch or so. Bring to a boil, reduce the heat, and simmer uncovered for 1 1/2 hours or until the chicken is tender. Remove the meat, leaving the broth in the pot. Dice the bacon. Take the chicken off the bones, discard the skin and bones, and shred the meat with your fingers.

Put the bacon and chicken back in the broth and add the potatoes and onions, 1 tablespoon butter, 1 1/2 teaspoons each salt and sugar, and slight pinches black pepper and cayenne. Return to a simmer and cook for about 1 hour, stirring at least

every 15 minutes, until the potatoes are very tender. Remove the quartered potatoes, mash roughly with a fork, and return to the broth.

Add the tomatoes and their juice, 1 tablespoon butter, 1 1/2 teaspoons each salt and sugar, and slight pinches black pepper and cayenne. Return to a simmer and cook for about 1 hour, stirring at least every 10 minutes.

Add the lima beans, 1 tablespoon butter, remaining 2 teaspoons each salt and sugar, and slight pinches black pepper and cayenne. Return to a simmer and cook for 1 hour, stirring at least every 10 minutes.

Add the corn and 1 tablespoon butter, return to a simmer, and cook, stirring constantly, for 15–20 minutes, until the stew is very thick. Serve hot.

If you want your stew a little darker and stringier, throw in a ham hock, 1 pound of round steak, or a squirrel.

OPTIONAL SIDE DISHES

"Side dishes are generally designed not to distract from the main event. ... The meal is not about balance. It is about focus, and the focus is on barbecue." (Wilber W. Caldwell)

If you ask North Carolinians what foods go with barbecue, they'll nearly all say slaw and some sort of cornbread (usually hushpuppies). After that, there'll be less agreement. Many will add Brunswick stew, and Easterners will probably mention boiled potatoes (boiled to death, sometimes with a little paprika or barbecue sauce or Texas Pete in the water to give them a hint of color and flavor). If there's anything else, it's probably something that would appear on the menu of a good country buffet, including (as we said earlier) chicken as a sort of side dish and, of course, cobblers and banana pudding.

We want you to be able to create a classic North Carolina barbecue meal, so here are recipes you might could use, along with a bit of their history. We haven't tried to include every dish you might want, just the most likely.

GREENS

Greens are essential for any down-home buffet and are served in most barbecue places that can be called restaurants rather than

Potatoes for a crowd, Braswell Plantation, 1944

joints. You probably don't need a recipe, but we keep thinking about poor, homesick expatriate North Carolinians trying to re-create a real pig-picking. Once when we were putting on a Southern New Year's feast in England, we had to use a leafy variety of bok choy for greens. It acted a lot like greens—a great armful cooked down to almost nothing—and with lots of smoked pork it tasted pretty good, too, but if we hadn't been cooking greens for years, we wouldn't have known where to start. North Carolina restaurants tend to serve turnip greens or collards or sometimes a mix of two or three greens. Mildred Council of Mama Dip's Kitchen in Chapel Hill says, "We didn't grow collard greens on our farm in Chatham County. Collards came to this area after World War II, maybe in the 1950s. This is a cold-weather vegetable—the flavor is best after October." (Several friends have said that when nature hadn't yet obliged with a frost, their mothers put fresh collards in the freezer.) *Marion Brown's Southern Cook Book* (1951) mentions collards but gives recipes for only turnip and mustard greens.

Southerners figured greens out early and haven't messed with success. Mary Randolph, in *The Virginia Housewife* (1824), says, chauvinistically but correctly, that turnip greens are "better boiled with Bacon in the *Virginia Style*." Lettice Bryan, in *The Kentucky Housewife* (1839), says much the same thing, though she ignores the Virginia pedigree: "They should always be boiled with bacon, it being the only good way they can be prepared." She also mentions another critical development: "Have salt, pepper and vinegar to season it

> ## From "The First Mess of Greens"
>
> I have never tasted meat
> Nor cabbage, corn nor beans
> Nor fluid food one half as sweet
> As that first mess of greens.
> —Cotton Noe, 1912

One pound of raw collards

One pound of stemmed collards, cooked

at table." We're not sure when people started adding onions, either cooked in the dish or raw on top. They're common but not essential. No early writer mentions sugar, but many folks now add a pinch or two. We don't think it's simply the Southern addiction to sugar—it does soften the flavor a bit.

You'll need a lot of greens. John Egerton quotes Tennessean Ben Hutcherson: "A grocery sack full of greens will cook down to a nice mess, plenty for four to six hungry people." We've seen recipes that say three pounds for six servings and recipes that say six pounds for six servings. A pound is plenty for four people as a side dish, but you should err on the generous side because no one minds having leftover greens and you can always make pot likker soup. The proportion of water to greens is crucial—you don't want too much because you don't want to dilute your pot likker, but all the old-timers say that too little leaves the greens bitter. The following recipe gives you some proportions, but feel free to play it by ear.

Your Mama's Basic Greens

Serves 4

1 pound greens
Turnips, peeled and diced (if they came with greens)
1–2 strips bacon, 1/2 cup chopped ham, or 1/4 pound salt pork
   or streak-o-lean
1 dried red pepper pod (optional)
Pinch of sugar (optional)
1 teaspoon salt

Wash the greens very well by dunking them in a big bowl of water and shaking them around. Repeat until you no longer see grit at the bottom of the bowl. Cut out the large stems and chop or shred the leaves. If you're using bacon or ham for seasoning, fry it in a large pot, remove it from the pot, and reserve, then place the greens and turnips in the pot and cover with water. Add the dried red pepper pod, sugar, and salt. If you're using salt pork, add it now, or add crumbled bacon or ham when the greens are nearly done. Cook until done, then taste for salt.

How long until they're done? Mrs. S. R. Dull, in *Southern Cooking* (1928), says to cook greens for two hours, which is just what Bill Smith of Crook's Corner in Chapel Hill advises, but Mama Dip says about forty-five minutes is enough. You can only decide by tasting, and a lot depends on the age and quality of your greens. Just allow extra time in case you need it. North Carolinian Robert Stehling of Charleston's Hominy Grill says, "I want to cook them until they taste like a mouth full of crushed velvet." He cooks them in chicken stock with garlic, onion, red pepper, and a ham hock for about three hours.

"You don't win friends with salad."
(*Homer Simpson*)

In Ayden, "The Collard Capital of the World," they grow cabbage collards, *Brassica oleracea*. We think they're sweeter than regular collards and have a bit of a broccoli taste. The *Southeast Farm Press* reports that local farmer and entrepreneur Benny Cox, operator of a roadside stand called the Collard Shack, sells up to 500 pounds a day. Cox says it takes about a pound per person to make a meal. Here's how they cook them at Bum's in Ayden, quoted from a handwritten recipe kindly given us by Shirley Dennis:

Bum's Restaurant Collards

We use our home grown Collards.

1/3 pot boiling water
Piece of corned meat
Fresh collards
Salt—to taste
Bacon grease or ham drippings

Fill large pot 1/3 full of water. Bring to a boil. Check collard leaves for trash and insects. Cut large stem ends off. Wash collards in 3 or 4 waters—til water is clear. Add meat to water. Then add collards. Then add salt and seasoning drippings. Cook for 1 1/2 hours or til tender. With slotted spoon, lift collards into a colander, then into a pan and chop the leaves. Skim a little of the drippings off top of water and pour over collards.

This recipe is for Summer Collards.

After frost, the leaves will cook in 30 to 45 minutes of boiling.

At Crook's Corner, Chef Bill Smith knows greens need pork.

Notice that she says "corned meat." Ayden seems to be an island of tradition in the aggressively modernizing down east barbecue world. Folks there have kept the old way of cooking pig, they've kept their old-style cornbread, and this reminds us that they've kept other things the rest of us have lost. "Corned" just means salted: corn in Old English meant grain or seed and was then extended to mean things shaped like grain or seed, including salt and gunpowder, and East Carolinians still talk about corned meat. A favorite holiday dish there, according to Bill Smith, is corned ham. Bill cooks collards every day. Here's his recipe:

Bill Smith's Collards

Serves 4–6

2 bunches (about 5 pounds) fresh collards
6 strips bacon, diced
1 large onion, diced
1 ham bone
1 teaspoon crushed red pepper
2 teaspoons salt

Remove the tougher, woody stalks from the collard leaves. Smaller stems are okay. Wash the leaves and cut them into 1/2-

inch-wide strips. You can roll them into cigars to speed this up. Put the bacon in a stockpot on high heat to render its grease, 3 or so minutes. Add the onion and cook until translucent but not brown, about 5 minutes more. Add the collards and cover with cool water. Add ham bone, crushed red pepper, and salt. Bring to a boil and cook for at least 2 hours. Taste for salt.

Bill notes that even people who love collards complain about how they stink up the house. "People have different cures for this," he says. "Place four pecans in the pot. Cover the top of the collards with slices of white bread. None of this works."

We can't resist including this recipe to go with your collards:

Carroll Leggett's Eastern North Carolina Cornmeal Dumplings

Makes about 8 dumplings

1 cup white or yellow fine or medium cornmeal (white and fine
    seems to be most widely used; add a spoonful of flour if the
    cornmeal is coarse)
1/4 teaspoon salt
1 to 1 1/4 cups water

Mix the cornmeal and salt. Add the water a little at a time while stirring until the batter is smooth but stiff enough to hold together. Set it aside a few minutes. Wet your hands. Pinch off dumplings in balls a little bigger than golf balls and flatten them a bit so they're about 3 inches across and 1/2-inch thick. Lay them on top of the greens in the pot, cover, and boil gently until done.

Bill Neal made his dumplings with boiling water, starting with half a cup for a cup of cornmeal and adding a tablespoon of melted bacon fat or lard. He liked his dumplings much smaller, the size of checkers, and thinner in the middle.

OKRA

Fried okra is served in many North Carolina barbecue restaurants, and we always order it when we find it. There are plenty of early recipes for okra, by itself or in soups, but we haven't been able to discover when people began frying it, probably because it was something everyone knew how to do. In 1870 Annabella Hill published a recipe for okra fritters, made with mashed okra, flour, and egg, which is fancier but probably not better than plain fried okra.

Fried okra is nearly as variable as hushpuppies. It can have a crisp, firm crust; a tender, tempuralike crust; or something in between. Marion Brown doesn't bother to give a recipe in her cookbook. She just says this: "Annie, our cook for many years, slices the okra into sections about 1/2 inch long, dredges the sections in flour, and fries them in hot fat." Mrs. Dull gives pretty much the same directions but reminds readers to salt the fried morsels. Here's a recipe with a little more detail, from our Southern food guru, John Egerton:

Simple Fried Okra

Serves 2–4

Slice off the thick stem ends of 1 pound of okra pods, cut into 1/4-inch rounds, place them in a large bowl, sprinkle liberally with salt, cover with ice water, and refrigerate until quite cold. Drain well. Roll slices in cornmeal seasoned with salt and pepper, and when well coated, fry them in hot fat about 1/2-inch deep in a black skillet. When brown and crisp, drain on paper towels and serve hot.

One day, to go with our tomato sandwiches, we tried most of the flour and cornmeal variations we could think of with some tiny, beautiful okra from a roadside stand. We soaked half in good buttermilk and half in ice water, then breaded each kind in cornmeal, corn flour, flour, or a half-cornmeal/half-flour mixture. Surprisingly, buttermilk made a tougher crust than water. Last, we even tried sprinkling the slices with flour, then water, then flour, then water again, but they were a little tough and it seemed a waste of energy. We liked plain corn flour best. This ultra-fine-ground cornmeal can be ordered on the web, or you can make a reasonable facsimile by pulsing cornmeal in your food processor until it's as fine as flour. If you like a delicate coating, you could also try

"There is a documented case in a Little Rock household of a transplanted New Yorker who declined a serving of fried okra on the ground that he was a vegetarian." (Mike Trimble)

Fried okra at the A&M in Mebane—also thick red sauce and pale pink slaw

plain flour, which makes a tempuralike crust. Some folks swear by a mixture of self-rising flour and cornmeal, but it didn't seem an improvement to us.

We fried ours in peanut oil at about 370°. There might be occasions when you'd like to add a little bacon grease to the frying oil—maybe a quarter of a cup to your skillet of oil. Check after frying to see if it needs more salt and pepper. A little cayenne is always good, either in the breading or sprinkled on afterward. We're told on good authority that frozen okra works perfectly well.

If you want something less traditional, you could try blanching whole tiny okra pods (1 1/2 inches or so) in boiling water for three or four minutes and then frying them as above. They're very pretty, but our taste is mostly in our mouths, so we personally like sliced okra better, to get more crunch to the munch.

BAKED BEANS

Baked beans have no Southern pedigree at all, as far as we can tell. They are said to have come from Indians in New England who cooked them with bear fat and maple syrup. The Puritan settlers found them a useful aid in keeping the Sabbath—the *American Heritage Cookbook* says that "the bean pot could be kept in the slow heat of a fireplace to serve at Saturday supper and Sunday breakfast," serving the same purpose as a Jewish cook's cholent. In the South's

Deviled Egg   **VEGETABLES** Pasta Salad
String Beans   Potato Salad
Pickled Beets   French Fries
Tossed Salad   Cole Slaw
Apple Sauce   Turnip Greens
Stewed Corn   Macaroni Salad
Fresh Fruit Salad   Macaroni & Cheese
Au Gratin Potatoes Stewed Apples
Fried Okra   Garden Peas & Potatoes
Butter Beans   Rice W/Gravy

rural culture, though, keeping the Sabbath by avoiding work was nearly impossible since the cows always needed milking. (We seem to have salved our consciences by trying to avoid pleasure on the Sabbath instead.) James Beard claimed that early-nineteenth-century Southerners adapted the recipe by using molasses and adding onion, tomatoes, and ginger, but we haven't found his source for this assertion—the earliest Southern recipe we've found is Mrs. Dull's in 1928. As soon as canned baked beans were readily available, however, Southerners added them to our large repertoire of outdoor meals, from the classic "store lunch," with saltines and Vienna sausages and other packaged foods; to camping trips, where the opened can went on the edge of the coals to heat; to proper picnics and backyard cookouts, where we almost always add onion, mustard, ketchup, and brown sugar (a little more sugar is always good).

Southerners may have come to baked beans late, but we've taken them to our hearts, and Bush Brothers in Tennessee is the leading producer of baked beans in the United States. Its website claims that "the Bush family holds a family reunion every summer at the old family home. Of course, there is always plenty of barbecue and Bush's Baked Beans." Of course.

Here's our favorite recipe. You can use any combination of beans, preferably with a mix of textures—we've tried almost everything, including chickpeas and black-eyed peas.

Lydia's Barbeque Beans

Serves about 8

4 strips bacon, fried, grease reserved
3 onions, chopped
1 clove garlic, minced
1 16-ounce can kidney beans, drained and rinsed
1 16-ounce can pork and beans, drained and rinsed
1 16-ounce can small lima beans, drained and rinsed
1/4 cup vinegar
1/2 cup ketchup
1 teaspoon prepared mustard
1/2 cup brown sugar
1/2 teaspoon black pepper
1/2 teaspoon salt

Preheat the oven to 350°. Brown the onions and garlic in bacon grease. Mix the beans, then add the cooked onions and garlic with their grease and the remaining ingredients. Mix well and pour into a greased casserole. Crumble the bacon on top. Bake for 45 minutes.

POTATO SALAD

We've already mentioned Southerners' taste for Duke's mayonnaise. Here's that company's own classic potato salad recipe:

Duke's Potato Salad

Serves 12

2 pounds red potatoes, boiled and cubed
3 hard-boiled eggs, chopped
1 2.2-ounce can sliced black olives
1/2 cup finely chopped red onion
1/2 cup chopped celery
1/2 cup finely chopped sweet pickles
1/2 cup finely chopped cooked bacon
1 cup Duke's mayonnaise

1 tablespoon Sauer's mustard

1 1/2 teaspoons sweet pickle juice

1 1/2 teaspoons white vinegar

1/2 teaspoon Sauer's black pepper

1/4 teaspoon salt

Mix all ingredients. Refrigerate for at least 1 hour.

MACARONI AND CHEESE

Mac and cheese goes way back. The first known English cookbook, *The Forme of Cury*, published about 1390, contains this recipe for "Macrows": "Take and make a thynne foyle of dowh. and kerve it on peces, and cast hem on boillyng water & seep it wele. take chese and grate it and butter cast bynethen and above as losyns. and serue forth." Got it?

Obviously, despite the legend, Thomas Jefferson did not invent macaroni and cheese. Nor was he the first to bring pasta to what became the United States—it seems to have come with the English. But Jefferson did love the dish and served it often, using imported macaroni and Parmesan cheese from Marseilles. The inventory taken at his death showed 112 3/4 pounds of "Maccaroni."

Here's his cousin Mary Randolph's 1824 macaroni recipe, which is probably very much like his: "Boil as much macaroni as will fill your dish, in milk and water, till quite tender; drain it on a sieve[,] sprinkle a little salt over it, put a layer in your dish then cheese and butter as in the polenta [in layers, with the top layer being thin slices of cheese and butter], and bake it in the same manner ['in a quick oven; twenty or thirty minutes will bake it']."

Finally, here's a good modern recipe.

Macaroni and Cheese

Serves 2–4

8 ounces elbow macaroni

4 1/2 tablespoons unsalted butter, divided

1 small yellow onion, minced

2 tablespoons flour

2 cups whole milk

2 heaping teaspoons salt

Freshly ground black pepper to taste

Freshly grated nutmeg to taste

1/8 teaspoon crushed red pepper

2 1/2 cups grated sharp cheddar cheese

2 tablespoons breadcrumbs

Preheat the oven to 350°. In a large pot, bring 3 quarts salted water to a boil. Add the macaroni and cook until the pasta is al dente—it will cook a bit more in the oven. Drain.

In a large saucepan, heat 3 tablespoons butter. Sauté the onion on low heat until soft, then add the flour and cook, stirring, for about 5 minutes. Add the milk all at once, then the salt and pepper, and cook on medium heat, stirring constantly until it begins to thicken. Simmer for 2 minutes and take off the heat. Add the nutmeg, crushed red pepper, and all but 1/4 cup of the cheese. Stir. Add the macaroni and mix well.

Pour into an 8″ × 8″ baking pan and sprinkle with the remaining cheese, then the breadcrumbs. Dot with the rest of the butter. Bake for 20–25 minutes or until the top is brown.

OTHER INTERESTING SIDE DISHES

Dillard's Barbecue in Durham serves a carrot soufflé that is a classic example of the Southern sweet tooth at work. It's very similar to the dish produced by this recipe, which is all over the web, attributed to Michael D. D'Amico of the Piccadilly Cafeteria:

Original Piccadilly Sweet Carrot Soufflé

Serves 10

3 1/2 pounds peeled carrots

1 1/2 pounds sugar

1 tablespoon baking powder

1 tablespoon vanilla extract

1/4 cup all-purpose flour

6 large eggs

1 cup butter, softened

Sifted powdered sugar

Preheat the oven to 350°. Lightly grease a 9″ × 13″ baking dish. Steam or boil the carrots until very soft. Drain well. While the carrots are warm, add the sugar, baking powder, and vanilla. Beat with a mixer until smooth. Add the flour and mix well. Beat the eggs, add to the flour mixture, and blend well. Add the butter to the mixture and blend well. Pour the mixture into the baking dish; the dish should be about half full since the soufflé will rise. Bake for about 1 hour or until the top is a light golden brown. Sprinkle lightly with powdered sugar before serving.

And what's more Southern than black-eyed peas? The Barbecue Joint in Chapel Hill is a nouvelle barbecue place that we view with mixed feelings on cultural grounds, but there's no question that it serves some great food. Co-owner Damon Lapas shared this rendition of the Southern staple with the *Raleigh News and Observer*.

Barbecue Joint Black-Eyed Peas

Serves 10

1 tablespoon lard or vegetable oil
1 cup diced onion
1/2 cup diced celery
1/2 cup diced carrot
1 teaspoon thyme
2 bay leaves
1 teaspoon salt
1/2 teaspoon black pepper
1/2 pound dried black-eyed peas
1 ham hock
3 cups water

Heat the lard or oil in a large, heavy-bottomed pot over medium-high heat. Add the onion, celery, carrot, thyme, bay leaves, salt, and pepper. Sauté for 3–4 minutes until the vegetables are tender and translucent. Add the peas, ham hock, and water, and bring to a boil. Reduce to a simmer and cook, stirring occasionally, for 1 to 1 1/2 hours or until the peas are tender. Remove the bay leaves before serving.

On the other hand, what's *less* Southern than brussels sprouts—even with bacon? But the Barbecue Joint has a great version of that decidedly untraditional vegetable. To do it right, you need bacon like theirs (brined for a week in water, salt, molasses, and brown sugar, then cold-smoked for twelve hours), but you can get the idea with any good thick-sliced country bacon.

Barbecue Joint Brussels Sprouts (or Green Beans) with Bacon

Serves 6

1 pound fresh brussels sprouts (or green beans)
1/2 pound bacon, diced
3–4 cloves garlic, minced
Salt and black pepper to taste

Blanch the brussels sprouts (or beans) in salted boiling water for about 5 minutes until tender. Drain and plunge into ice water to stop cooking. Slice the brussels sprouts very thin (about 1/8 inch) and set aside. (Leave the green beans whole.)

In a heavy-bottomed pan over medium heat, cook the bacon for 8–10 minutes until crisp. Remove the bacon, leaving the rendered fat in the pan. Add the garlic and sauté until lightly browned, being careful not to burn. Add the brussels sprouts (or beans) and heat through. Toss in the diced bacon and season to taste with salt and pepper.

Finally, there are desserts. Lots of barbecue places don't have them, but when they do, they're so sweet they'll make your teeth ache. Many places proudly announce that theirs are homemade, and even if they're not homemade, they're usually good enough to fool you (like the cobblers at Carolina Barbecue in Statesville). Peach cobbler and banana pudding are the most common, but there's a broad range. Some pies are also favorites, and a few cakes. Most places have ice cream, a necessity for topping cobblers and not a bad finish on its own to a greasy, salty meal.

COBBLERS

Cobblers are pies for relaxed, not to say lazy, cooks. They usually lack a bottom crust, and they tend to be deeper than normal pies. The variations are endless. Older versions often had a crust around the sides and one on top, but cobblers now can also have bottom crusts, and even middle crusts, usually cut in strips, that add a nice dumplingy texture. (This last variation isn't in the early cookbooks, but Mrs. Dull suggested it in 1928 and you often find it on down-home country buffets.) The top crust doesn't have to be rolled pas-

The dessert board at Allen & Son, Chapel Hill

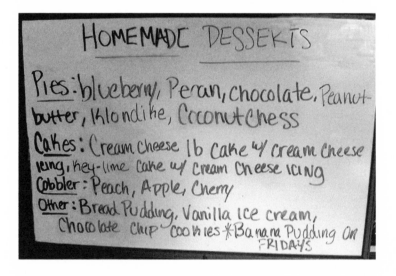

try; sometimes it's just blobs of sweetened biscuit dough. There are also "magic" cobblers that create their own top crusts while cooking (see Dori's Easy Peach Cobbler on the next page).

The word "cobbler" is probably from "cobble," meaning to mend clumsily, because a cobbler is not constructed properly like a pie. The earliest recipe we've found that uses the name is in Lettice Bryan's *Kentucky Housewife* (1839), and it's for "a Peach pot pie, or cobler, as it is often termed," one of the classic desserts at North Carolina barbecue restaurants. The recipe says to "put a paste over the top, and bake it with moderate heat" until it is brown, then "invert the crust on a large dish, put the peaches evenly on, and grate loaf sugar thickly over it." That bit about turning it out on top of the crust seemed weird to us, but it appears again in Georgian Annabella Hill's cookbook (1867), and it certainly makes it easier to judge how much sugar you need. As late as 1913 Martha McCulloch-Williams, in *Dishes and Beverages of the Old South*, still called for removing the top crust, inverting it on a plate, and spooning the seasoned fruit on top.

Here are Mildred Council's directions from *Mama Dip's Kitchen* for the peach cobbler she serves at her Chapel Hill restaurant:

Mildred Council managed Bill's Barbecue, her father-in-law's place, before she opened Mama Dip's Kitchen in Chapel Hill in 1976.

Mama Dip's Cobbler Crust

3 cups flour
1/2 teaspoon salt
2 tablespoons sugar
1 cup shortening
1/4 cup cold water
Melted butter (optional)
Sugar (optional)

Preheat the oven to 375°. Put the flour, salt, and sugar in a bowl. Add the shortening and mix everything together well, using a fork or your fingertips, until crumbly. Add the water and mix to form a moist ball of dough. On a floured board, roll out half of the dough to make a crust that fits the bottom of the baking dish, prick it with a fork a few times, and bake for 10 minutes. It should look done but not brown. Cool for 10–12 minutes, then put the fruit mixture on top. Roll out the rest of the dough, place it on top of the fruit, and prick it with a fork a few times. Or roll it out, cut it into strips, and make a lattice crust over the fruit. If you like, brush the top crust with melted butter and sprinkle with sugar. Bake as specified in the recipe, until the crust is well browned.

Mama Dip's Fresh Peach Cobbler

Serves 8

When making peach cobbler, be sure to taste the peaches. The riper the peaches, the sweeter they will be, which means you should use less sugar. If the peaches are tangy, add a pinch of salt.

2 tablespoons self-rising flour
1/4 teaspoon ground ginger
1 cup sugar
6 cups sliced fresh ripe peaches
6 tablespoons butter
Cobbler crust (above)

Preheat the oven to 375°. Mix the flour, ginger, and sugar, pour over the peaches, and mix well. Put the peach mixture over a bottom crust in a 9" × 13" baking dish. Dot the peaches with butter. Place a top crust over the peaches and bake on the lower rack of the oven for 35–40 minutes.

Dori Sanders is a South Carolina peach farmer and writer who lives so close to North Carolina that it was only a tiny stretch to include her here. *Dori Sanders' Country Cooking* includes this great recipe. Pork shoulder's not the only thing with tasty "outside brown"—check this out (especially the corners).

Dori's Easy Peach Cobbler

Serves 6–8

1/2 cup unsalted butter, melted
1 cup flour
2 cups sugar, divided

1 tablespoon baking powder

Pinch salt

1 cup milk

4 cups peeled, pitted, and thinly sliced fresh peaches
    (5–6 medium peaches)

1 tablespoon fresh lemon juice

Several dashes cinnamon or nutmeg (optional)

Preheat the oven to 375°. Pour the melted butter into a 9″ ×
13″ baking dish. In a medium bowl, combine the flour, 1 cup of
the sugar, the baking powder, and the salt and mix well. Stir in
the milk, mixing until just combined. Pour this batter over the
butter but do not stir them together.

In a saucepan, combine the peaches, lemon juice, and
remaining cup of sugar and bring to a boil over high heat,
stirring constantly. Pour the peaches over the batter but do
not stir them together. Sprinkle with cinnamon or nutmeg,
if desired. Bake for 40–50 minutes or until the top is golden
brown. Serve warm or cold.

You could use self-rising flour and leave out the baking powder. You
could use frozen peach slices or, in extreme circumstances, a 29-
ounce can of peaches or any other fruit, with its juice.

If you want to branch out from peaches, try this recipe:

Lexington Barbecue's Berry, Berry, Berry Cobbler

Mama Dip's Blackberry Cobbler

Serves 6–8

3 cups blackberries
3/4 cup sugar
1 tablespoon flour
Pinch ginger
Pinch salt
4 tablespoons butter
Cobbler crust (pages 165–66)

Preheat the oven to 375°. Wash the blackberries, drain them, and put into a 10″ × 10″ baking dish (over a crust if you like). Mix the sugar, flour, ginger, and salt. Pour over the berries and stir to mix well. Dot the berries with butter. Place a crust over the berries and bake for 35–40 minutes.

Sweet potatoes make good cobblers, too. North Carolina is the leading producer of those tubers in the United States, with about 36,000 acres producing roughly 40 percent of the total U.S. crop. Tabor City celebrates this fact with an annual Yam Festival. Cobblers made with sliced sweet potatoes turn up early and late in the South. Mrs. Cole's handwritten recipe in Virginia in 1837, sent to her by a friend, ends, "Cook it well and send me a piece." Lettice

Bryan's and Annabella Hill's nineteenth-century books include recipes for sweet potato cobbler, as do Mrs. Dull's 1928 *Southern Cooking* (she puts layers of pastry inside as well as on the top and bottom) and Mama Dip's recent best seller, where she describes the dish as a "real down-home dessert." After eating a great one at the Old Place near Siler City, we went looking for a recipe and found one for "Aunt Esther's Sweet Potato Pie" from the Sutherland family of Shelby in Vince Staten and Greg Johnson's *Real Barbecue*. Here's our version:

John's Sweet Potato Cobbler

Serves 6–8

5–6 medium sweet potatoes, peeled and sliced (you want
    something that looks like the slices of apple in apple pie)
Pecans, chopped or halves, to taste (optional)
2 cups sugar (or 1 1/2 cups sugar and 1/2 cup sorghum added
    with liquids)
2 tablespoons cornstarch
1/2 cup butter
Nutmeg
Baptist version: 1 cup water or 1/2 cup water and 1/2 cup
    sorghum molasses
Episcopalian version: 1/2 cup water and 1/2 cup bourbon or 1/2
    cup bourbon and 1/2 cup sorghum
Splash vanilla extract (optional)
Cobbler crust (pages 165–66 or use your favorite)

Boil the sliced sweet potatoes (just give them a head start: leave them somewhat firm). Drain them and spread them over a bottom crust in a 9" × 13" baking dish. Sprinkle the pecans on top, if desired. Mix the sugar and cornstarch and sprinkle on top. Dot with butter and sprinkle with nutmeg. Mix the liquids (and vanilla, if desired) and spoon over the top. Place a top crust over the sweet potatoes and bake for 1 hour or so, until the crust is done.

BANANA PUDDING

Banana pudding, the other classic dessert with North Carolina barbecue, has evolved from English trifle, which is made with layers of fruit, cake, spirits, and custard. Referring to the booze, American recipes often call it Tipsy Cake, Tipsy Parson, or Tipsy Squire (Annabella Hill calls it, delightfully, Gypsy Squire). The banana variety is fairly recent since bananas weren't commercially available in the United States until the 1870s. Early versions stuck with the traditional boiled custard and cake but omitted the spirits, as you would expect in the Baptist-Methodist South. They were often topped with meringue, a way for thrifty cooks to use egg whites left over from the pudding.

A 1901 recipe from *The Picayune's Creole Cookbook*, published in New Orleans, calls for "Stale Cake" and uses a custard made from egg yolks with the whites whipped stiff and folded in. Mary Harris Frazer, in her *Kentucky Receipt Book* (1903), omits the cake but otherwise uses exactly the same ingredients, making the custard with the egg yolks and using the whites for a meringue, baked on top. Removing the egg whites from the custard makes it more like a pudding.

So, by about 1900, we had the custard, bananas, cake, and meringue. In 1901 Nabisco (a conglomerate even then, with no regional identity) began selling Vanilla Wafers, and soon thereafter, some inspired, or just tired, cook put them in her trifle, where they have stayed ever since. By about 1920, Nabisco was printing the recipe on its Vanilla Wafer box, where you can still find it, virtually unchanged (although inside a box we bought in 2007 was a recipe for something called "Easy Southern Banana Pudding" with instant pudding and whipped topping—more about that later). How the dessert became so associated with the South is a mystery, but when you find it elsewhere, it's usually in Southern-themed restaurants.

In the past, some folks made what they called winter pudding, topped with meringue, and summer pudding, topped with whipped cream. Meringue tends to break down rather quickly without refrigeration, but air-conditioning has made the question moot, and it never seemed like a problem to us anyway since there aren't usually

Seventeen shipwrecked Ukrainian sailors rescued off the coast in 2003 were taken to Jackson's Big Oak Barbecue for pulled pork, Brunswick stew, and banana pudding. "Wilmington good," said ship's engineer Vladimir Bqan.

a lot of leftovers. (If you want to make meringue more stable, however, try a hint of vinegar, as in Bill Smith's recipe below. And if you're worried about salmonella, the Pennsylvania Department of Agriculture says you should be safe if the dish has been baked at 350° for 15 minutes.)

You can find Nabisco's banana pudding recipe on any box of their Vanilla Wafers. Basically, it's the same as the New Orleans pudding, if the egg whites are made into a meringue. (By the way, any of these recipes can be returned to their trifle roots by adding a couple of tablespoons of rum or bourbon.) We prefer the unctuous combination of pudding and whipped cream to the standard meringue-topped dish. If you agree, freeze the leftover egg whites in an ice cube tray to use later, or if you like a custardy dessert, just beat the whole eggs with the sugar and follow the rest of the recipe, adding 1/2 teaspoon vanilla extract.

Or you could skip the eggs and make a pudding with cornstarch—maybe this one:

Eggless Banana Pudding

Serves 8

2 pounds ripe bananas (about 5 large bananas)
Vanilla wafers (about 3 dozen)
2 1/2 cups half-and-half (or 2 cups half-and-half and 1/2 cup
     milk, for convenience), divided
2/3 cup sugar
Pinch salt
3 tablespoons cornstarch
2 tablespoons unsalted butter
1/2 teaspoon vanilla extract, or a bit more to taste

Slice the bananas and layer them with the vanilla wafers in a 1 1/2-quart dish. Combine 2 cups of the half-and-half with the sugar and salt in a saucepan. Cook over medium heat until it starts to steam. Meanwhile, combine the cornstarch and remaining 1/2 cup half-and-half (or milk) and whisk until blended. Add to the pan and stir until it starts to thicken and

begins to boil, perhaps 5 minutes. Turn the heat to simmer and cook, stirring, until thick. Stir in the butter. Remove from the heat, stir in the vanilla, and pour over the bananas and vanilla wafers. Serve warm. (If you don't, you'll need to put plastic wrap right on the pudding, to keep a skin from forming.)

(opposite) Banana pudding and pecan pie at Hill's, Winston-Salem

For that matter, you could use packaged cook-and-serve pudding mix, the way "Mama Dip" Council does. She makes it even more Southern by adding that old Southern favorite, sweetened condensed milk, in one of her versions of the pudding:

Mama Dip's Banana Pudding

Serves 8

2 pounds bananas, ripe but not mushy (about 5 large bananas)
Vanilla wafers (about 3 dozen)
2 cups milk (skim milk if you like)
14-ounce can sweetened condensed milk
4.6-ounce box cook-and-serve vanilla pudding mix
1 teaspoon vanilla extract

Slice the bananas and layer them with the vanilla wafers in a 1 1/2-quart dish. Mix the milk and sweetened condensed milk in a saucepan and let them get hot over medium heat but do not let them come to a boil. Using a wire whisk, stir in the pudding mix. Cook only until the pudding begins to thicken. Remove from the heat, add the vanilla, and pour over the bananas and vanilla wafers. Crush a few vanilla wafers and sprinkle them over the top. Serve warm.

And you definitely won't be alone if you decide to use *instant* pudding. You could use a 5-ounce box in Mama Dip's recipe, for instance. But here's a pedigreed recipe that Vince Staten and Greg Johnson got from Wilber's in Goldsboro. Wilber Shirley says: "People think it's a complicated recipe, and I don't tell them otherwise. There ain't nothing to it. My granddaughter could make it if she didn't eat all the cookies first." It's no longer a secret, but people seem to love it just the same.

Wilber's Secret Banana Pudding

Serves 6–8

1 (4-serving) box instant vanilla pudding
2 cups milk
4 medium bananas, sliced
12-ounce box vanilla wafers

Make vanilla pudding according to the package directions. Stir in sliced bananas and vanilla wafers to taste.

Most recipes use two boxes of instant pudding per box of wafers, but Wilber says, "We like to use a lot of wafers to give it a kind of cakey taste."

Notice that Wilber neatly sidesteps the question of meringue versus whipped cream. So do most other folks who use instant pudding—it's supposed to be easy, after all. But the ne plus ultra of convenience is this recipe, from another of Vince Staten's books, *Jack Daniel's Old Time Barbecue Cookbook.* It ought to taste entirely like chemicals, but it's surprisingly good.

Judy's Banana Pudding

Serves 10–12

3 3-ounce boxes instant vanilla pudding
5 cups milk
9-ounce container frozen whipped topping, thawed
8-ounce container sour cream
5–6 bananas
12-ounce box vanilla wafers

Add the pudding mix to the milk and stir until thick. Add the whipped topping and sour cream and stir well. Place 1 layer of wafers in the bottom of a large bowl and cover with 2 sliced bananas. Pour in 1/3 of the pudding. Repeat the layers twice more. Chill.

Finally, for an uptown version of the down-home favorite, try this luxe staple of Bill Smith's kitchen at Crook's Corner. (Bill credits Rose Levy Beranbaum for the pastry cream.)

Crook's Really Good Banana Pudding

Serves 5 plus

4 cups half-and-half, divided
1 vanilla bean, split
6 tablespoons cornstarch
4 large eggs
1 cup sugar
1/2 cup unsalted butter
1 box vanilla wafers (not artificially flavored)
2 1/2 pounds ripe bananas
Meringue

Scald 3 cups of the half-and-half with the split vanilla bean in a heavy-bottomed pot until it just steams and begins to form a skin, about 5 minutes over medium-high heat. Do not boil. Meanwhile, beat the cornstarch into the remaining cup of half-and-half to dissolve it. Then beat in the eggs. Whisk the hot half-and-half into the egg mixture in a slow stream. Strain all this back into the heavy-bottomed pot. Return the vanilla bean to the mixture. Cook over medium-high heat, stirring constantly. In 3–5 minutes, the custard will begin to thicken and to tug at the whisk. Continue to stir for a few minutes more, being sure to move the whisk over the entire bottom of the pot. When the surface begins to steam a little, gradually stir in the sugar. Be careful because this will make the custard more likely to burn on the bottom. Remove from the heat and beat in the butter, 2 tablespoons at a time. Stir constantly so that the butter is absorbed before it separates. (This will temporarily thin the custard. Don't worry about it.) Discard the vanilla bean.

Pour a cup of the hot custard into a 9-inch glass pie pan. Line the bottom and sides with vanilla wafers. Slice the bananas over the cookies, then layer any remaining cookies over the bananas.

Gently fill the casserole with the rest of the custard. While the pudding settles, make the meringue.

Meringue

2 tablespoons cider vinegar
1/4 teaspoon salt
3/4 cup egg whites (from about 8 large eggs)
1/4 teaspoon cream of tartar
1 cup sugar, divided

Preheat the oven to 300°. Put the vinegar and salt in a mixing bowl. Swirl the bowl around and dump it out over the sink. The amount of vinegar and salt that clings to the bowl is the right amount. Add the egg whites and beat with a mixer at medium speed. Add the cream of tartar. Increase the mixer speed a bit and drizzle in 3/4 cup of the sugar. When the sugar is absorbed, increase the speed to high and beat until stiff peaks form. Spread the meringue over the top of the pudding with a spatula, making lots of dramatic swirls and curlicues. Sprinkle the rest of the sugar evenly over the top.

Bake for 30 minutes at 300°, checking from time to time for browning. When it begins to color, turn up the heat to 325° and cook for 10 minutes more or until the points of the meringue are toasty. Serve hot, warm, or cold—this can be served at once or day-old.

BREAD PUDDING

Bread pudding is a common dessert in barbecue restaurants. It's an old, probably ancient, dish that fits the rural Southerner's waste-not-want-not worldview, and it's found in all the old Southern cookbooks. The distinction between bread pudding (made with bread crumbs) and bread-and-butter pudding (made with buttered slices of bread) seems to have been lost in the modern South, although it still hangs on in England.

To give this dessert a Tar Heel twist, why not make it with Krispy Kreme doughnuts? The Krispy Kreme as we know it was born in Winston-Salem in 1937. It has become iconic for Southerners, and if there's any justice, it should become as well known as Coca-Cola worldwide. Roy Blount wasn't exaggerating when he said, "When they're hot, they are to other doughnuts as angels are to people."

Still, sometimes we buy more hot ones than we can eat at one sitting. Cold ones can be microwaved for eight seconds to restore some of that classic flavor, but bread pudding offers another use for leftover doughnuts. As usual, the folk process has been at work, and recipes are now everywhere, with lots of variations (Raleigh's Falls River Smokehouse adds chocolate chips).

Here are two versions. Use either the ingredients listed on the left or those listed on the right with the doughnuts.

Krispy Kreme Bread Pudding

Serves 8

3 cups whole milk	1 cup heavy cream plus 1 cup whole milk
2 egg yolks	5 egg yolks
2 whole eggs	1 whole egg
1 tablespoon sugar	1/2 cup sweetened condensed milk
1/4 teaspoon nutmeg	
1/2 teaspoon salt	
1 teaspoon vanilla extract	

9 day-old Krispy Kreme doughnuts, cut into sixths (for a slightly firmer pudding, bake the doughnuts at 250° for about 30 minutes—the outsides should be firm but the centers still soft)

Preheat the oven to 350°. Butter an 8″ × 8″ pan. (You can double the recipe and bake it in a 9″ × 13″ pan or whatever you have that's approximately the right size—just cook the pudding until a knife stuck into the center comes out clean.)

Mix everything but the doughnuts well. Pour the mixture over the doughnuts in a large bowl and allow to stand for 30 minutes to 1 hour, stirring occasionally. Pour into the buttered pan and bake, uncovered, for 45 minutes to 1 hour. (Some folks place the pan in a bigger pan and add hot water to go about halfway up the pudding pan, but we don't think it makes any difference and it's a pain.)

For the sauce:

1/2 cup salted butter (or 1/2 cup unsalted butter and pinch salt)

1 cup sugar

1/2 cup whipping cream

4 tablespoons rum, scotch, or—why not go all-Southern?—
    bourbon (or you can be Southern in a different way and avoid
    the alcohol altogether by substituting 1 teaspoon vanilla
    extract or 2 or more tablespoons lemon juice plus some
    grated rind)

Melt the butter in a small saucepan over medium heat, then
stir in the remaining ingredients and simmer, stirring, until the
sauce thickens a bit. Serve warm over the pudding.

PIES

The most common pies in barbecue restaurants are probably pecan,
apple, lemon chess, and the classic lemon icebox pie made with
sweetened condensed milk. We also see a lot of chocolate, and key
lime seems to have moved north with the palmetto bugs. But after
that, it's hard to generalize.

Pecan pie is a Southern favorite—indeed, a Southern cliché—but
it turns out to be a pretty recent tradition, as traditions go. The nut
is native to North America (the name comes from an Algonquian
word meaning "all nuts requiring a stone to crack"), and Washington and Jefferson both grew pecans—so why can't we find any
pecan recipes in early cookbooks? We find almonds and walnuts
in desserts, and a recipe in the *Carolina Housewife* (1847) uses finely
pounded peanuts, but we don't find pecans.

That early peanut pie recipe, however, is almost the same idea as
the corn syrup–less pecan pie Dale grew up with. Here's the recipe,
from a family friend, which is said to be from Williamsburg:

Syrup-free Pecan Pie

Serves 6–8

4 tablespoons butter

2 cups brown sugar

3 large eggs

Williamsburg pecan pie

1 tablespoon cornmeal (optional)

1 1/2 to 2 cups pecans, chopped or halves (your call)

Unbaked pie crust

Preheat the oven to 350°. Melt the butter in the top of a double boiler. Whisk together the brown sugar and eggs and stir into the melted butter. Heat the mixture, stirring, until it's warm and thoroughly combined. (You could add a tablespoon of cornmeal for the crunch.) Pour into the pie shell. Arrange the pecans on top. Bake for 30 minutes.

By the way, don't use sugar made from beets—it doesn't set properly. Right now Dixie Crystals, Domino, C&H, and the Harris Teeter house brand are still made from cane, but read the label.

Pecan pie is clearly first cousin to chess pie and to nineteenth-century molasses pies, but the first actual pecan pie recipe we've found, from *Texas Siftings* in 1888, is a custard pie with pecans, not our sort of pecan pie. A similar recipe appeared in the *Dallas Morning News* in 1898, and the *Oxford English Dictionary*'s first citation of "pecan pie" also comes from Texas, from the *Lone Star Cook Book* of 1901: "Pecan Pie. 1 cup sugar, 1 cup sweet milk, 1–2 cup chopped pecans, 3 eggs, 1 tb. flour. Bake and spread meringue on top."

Karo syrup was introduced in 1902. The company says it was probably named after a woman named Caroline. Since it's pronounced "Kay-ro," however, we'd like to think it was named with the hope that customers would confuse it with a rival product, Roddenbery's cane syrup, produced in Cairo (pronounced "Kay-ro"),

Georgia, since 1889. Be that as it may, the Karo people claim that the wife of a corporate sales executive invented the pecan pie as we know it in the 1930s, and that might well be true.

If you don't already have a Karo pecan pie recipe, just look on the back of a Karo bottle. (It says to use margarine, but use butter.) Some folks use brown sugar and dark Karo, some use white sugar and light Karo, some folks only use two eggs, some use four. We add a tablespoon of cornmeal. You can mix and match and always come up with something pretty good.

Another Southern classic is chess pie. There's no doubt in our minds that the name comes from "cheese pie." (Other explanations, like "it's jes' pie," are cute but unnecessary.) "Cheese" was commonly applied to anything that resembled cheese (head cheese, liver cheese). A Williamsburg cookbook from 1742 includes "Lemon Cheesecakes"—little pies made with sugar, eggs, butter, and lemon juice and with bottom crusts—and another Williamsburg recipe from 1801 for "Chess Pie" calls for sugar, flour, egg yolks, milk, butter, and lemon juice beaten together and cooked in a pie shell. Kentuckian Martha McCulloch-Williams was still calling her chess pies "Cheese Cakes" in 1913. Most of the early recipes do have lemons; maybe plain chess pie is a latecomer, born when someone failed to buy lemons.

Plain Chess Pie

1 cup brown sugar and 1/2 cup white sugar, or 1 1/2 cups white
    sugar
1 teaspoon flour
1 tablespoon cornmeal
2 large eggs, unbeaten
1 tablespoon milk
1 teaspoon vanilla extract
1/2 cup butter, melted
Unbaked pie crust

Preheat the oven to 325°. Mix the sugar, flour, and cornmeal. Beat in the eggs, then add the milk and vanilla. Add the melted butter and mix well. Pour into the pie crust. Bake for 30–35 minutes, until the pie is puffed and yellow.

Chocolate Chess Pie

Follow the recipe for chess pie above, but melt 1 1/2 squares unsweetened chocolate with the butter. You may also add some chopped pecans.

Lemon Chess Pie

Follow the recipe for chess pie above, but use 4 eggs instead of 2 and add 4 tablespoons fresh lemon juice along with the milk and vanilla.

Dale's Lemon-Almond Chess Pie

Follow the recipe for chess pie above, but use 4 eggs instead of 2 and 1/2 teaspoon vanilla extract instead of 1 teaspoon, and add 1/4 cup fresh lemon juice and 1/4 teaspoon almond extract along with the milk and vanilla. Sprinkle slivered almonds on top.

Allen & Son in Chapel Hill serves a great coconut chess pie, but this isn't their recipe:

Coconut Chess Pie

Serves 6–8

1/2 cup butter
1 1/2 cups sugar
3 large eggs, beaten
1 cup flaked coconut
2 teaspoons vinegar
1 1/2 teaspoons vanilla extract
Unbaked pie shell

Preheat the oven to 350°. Combine the butter and sugar in a saucepan and heat, stirring, until melted and well blended. Combine the remaining ingredients and mix well. Pour into the pie shell. Bake for about 1 hour, until a knife inserted in the center comes out clean.

Sweet potato pie is another Southern restaurant staple. We've been known to go to Mama Dip's and order only pie:

Mama Dip's Sweet Potato Pie

Serves 8

1 1/2 pounds sweet potatoes (about 2 medium potatoes)
3/4 cup butter, softened
2 cups sugar
3 large eggs, beaten
1/2 teaspoon ground ginger
1/2 teaspoon nutmeg
1/2 teaspoon ground cloves
Pinch salt
1 teaspoon vanilla extract
1/2 cup milk
Unbaked pie shell

Preheat the oven to 375°. Wash the sweet potatoes, place them in a pot, and cover them with water. Bring to a boil. When the potatoes are soft (after about 45 minutes), drain, cool, and peel. Using a fork or potato masher, mash the potatoes along with the butter and sugar, combining well. Add the eggs and stir in the ginger, nutmeg, cloves, salt, vanilla, and milk. Pour into the pie shell. Bake for 45 minutes, or until the center is firm.

Buttermilk pie is a wonderful use of a classic Southern ingredient that many Southerners don't actually like. Robert Stehling learned to make this pie when he was head chef at Crook's Corner, and it's a favorite now at his own Hominy Grill in Charleston. It's best with great buttermilk like the stuff from Maple View Farms outside Chapel Hill, but you can make it with ordinary grocery-store buttermilk and it will be delicious (if not transcendent).

Robert Stehling's Buttermilk Pie

Serves 8

6 tablespoons unsalted butter, at room temperature
1 cup sugar
2 large eggs, separated
3 tablespoons flour

Robert Stehling's buttermilk pie

1 tablespoon fresh lemon juice
1/2 teaspoon freshly grated nutmeg
1/4 teaspoon salt
1 cup buttermilk
Partially baked pie crust

To blind-bake the crust, put foil over the dough, weight with pie weights or dry beans, and bake at 325° on the bottom rack for 10 minutes. Remove the foil and weights and bake for 5 minutes more, until it looks dry but not at all brown. (We have been known to skip blind-baking without disaster.)

Preheat the oven to 350°. In a medium bowl, combine the butter and sugar until the sugar is completely incorporated. Add the egg yolks and mix well to combine. Add the flour, lemon juice, nutmeg, and salt. With the mixer running, slowly add the buttermilk. Mix well and set aside.

In another bowl, whip the egg whites until they form soft peaks. Pour a small amount of the buttermilk mixture into the whites. Fold gently to combine. Gently fold the egg white mixture into the remaining buttermilk mixture until just combined. Pour the custard into the baked pie shell. Bake in the middle of the oven until the filling is lightly browned and barely moves when the pie is jiggled, about 45–50 minutes.

This is great with fresh raspberries or pureed frozen raspberries, slightly sweetened, and some whipped cream on top never hurts.

Finally: Pie's good. Fried's good. Why not fry a pie?

A few Piedmont barbecue restaurants sell B&G pies from Winston-Salem—they're almost as good as homemade—but we don't know of any place that makes its own, and we don't understand why not. Fried pies are a natural for fingers already greasy from a nice, overfilled sandwich, they can be made ahead, and they don't require forks and plates unless you want ice cream on top.

Fried pies are sometimes called "half-moon pies," and Joe Dabney says they're called "mule ears" in parts of the Piedmont. We hope so. Beth Tartan's Old Salem cookbook calls the apple version "fried apple jacks." The first printed recipe we've found is from Kentuckian Lettice Bryan in 1839:

> Fried pies may be made of any kind of nice fruit, having prepared it in the proper manner, but dried fruit is preferable to green [she means fresh here, not unripe]. Stew it tender, mash it fine, and season it to your taste with sugar and spices. Roll out a sheet of plain or standing paste, nearly one fourth of an inch thick, cut it in as many circular pieces as you wish pies, making them as large as a common sized patty-pan; put your fruit in one half of each piece, and turn the other half over, in the form of puffs, or half moons; cut them smoothly round the edges, closing the paste together, to keep in the fruit, and crimping or notching them handsomely; lay them in a pan of boiling butter, having plenty to cover the pies without having to turn them over, and fry them till they are a nice brown on both sides; then raise them carefully, drain them on an inverted sieve, grate loaf sugar over them, and send them to table warm.

You could use those directions just as they stand, with your standard pie crust dough (perhaps with only half the shortening). You can cut the dough in squares and fold it over to make triangles, if that seems easier. Most pies will only need a tablespoon or two of filling. Dampen the edges with water before you crimp them. *Love* that pan of boiling butter, but peanut oil is probably better for frying, and 375° is a good temperature. (Don't bake them unless you want turnovers, which aren't the same thing at all.) Use fairly deep oil, so the entire pie is crunchy and the same delectable brown. It never hurts to dust the pies with sugar after they've drained.

For fillings, some fresh fruits work perfectly well. (Try blanching four firm, ripe peaches for a minute in boiling water; then peel them, cut them into smallish cubes, and cook them with 1/4 cup of sugar and a little lemon juice.) Good jams and preserves will work, too. But most people use dried fruit. (Sunmaid peaches from your grocery store are okay, but Sunmaid apples look like albinos and taste like nothing—dry your own or hit a health-food store.) Whatever you use—apples, peaches, pears, apricots, or a medley—use 2 cups of dried fruit stewed with about 2 cups of water for pastry using 2 cups of flour. Be stingy with the water at first, adding a bit at a time. You don't want to have to drain the fruit and lose some of the flavor. If you have to pour some water off, boil it down to a syrup and then put it back in the fruit. Add about 1/2 cup of sugar, 1 tablespoon of butter, and spices of your choice—lemon peel, ginger, cinnamon, or (our favorite) nutmeg. We always add some lemon juice, and a tiny bit of almond extract is nice for a change with peaches. With any fruit, you'll probably want to jab it a time or two with a potato masher to get a more mushy texture.

We leave you with Martha McCulloch-Williams's final words on fried pies: "Most excellent for impromptu luncheons or very late suppers—withal wholesome. A famous doctor said often of them, 'You would be only the better for eating an acre of them.'"

AND MOON PIE

Peter Batke says a Moon Pie "is not really a pie at all but just a reprehensible habit." He obviously never microwaved one. Try about 20 seconds for a classic chocolate. (Unwrap it first.) You can also go on the web and find a bunch of wonderfully over-the-top Moon Pie recipes, like Moon Pie ice cream, banana splits, brownies, strawberry shortcake, and Moon Pie Bienville. . . .

WINE JELLY

Wine jellies—think grown-up jello—are ancient and honorable desserts. (Thomas Jefferson served a Madeira jelly at Monticello.) Scuppernongs are our native grape, and you can get scuppernong wine from North Carolina vintners like Duplin Winery in Rose Hill, so why not try it in a jelly? You won't find this dessert at any barbecue place we know of, but maybe you should. Nancy King Quaintance, co-owner of Greensboro's Green Valley Grill, says this has been a holiday and special-event dish for generations of the King family of Fayetteville:

Scuppernong Wine Jelly

Serves 8

2 envelopes powdered gelatin
1/2 cup cold water
1 cup boiling water
9 ounces scuppernong wine
1 cup orange juice
1/2 cup fresh lemon juice
1 1/4 cups sugar
Pinch salt

In a large mixing bowl, sprinkle the gelatin on cold water and let it sit for 5 minutes. Pour the boiling water over the gelatin and stir to dissolve. Mix in the remaining ingredients and stir well. Pour into individual bowls to set, or let it set in the mixing bowl and spoon it out. Top with whipped cream, plain or barely sweetened.

If you want a cooling and different dessert, this is it. You can serve it in those lovely wide champagne glasses that wine snobs deplore.

CAKES

Pound cakes turn up a lot on the menus of barbecue restaurants. Layer cakes are much less common, but we once had a slice of heavenly caramel cake after a tray of nice smoky 'cue, and from time to time you may see red velvet or chocolate cake as well.

Pound cakes are among the oldest American recipes. They began in England as literally a pound of eggs, a pound of flour, and a pound of butter, and in the first cookbook written specifically for the American market, in 1796, Amelia Simmons provided that recipe. She followed it immediately, however, with one for "Another (called) Pound Cake," which changes the proportions and

All desserts are homemade at Allen & Son.

adds brandy and rose water, among other things. The folk process was already at work.

Pound cakes are relatively easy to make, especially since the spread of the ubiquitous and excellent cake mix/pudding mix recipes, and they keep well. Our all-time favorite pound cake comes from Dale's Aunt Eva. She wasn't really Dale's aunt. She was married to Dale's first cousin once removed, but being a generation older, of course she was called "Aunt Eva."

Aunt Eva's Pound Cake

Serves 16–20

8-ounce carton sweet whipped butter
3 cups sugar
5 large eggs
1/4 teaspoon baking soda
1 cup sour cream
3 cups flour
1 teaspoon lemon extract
2 teaspoons vanilla extract

Preheat the oven to 325°. Butter a bundt pan or tube pan *very* well, then flour lightly. (Aunt Eva used to butter the pan and then line the bottom with waxed paper and butter that.) Using either a mixer or a food processor, cream the butter with the sugar, then add the eggs one at a time, beating well in between. Add the baking soda, then add the sour cream and flour alternately, 1/3 at a time, ending with flour. Beat in the extracts. Bake for 1 hour and 25–30 minutes. Cool on a rack for 15–20 minutes and remove from pan.

A nice variation is to use 1 teaspoon lemon extract, 1 teaspoon vanilla extract, 1 teaspoon almond extract, and 1 cup toasted almonds.

Last time we noticed, North Carolinians led the nation in per capita soft-drink consumption. Not only do we drink them, but we cook with them. Websites and community cookbooks are awash in recipes that call for soft drinks, like the Sun-Drop cake served regularly at the Log Cabin Barbecue in Albemarle. There are also recipes that start with candy bars, like the Snickers pie at Bullock's in Durham, but we'll let you find those on your own. Here are a couple of recipes using indigenous soft drinks:

Pepsi-Cola Cake

Serves 15–20

For the cake:
2 cups flour
2 cups sugar
1 cup butter, melted
2 tablespoons unsweetened cocoa
1 cup Pepsi-Cola
1/2 cup buttermilk
2 large eggs, beaten
1 teaspoon baking soda
1 teaspoon vanilla extract
1 1/2 cups miniature marshmallows

For the icing:
6 tablespoons butter, softened
1 cup dark brown sugar
2/3 cup chunky peanut butter
1/4 cup milk
2/3 cup chopped peanuts, salted if you like

Preheat the oven to 350°. Grease and flour a 9" × 13" pan. Mix the flour and sugar in a large bowl. Combine the melted butter, cocoa, and Pepsi and pour over the flour and sugar mixture. Stir until well blended. Add the buttermilk, eggs, baking soda, and vanilla. Mix well. Stir in the marshmallows. Pour into the prepared pan. Bake for 40 minutes. Remove the cake from the oven, let it cool a bit, and ice while still barely warm.

To make the icing, cream the butter, sugar, and peanut butter. Beat in the milk, then fold in the nuts. Spread over the cake. Put the cake under the broiler just until it starts to bubble. Let it cool a bit before serving.

Alternative icing:
1/2 cup butter
1 tablespoon unsweetened cocoa
6 tablespoons Pepsi-Cola
1-pound box confectioner's sugar
1/2 cup chopped pecans (optional)

In a saucepan, bring the butter, cocoa, and Pepsi to a boil. Stir in the sugar and mix well, then stir in the nuts. Spread over the cake while both cake and icing are still warm.

Note: The flavor of this cake is surprisingly subtle, not intensely chocolate. For a small group, cut the recipe in half and use a 9-inch square pan. For groups of 50 or so, double the recipe and use a 12" × 18" half sheet cake pan.

Cheerwine Cake

Serves 15–20

For the cake:
1 box devil's food cake mix, plus the ingredients called for on the box:
Eggs (probably 3)
Vegetable oil (probably 1/2 cup)
Water (probably 1 1/3 cups) — replace with Cheerwine
1 teaspoon almond extract

For the icing:
1/3 cup Cheerwine

1/2 cup butter

1/4 cup cocoa

2 1/2 cups powdered sugar

1/4 teaspoon almond extract

1 cup chopped nuts

Preheat the oven to 350°. Grease and flour a 9" × 13" pan. Prepare the cake mix as directed, substituting Cheerwine for the water and adding the almond extract. Pour into the pan and bake as directed. Ice immediately.

To make the icing, combine the Cheerwine, butter, and cocoa in a saucepan and bring to a boil. Pour the hot mixture over the powdered sugar and blend until smooth. Stir in the almond extract. Mix in the chopped nuts. Cool, then spread over the cake.

Make what you will of the facts that the first man to sell barbecue commercially in Salisbury was named Blackwelder (originally Schwartzwalder) and one of the most famous German cakes is the Schwartzwalder Kirschtorte, which combines chocolate and cherries.

Everyone seems to have a recipe for "pig pickin' cake," but no one knows where it originated. We'd bet the name started in North Carolina, though maybe not the cake itself, which is a cousin of pineapple dream cake. But it has certainly naturalized here and it's flourishing. Here's the version Corbette Capps serves at his pig-pickings. He says he got it from a Baptist church cookbook.

Pig Pickin' Cake

For the cake:

1 box Duncan Hines yellow cake mix

4 large eggs

3/4 cup vegetable oil

5 1/2 to 6-ounce can mandarin oranges

For the topping:

9-ounce carton frozen whipped topping

3.4-ounce box instant vanilla pudding

Pig-Picking

North Carolinians have been going to pig-pickings for a very long time, but most didn't call them that until the 1970s. The first example we've found of the phrase in print comes from 1971, when North Carolina congressman L. H. Fountain was questioning an official of the Food and Drug Administration. "We cook hogs down my way," Fountain remarked, "and they taste awfully good. Especially when they have a pig-picking." (This was part of a long-winded prelude to a question about whether it's dangerous to eat hog kidneys. "Not usually," the FDA man replied. Your tax dollars at work.)

The congressman's use of the expression suggests that it was part of common speech down Tarboro way, but when newspapers reported in 1972 that the North Carolina Pork Producers Association had held a "Pig Pickin'" at the governor's mansion, they put the strange phrase in quotation marks. When the same organization sponsored a "Pig Pickin' Hoe Down" at the state fairgrounds the next year, the women's editor of the *Burlington Daily Times News* thought pig-picking had something to do with hog-killing.

High Point Enterprise, August 1976

"But my worries were quickly put to rest," she wrote, "when I arrived and realized that the only 'pig-picking' that would take place that night would be picking morsels of succulent meat from the sides of pork."

Within two or three years, however, the expression was cropping up statewide—from Guilford County's celebration of the Bicentennial to a wedding party in Henderson to the grand opening of Auto Mart of High Point (just for starters).

5 1/2 to 6-ounce can crushed pineapple

1/2 cup chopped pecans (optional)

Preheat the oven to 325°. Grease and flour 3 8" or 9" cake pans or a 9" × 13" baking pan. Add the eggs and oil to the cake mix and beat for about 2 minutes. Add the orange slices with the juice and beat for about 1 minute. Pour into the pans and bake for about 20–30 minutes. Cool thoroughly.

Put all topping ingredients in a bowl and whip until fluffy enough to ice the cake easily. Spread over the cake. Sprinkle chopped pecans on top, if desired. Keep cake refrigerated.

Note: If you're serving a crowd of, say, 50 people, you can double the recipe and bake it in a 12" × 18" half sheet cake pan for 30–40 minutes.

You'll need something to drink with your barbecue. There is, of course, a drink that traditionally goes with North Carolina barbecue.

TEA

Notice that we don't say "ice tea" or "sweet tea"—just "tea" will do nicely in most places. True, some restaurateurs have given in to people who don't know better and now offer "unsweet tea" as well (although you usually need to ask for it). We understand the pressures of the marketplace and will forgive them, but the classic tea to drink with North Carolina barbecue is sweet.

Real sweet. What the Reverend Grady Nutt used to call "40-weight tea." David Gibson wasn't exaggerating much when he wrote in *Chile Pepper* magazine that "Carolina sweet tea coats the back of a spoon. Left undisturbed, rock candy will form in the glass. Were it much thicker, you could pour it on waffles." Alan Richman concurs. "Sweetened ice tea in North Carolina isn't a beverage," he concluded, after drinking a lot of it. "It's an intravenous glucose drip."

There's a reason for this. The vinegar base of most North Carolina sauces cries out for something sweet to complement it. It's not just the Chinese who like sweet-and-sour.

Sweet tea is not just for barbecue, of course. Indeed, as John T. Edge puts it, it has become for many Southerners "a kind of culinary-cultural Global Positioning System, an indicator of where we are and, yes, who we are." How did this happen?

The history is sketchy at best, but we can pick it up in the nineteenth century, when cold green tea was a common ingredient in punches. England had Regent's Punch, Charleston had St. Cecelia Punch, and Savannah had its lethal Chatham Artillery Punch. In 1839, our reliable source Lettice Bryan published a recipe for "tea punch" that called for hot tea to be poured over sugar to dissolve it, then mixed with cream and champagne or claret, and served hot or cold. By 1879 we find a recipe for proper ice tea in Marion

"The rhythmic crack of cleaver on cutting board, the glorious vision of wood smoke belching darkly into the sky, the heady scent of vinegar infused with Texas Pete Hot Sauce. . . . It would be me, a sweating pitcher of sweetened ice tea, a fat sandwich wrapped in wax paper, and a few flies torpid from the heat." (Alan Richman)

Cabell Tyree's *Housekeeping in Old Virginia*—although the sugar and tea are married late: "Fill the goblets with ice, put two teaspoonfuls granulated sugar in each, and pour the tea over the ice and sugar. A squeeze of lemon will make this delicious and healthful, as it will correct the astringent tendency."

You might assume—most people do—that ice tea has always been a Southern thing, but in the nineteenth century it may have been at least as prevalent in the North, probably because reliable supplies of ice were hard to come by in much of the South. (We've never said Southerners invented everything important, just that we know a good thing when we find it.) Here are a few of the stories we turned up.

In 1863 the *New York Herald* wrote about the steamer *Rome*, where Union sailors in the Charleston blockade went for R&R: "There are three large iceboxes in the vessel, which are capable of containing about thirty tons of ice, besides stowing away a large quantity of fresh meats, &c. Tanks have been placed in different parts of the vessel, which are to be filled with iced tea and coffee, and in fact everything has been done to make her indeed a 'home.'" In August 1868 something odd was going on: did tea importers launch a newspaper campaign to counter a summer slump in sales? Anyway, first the *New Orleans Times* wrote that "iced tea with lemon juice is said to be a popular and healthy drink at the North," then a few days later papers in Janesville, Wisconsin, and Alton, Illinois, carried an identical item: "Iced tea is becoming very popular. It is a beverage easily prepared, costs little, does not intoxicate, and can be taken at any hour. Sweeten the hot tea to suit your taste; then pour it, spoonful by spoonful, into a tumbler filled with ice." (Notice that they got the method right.) Connecticut was a bit behind the times, it seems: it wasn't until 1872 that the *Middletown Constitution* suggested that "the practice of drinking iced tea, without milk, is becoming very usual. Some persons add a slice of lemon to it, which is said to be an improvement." By 1880 ice tea seems to have been well established in the Midwest—at least in Ohio, where the *Summit County Beacon* listed the menu of a huge celebration for employees of a local mower and reaper factory: the dessert course, after the pastries, included "almonds, filberts, pecans, watermelons, raisins, Brazil nuts, English walnuts, ice tea, tea, coffee, vanilla ice cream."

The South wasn't totally out of step, though. An 1872 story in the *Dallas Herald* about a train ride to Galveston shows that Southerners understood the cooling effects of ice tea. The writer complained about the fare on the refreshment cart, saying, "We would have enjoyed an occasional drink of ice water and would have gladly exchanged coin for ice cream, sherbit, soda, iced tea or coffee." And Saul's, an Atlanta soda fountain, was advertising in 1883 in the *Atlanta Constitution* "Ice Tea, all flavors, on draught at Saul's, only five cents a glass" and "Ice Tea, the most healthful and pleasant drink on draught, at Saul's." (Draft ice tea? And what could the flavors have been?)

In those days, it seems, ice tea was an all-American drink. Washington was a Southern town, but congressmen came from all over, and in 1874 the *Washington Star* reported that "it costs the country about thirty-six dollars per day during the heated term to supply the House of Representatives with iced tea and lemonade."

It's hard to say when ice tea became a specifically Southern drink—indeed, an icon. It's also hard to trace the transition from green tea to black tea, but after 1900, inexpensive black tea was increasingly available and used for ice tea, as it is now. Yes, we know green tea is making a comeback, and there are all sorts of bottled teas, but we've already gone on long enough about what should go without saying.

Here's how to make what Raleigh food writer Fred Thompson calls "the house wine of the South," from his book *Iced Tea*:

Sweet Tea

6 regular-size tea bags

1/8 teaspoon baking soda

2 cups boiling water

1 1/2 to 2 cups sugar (if you are new to sweet tea, start with 1 1/2 cups)

6 cups cold water

In a glass measuring cup or ceramic teapot large enough to accommodate the boiling water, place the tea bags and baking soda. Pour the boiling water over the tea bags. Cover and let steep for 15 minutes. Remove the tea bags, being careful not to

"Waitresses who work the barbecue circuit have a routine. Once you're seated, they take your order within thirty seconds. A minute later they're back with tea, utensils wrapped in a paper napkin, and an apology for keeping you waiting for your meal. Two more minutes pass and your sandwich arrives." (Alan Richman)

There's plenty of tea at Wink's, Salisbury

squeeze them (squeezing the bags will add bitterness). Pour the concentrate into a 2-quart pitcher and add the sugar. Stir until almost dissolved. Stir in the cold water. Let cool, then chill and serve over ice.

If, for some reason, you want to serve both sweet and unsweet tea, Crook's Corner in Chapel Hill has a brilliant solution—literally. On each table, chef Bill Smith puts a pitcher of a delectable concoction that's so good it almost reconciles us to the idea of unsweet tea:

Bill Smith's Elixir

Makes about 6 cups

4 cups sugar
4 cups water
4 cups fresh mint leaves, tightly packed
Grated zest of 2 lemons
1 1/2 cups fresh lemon juice

Bring the sugar and water to a boil in a large nonreactive pot with a tight-fitting lid. Remove from the heat when the sugar is completely dissolved. Add the mint leaves and lemon zest, making sure that the leaves are all submerged. Cover and let them steep for at least 15 minutes. Longer is fine. Add the lemon juice and strain. Use the syrup to sweeten tea.

Smith also adds this to sparkling water for a spritzer and notes that if you reduce the sugar to 2 cups, you can churn it in an ice-cream maker to make a mint sorbet.

SOFT DRINKS

The Statesville Landmark reported that a 1922 Chamber of Commerce meeting consumed "several tubs of barbecue . . . together with about one week's output from the Coca-Cola and Orange Crush Bottling plants and the McElwee-Martin Cigarette Co."

The other sweet choice to go with North Carolina barbecue is a soft drink of some sort. It's almost as traditional as tea. In fact, until recently that bastion of Eastern-style tradition, Ayden's Skylight Inn, didn't offer tea at all—just soft drinks from a cooler, until tea came bottled and could be put in the cooler with the soft drinks.

If you're going to drink a soft drink, why not drink those local ones we mentioned? Devotees of Eastern-style might wish to consider Pepsi-Cola, originally concocted as "Brad's Drink" in New Bern in 1893 by a pharmacist named Caleb Bradham. "Doc" Bradham renamed his product in 1898, set up a bottling company in 1902, and franchised bottlers in Charlotte and Durham three years later. After a number of reversals and changes of ownership, the company's headquarters moved to New York in 1935. Nevertheless, Pepsi is, as advertised, a "Taste Born in the Carolinas."

Old Pepsi sign at the Skylight Inn, Ayden

For Piedmont-style barbecue, the obvious carbonated complement is Cheerwine, formulated in 1917 in the basement of L. D.
Peeler's wholesale grocery store in Salisbury. (The family name,
by the way, was originally Bühler.) The Carolina Beverage Corpo-
ration is still in the family: L. D.'s son, Clifford, was chairman of
the company until his death in 2000 at age ninety-six. Cheerwine
has the same relation to wine that ginger ale has to ale: that is, it's
roughly the same color. If you buy this (very) fizzy cherry-flavored
drink in glass bottles, it will be sweetened with real cane syrup,
not the corn syrup everyone else uses these days. Food writer Alan
Richman describes Cheerwine as "pretty much the sweetest soft
drink ever made, and in my opinion the greatest accompaniment
to barbecue ever produced." If you want something lighter, Fred
Thompson, in *Iced Tea*, has a Cheerwine and tea spritzer that combines both Piedmont favorites.

BEER

In North Carolina—unlike, say, Texas—old-fashioned barbecue
places rarely serve beer. This is not just because most of them seem
to be run by Baptists (who also close on Sundays). For all the chat-
ter about barbecue and beer, beer goes best with a sweet sauce, like
what they use in Memphis or Kansas City. So if you want beer, drink
it while you're cooking. When it comes time to eat, stick with tea
or a soft drink.

If you're going to ignore that advice, however, at least drink
cheap domestic lager with your barbecue. These days there are
some fine North Carolina microbrews—the Belgian Amber Fram-
boise from Boone's Cottonwood Brewery, for instance, which won
top honors at the Great American Beer Festival—but there's a time
and a place for designer beer, and when you're eating barbecue is

These Charlotteans didn't get the memo: they're drinking beer.

not one of them. You want Old Milwaukee for the same reason you want Wonder Bread for sandwiches: It lets you keep your focus.

WINE

As for wine—well, that strikes us as somehow deeply wrong. But Richard Childress disagrees.

Childress was born in Winston-Salem and presumably grew up with ice tea, but when his career as a NASCAR driver and team owner took him to Sonoma County, California, he got interested in wine. In 2004 he opened Childress Vineyards in Lexington, catching the wave of the remarkable renaissance of North Carolina winemaking. The next year, he paid tribute to Lexington's better-known culinary tradition by producing a limited bottling of "Fine Swine Wine" for the 2005 Lexington Barbecue Festival. North Carolina artist Bob Timberlake designed the label for this blend of cabernet sauvignon, cabernet franc, and merlot from grapes grown at the vineyard.

Asked what the wine is like, vintner Mark Friszolowski told the *Winston-Salem Journal* with a straight face, "It smells like slaw." No, seriously, it's "heavy, with hints of plum and cherry, the aroma of cedar and the toastiness of oak." Choosing his words carefully, he said that the "semi-sweet, fruity flavor" of this "porcine little wine" is just right to go with barbecue. "This wine is a wine you could do in a paper cup." It's sweet, like—are you ready for this?—"sweet tea with a kick."

The wine seems to have become an annual feature of the festival, but so far there are no plans to market it more generally. Until that happens, you might take the advice of Durham-based wine journalist Barbara Ensrud, who says that "well-chilled white Zinfandel or Sangria really cools the heat." (Designer Alexander Julian, a Chapel Hill native, concurs. Kunde Zinfandel, he says, is "designed in heaven to go with Carolina barbecue.") In general, Ensrud recommends dry or fruity rosés to go with vinegar-based sauces. If you want to go native, she recommends Carolina Blush from Westbend Vineyards in Lewisville or Childress's Classic Blush (since Fine Swine Wine is hard to find). Ensrud also urges adventurers to try McRitchie Hard Cider, made from North Carolina apples.

But as with beer, if you insist on drinking wine, stick with the cheap stuff. Greensboro wine buff Edward Tewkesbury observes that drinking wine with barbecue is pretentious enough without drinking *expensive* wine.

THE PEOPLE

Michael Conrad of the Barbecue Center in Lexington observes that "you cannot learn barbecue, you *live* barbecue." We want you to meet some of the folks who make North Carolina barbecue for a living, most of whom have made it their lives, as well. We've talked with a lot of barbecue men (and a few women), and many talk almost as well as they cook. Here's some of what we heard. We haven't included everyone we talked to—not by a long shot—but we've gone for a representative sample of Eastern and Piedmont, young and old, entrepreneurs and heirs. All of these people are in the tradition, and all of them know it. All are keepers of the flame, Nobles of the Mystic Swine. They're not the only North Carolinians who cook good barbecue, but all of them sure do.

(overleaf) Wilber's still
burns wood.

The small Pitt County town of Ayden is easy to miss. Once you get there, though, it's hard to miss the Skylight Inn. Look for an unassuming building with a replica of the U.S. Capitol dome on top of it, put there after *National Geographic* in 1979 called the place "the barbecue capital of the world." The Skylight was founded in 1947, but founder Pete Jones came from a long line of barbecue men. (Family lore dates their barbecue pedigree to the 1830s.) It is owned today by his nephew Jeff, his son Bruce, and Bruce's son Samuel, who cook the way the family has always cooked: whole hogs over smoldering hardwood coals. (The bill for the oak and hickory burned in 2000 amounted to $23,000.) This devotion to the old ways earned the Skylight Inn an America's Classic Award from the James Beard Foundation in 2003.

"When you come here, it's not what you want, it's how much of it."

The Skylight Inn proudly displays its James Beard award.

SAMUEL JONES

My granddad worked with his uncle Emmitt Dennis, went to work with him at eight or nine years old, and he built this place and opened it when he was eighteen years old. He sold barbecue but not exclusively. This place was built as a hangout. I mean, eighteen-year-old running his own place, right? It was anything goes. Everybody came and hung out all the time and he served beer. This place stayed open until midnight back then—neon lights, the whole nine yards. They had an airstrip out back, and he and some of his friends flew planes. The name Skylight comes from the airstrip. It was crazy then, [but] in the mid-1970s he focused more on his barbecue. In the late 1970s, *National Geographic* came through and said we had the best barbecue in the country, and that put us on the map, so to speak.

In 1985 the place didn't have air-conditioning. My dad told my granddaddy, "Supposedly we have the best barbecue in the country, but you got to sweat to eat it." So they remodeled. They added the two extra dining rooms, the kitchen, and that was when they added the rotunda—the replica of the U.S. Capitol building on our

roof. Ain't neither my dad or granddad going to let the other one take credit for coming up with the idea of putting the dome on the building.

I started working here when I was about nine or ten years old. When I was younger, all I did was wipe tables, sweep floors, and stuff. My grandfather wouldn't turn me loose in the pits until I was eighteen or nineteen years old, and once I was back there, he was questioning me all the time. Anybody that knew him would know that was his way.

When I was a freshman in high school I quit working here. I hated it with a passion. A man named Glen Bowen came in here one day while we were making slaw. My granddaddy kept it so hot that it felt like a hundred degrees all the time—we were sweating. And Mr. Bowen said, "I just opened a gun and pawn shop up in Greenville. You want to come work with me?" I said, "When do I start?" I worked with Mr. Bowen through high school, [but] when my granddaddy started talking about retiring, around 1998, I came back. My granddaddy didn't retire until 2004. There were many years of alluding to his retirement, but it wasn't until he had a heart

attack that he stopped working here. He worked the place for fifty-seven years, and when he stopped working, it wasn't because he didn't want to.

The last week my granddaddy worked, he would work me and you to death. He was seventy-six years old, and you could not keep up with him. When you would give out and want to take a break and sit down, he would find something for you to do. That's because he was on his feet—he was like a robot. He came from a different generation. He was raised in the 1930s and 1940s when there wasn't a lot of money and everything was smarts, hard work, and long days. He grew up on the farm where you fell out in the morning when the sun came up, and it wasn't until five or six o'clock in the evening you came home.

This was his life. There wasn't anything he loved, outside of my grandmother, more than this barbecue place. He lived across the street, and the restaurant is on our old family farm. On the holidays, Thanksgiving and Christmas, when we all got around the table to eat, my grandmother would say, "One of those grandyoung'uns, go over across the street and tell Granddaddy it's time to eat." And we would come over here and he wouldn't be doing anything but standing at the counter, propped up smoking a cigarette and looking out the door. He just loved this place; it was all he thought about. He took it from its inception to what it is now, and that's one reason why I don't look at it so much as a job but that there's family history here. I would hate to know that my granddaddy spent his whole life building something and I pissed it away, pardon my French. There're a lot of businesses that have been passed along to this generation and they go to pot. They want to change over to something easier. Cooking with wood is a good example—that would be an easy thing to do away with—[but] I think we would probably be out of business in a year if we did that. Then there wouldn't be anything that sets us apart. And to me, cooking over gas isn't barbecue, that's cooked pork. The definition of barbecue is the whole hog cooked over wood coals. Maybe I'm not very smart, but in my mind anything less than that isn't barbecue.

Everybody thinks that when you have your own place you got it made, but working at any kind of retail store or textiles, you're guaranteed some time off. In this kind of business, you got to work when everybody else is off. My dad Bruce, my uncle Jeff, and I put in six days a week. We do take the week following Christmas off, [but] Christmas Eve is our busiest day of the year; we do about twenty-five hogs that day, and that's a lot of work. We still chop the barbecue by hand then, so I'll get some friends and family to come in and help out.

We average on a week thirty to forty hogs. We've been buying from the same guy since as far back as I can remember, the same folks my granddaddy bought from, a company out of Richland, Barbecue Pigs Incorporated. Weight is the main thing we look for in a pig because pigs are not like they used to be. Pork is not a fatty meat like it was before. They'll top a pig out at four or five months from birth to market, and the way they feed it, there's no chance for it to get fat. For cornbread pans we're dependent on lard. Down here people used to raise hogs and have hog killings; back then you'd get three to four buckets of lard out of a homegrown hog. Now on a Saturday, we'll cook eight to ten pigs and we won't have

Samuel, Jeff, and Bruce Jones

a dishpan full of grease. We don't cook anything under 140 pounds because any less just doesn't turn out good barbecue. I won't cook one for anyone anymore that weighs less than a hundred pounds.

Our family is not subject to change at all. We hold on to something until the bitter end. We sold Pepsi bottle drinks for years and years, recycled glass bottles. We didn't have tea then; bottle drinks was it. We did that because it was quick. When Pepsi announced they would stop doing bottle service, my granddaddy bought eight truckloads of Pepsi products. He stocked them up from floor to the ceiling; if my family owned a building, you would walk past bottles in it. We sold bottle drinks for a year and a half after Pepsi stopped selling them. A lot of the magazines were always commenting that we were the only place that didn't have sweet tea, but we didn't start selling it until my granddaddy retired. We get it through Pepsi—Minges Bottling right here locally. We still pretty much deal with the folks we always dealt with, outside of the suppliers who've died off. I'm kind of like my granddaddy; if I'm doing business with somebody and feel like I can trust them, then I'm not going to go anywhere else.

Now the wood is something that's getting harder to come by because that's something that's labor-intensive—splitting the wood and all that. The guy I've been buying from for the past year and a half has been pretty easy to deal with. [He] splits the wood and brings it on a dump truck—fortunate for us, not for him. We use about two and a half cords of wood a week. When I was a boy, we stacked the wood as tall as our building, probably six or eight rows, twenty feet high. Now you can't find that much wood. When the town cuts down oak trees, they'll give them to us to use.

Usually we use the cardboard boxes the groceries came in to start our fires. My uncle has a fruit stand next door, and a lot of times we use those wax boxes they ship cabbage in and those things burn hotter than hell. They do the trick. The greener the wood we use, the harder it is to burn it down. It'll take about thirty to forty minutes to burn the wood down. That's why we try to chop it small, for the coals.

On days our story runs on a TV show, I'll get calls from all over the country to ship barbecue they saw on television. We ship barbecue all the time, frozen, by next-day air. To me it's always been weird. I think about my granddaddy, who was a simple boy, all business, and we're getting all this recognition. But we're really still a small business. And my granddaddy wasn't a very educated man; he came from that generation, born in 1928, where there wasn't the option of finishing high school. So right out of the gate, there was the Depression, and I see what he did just from hard work. Even now, we do not have the nicest décor—it's just simple. If you have a good product, halfway decent service, and consistency, you don't need this, that, and the other.

We got barbecue, slaw, and cornbread. That's it. When you come here, it's not *what* you want, it's how much of it. If we don't do a good job one day, then we're out. There may be times when you come in and you have to stand and wait to get food here, but that's because we're chopping up a new piece of barbecue. We don't like to let quantity get over quality.

We don't have a big catering business, but we'll do fifty to eighty events a year maybe. When we cater, we'll also do barbecued chickens. In my opinion, cooking chickens is easier than cooking pigs. You got to tend to the chicken a little more because the time span is shorter—you don't have the leisure between firings that you do with the pigs—[but] I can cook fifty chickens in one-third the time it takes to cook a pig. We cook the chickens the same way we do the pigs, on the coals. I reckon everybody got their own style, but I do

How to find a North Carolina barbecue place: "Just drive. Preferably on back roads, and definitely with the windows down. When you smell hickory smoke, slow down; there's a pit coming up. If you find yourself passing a pig farm, though, you might want to roll up the windows." (David K. Gibson)

not flip a chicken until it's done, and that's for just enough time to blister the skin on it. The way I cook them, if I turn them a lot they'll fall to pieces. Cooking them slow, the meat is so tender, if I pull a leg on the chicken it will fall right out.

We don't own a thermometer in the restaurant. My granddad, when he was showing me how to cook pigs (that's not a one-day lesson, I might add; it's like an internship) — my granddaddy would say if you can put your hand to the pig's back you need to put some heat to it. He did not cook pigs a whole lot himself in the last ten years, [but] at Christmas time, he would cook for the people who tended our farmland, and when he would do that, I always made sure I followed him. I mean, who better to learn from than the man himself? The pigs he would cook for them were a little bit smaller, so he would put them on first thing in the morning and cook them all day long. Here, we cook all night to have them ready for the morning.

Most of the time, it's my uncle Jeff who handles the pigs at night. He's really my father's first cousin, but you can't call someone who's sixty years old "cousin," so he's Uncle Jeff. He lives close by and will come by and check at night that things are on the up-and-up for the next day. Not tooting our own whistle, [but] between my father Bruce and Jeff, we got keeping the pits at the right temperature down to a science.

My granddaddy had the pits built to be just like the ones his uncle had, just on a bigger scale. We clean the pits depending on how much we use them. You don't want to clean the pits the whole way out because you're losing all that insulation. Our chimney is firebrick, but the pits are just normal brick. We burn 125 cords of wood a year, so it creates some wear and tear. Our chimney bricks never even get cool, really. In the summer, it's hotter than the vestibule of hell in here. Our cookhouse has caught on fire about a dozen times, but that's just how it works.

One of our smokehouses will cook eleven hogs, and the other will cook fifteen. The only thing we do prior to cooking them is split the head; otherwise we receive them already butterflied. Most times we give the feet away—a lot of people around here cook them and the ears up. We use some brick to keep the grills cracked open a little bit because if you keep the lids all the way sealed, you'll burn

"If we can all agree that eating barbecue is like firing a cholesterol bullet straight into our own hearts, we can simply note that Pete's merely packs a heftier slug." (Bob Garner)

James Howell prepares pigs for the pit.

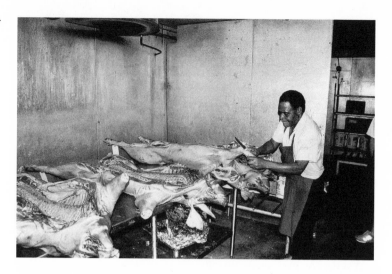

the pigs. My granddad, I've seen him push one a little bit by closing the lids when he needed to. But you got to be careful or you'll burn it. Pork's not like beef where you can sear it—you really got to cook it for a while. Our pit man, James Howell, has been cooking pigs for fifteen or eighteen years here, and it's an art to cooking them. It's like second nature to him: he knows how much to put and where. I couldn't tell how much coals to add or where to add them, because it's different each time. We put the coals in on the edges of the pit on each side. We end up warping the shovels because the heat wears them out.

We let the pigs sit [in the pit] all night, then the meat will be done for the most part around 6:30 A.M. and we'll turn them over. You don't wait too long to turn them because you don't want it to be too tender. Sometimes if we slip up and cook one that weighs less than we thought, when I come out to flip that smaller one, the meat will go all over the place.

When it's done, we'll pull the ribs out so as not to burn them, then we'll cut the pigs as we need them. They stay warm by sitting on the grill until we need to chip them. My favorite part of the pig is right in the shoulders. The ham is the driest part. So when we pull them off the grill, first thing we do is split the hog in quarters. Then we'll mix the hams and shoulders so we serve an even mix.

We don't put much on them, a little vinegar and some Texas Pete. Cooking them on the grill is what does it. I watch some of those television shows on barbecue, like on the Travel Channel, where people put a lot of stock in their sauces, and it don't make no sense to me. You can eat a cardboard box with enough sauce. Every barbecue [place] you go to, go out to the smokehouse and try the meat without the sauce. I may not be the best every time, but I'll be in the top two, I guarantee you. There probably ain't twenty-five people in North Carolina that cook like this. I always try barbecue while traveling, and not to say this isn't a biased opinion, but I've never had it as good as it is here. The whole hog is the best barbecue; if it's anything less than that, you need to call it something else because that's false advertising. If you cook Boston butts, then that's what you got—but you don't got barbecue.

I wouldn't live anywhere else. It's nice to drive to work every day and wave at the same people. I'm also assistant chief of the Ayden Fire Department. If the fire alarm goes off, I can break out and go check on it. Most of the time you know the folks, and it's nice you can go help them, your own community. When there's a death in our community, we always send food. We probably send food a couple of times a month. Because a lot of our business is from out of town, I've been as far as the beach to carry food for someone's funeral.

BRUCE JONES

I was probably a teenager—been in here about ten years—before I really got a grasp on how to run the place. When I started working here, there were three tables and a counter with eight stools. We could seat about twenty people, grand total, and no air-conditioning. Daddy's big day was Saturday, and we sold about three pigs. Now we sell two times that on Monday, which is our slow day, and almost twelve on Saturday. Our chopping blocks we switch out every six months. The last one we got custom-made over in Wilson out of Arkansas rock maple.

I took off to go to college because I hated the place, and when I got to college [at] Mt. Olive our [history] professor was from a little town called Turkey, down near Faison, and I don't care what history he taught, it came back to the Civil War in eastern North Carolina. And he was talking one day about Lakeside Mills, up on Highway 70. He said the mill had been burned twice, once in the Revolu-

tion and once in the Civil War, and I was thinking, "Wait a minute. That's where we buy our cornmeal!" So then I loved history, and I started remembering Daddy and his mama talking about how long the barbecue business has been in our family, and then, rather than being a job to come to, it became a family tradition. And I wanted to see that keep going.

They were talking one day [on the radio] about who had the better barbecue, South Carolina or North Carolina, in reference to a cook-off that was going to happen in Washington, D.C. The two entrants were from Columbia and Greensboro, and neither of them had real barbecue. So I called up to one of the North Carolina congressmen at the time and said we needed to be in that competition. I said *National Geographic* said we had the best barbecue around. So we got invited and set up a table that said, "World's Best Barbecue." Senator Strom Thurmond from South Carolina came through and had about five or six different types of barbecue on his plate, and when he ate ours, he dropped that other plate in the garbage can and said to an aide, "Go get me a clean plate. I want this one." I said, "Now I know why you been in the Senate so long: you're a smart man."

An Eastern Dynasty

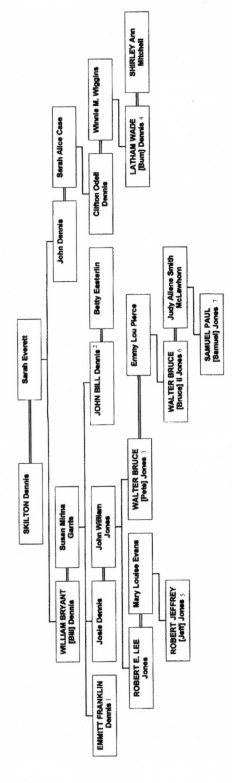

Note: The names of those in the barbecue business are in capital letters.

1. Emmitt Dennis had his own restaurant.

2. John Bill Dennis is said to have been selling barbecue on the street in Ayden in the 1920s. He opened a restaurant in 1941 and a couple of decades later sold it to Bum and Shirley Dennis.

3. Pete Jones worked for his uncle Emmitt, then opened the Skylight Inn in 1947.

4. Bum and Shirley Dennis run Bum's Restaurant in downtown Ayden.

5. Jeff Jones, Pete's nephew, is now running the Skylight Inn with his cousins Bruce and Samuel.

6. Bruce Jones runs the Skylight Inn with his cousin Jeff and his son Samuel.

7. Samuel Jones is now running the Skylight Inn with his father and his cousin Jeff.

THE ESTABLISHMENT (EASTERN)
WILBER'S, GOLDSBORO

"That grease hitting those coals makes the smoked flavor. . . . You can't spray it on there, paint it on there, put it on there—that's the natural way to cook it to get the smoke taste."

Wilber Shirley opened his restaurant (it's too nice to be called a joint) on Highway 70 in Goldsboro in 1962. Since then it has become a regular stop for flyers from nearby Seymour Johnson Air Force Base and so much a part of many people's beach trips that you wouldn't be surprised to see patrons in bathing suits. Mr. Shirley cooks split halves of whole hogs over oak coals in closed pits and serves his barbecue with a simple Eastern-style sauce.

The first thing I remember about barbecue was my dad used to cook for family reunions, and we'd dig a hole out under a shelter and take a piece of wire and put across it and cook the pig down in the hole. That's just an old tradition that we've had as long back as time, I reckon since they first started cooking a pig. You know, there wasn't a lot of commercial barbecue places around.

Later I came to Goldsboro. I went to work at a place called Griffin's Barbecue. They had a pit, of course, a cooking house, and they had rods [they put across the pit]. That's how I first learned to cook

Wilber Shirley

it, and that's just the only way I know to cook it, really. It's the most expensive way you can cook it.

[Our pigs weigh] between ninety and one hundred pounds. We used to raise pigs in the country, and they'd be two years old before you got them to weigh one hundred pounds dressed. Now they're grown so fast, a pig that will dress out at one hundred pounds is probably not half as old as when they grew so slow. These pigs here, they're grown just like you would raise a baby in a nursery at Chapel Hill. They get dietary food; they've got medication. These mills have formulas where they feed them, and it cuts down the fat content. If you've got one that's grown fast and it's a younger pig, he'll cook better than one that's real old. If you're talking about a pig eight months old or less, he'll cook faster than one that's a year and a half old, like back when we first started. And the skin looks different, and the meat texture looks different.

This time of the year [summer], we're running probably 100 to 125 pigs a week. Woodwise, it's supposed to be a cord and a half or something, anywhere from twelve to fourteen loads a week. We try to keep it not piled up. If you get too much ahead and it dries out, when you burn it to make the coals you got ashes, so you got to have it kind of green.

I've got a man that's been cutting wood for me for thirty years and I don't know what I'll do when he retires or dies. I don't know a thing about cutting wood. We use oak. That's predominantly what you find around here. You can use any kind of hardwood, but predominantly in this area it's oak. You'll find a little hickory, but I could burn all the hickory in this county in a year's time. Some years ago, [my wood supplier] got to buying behind the timber buyers. You know how these timber buyers go in and they cut the pine and all that, and we go behind them and cut the hardwood. So there's been a supply of wood. That's not a real problem.

I think it's a better product [with wood]. See, you cook it with gas and electricity, your cooking process starts out different. In most cases you have the flame at the top, so you put [the pig] with the skin down and the ribs and meat up. As a result, that skin holds the grease and it sits there and boils. If you cook them like we do, with the skin up and the meat down and you fire coals underneath, it drips. And when it does that, it's doing two things. One, it's get-

"There's more imitation barbecue served these days than real barbecue. Look for a pile of logs out back, or at least some kind of pit cooking facility on the premises. You won't find these often." (John Batchelor)

Postcard from Wilber's

"You can't beat the old way of cooking. When the pork drips grease, it hits that wood and just smokes right back up.... But putting it in a gas cooker? That's like putting barbecue in the stove in your house." (Mark Johnson, Hillsborough Hog Day cook-off winner, 2005)

ting the grease out and it's not sitting there boiling in the meat. The second thing, that grease hitting those coals makes the smoked flavor that you won't get any other way. You can't spray it on there, paint it on there, put it on there—that's the natural way to cook it to get the smoke taste. And it's what people in this area grew up accustomed to. [Our sauce] is just a recipe we had down there that we use—just vinegar and pepper and hot water and boil it.

[Changing to gas] goes through my mind sometimes because of the cost and the labor. They can take a thermostat and they can put their pigs on there, and if it takes seven or eight hours, they can go home and go to bed. Ours, you stay there with them from the time you put them on until the time you get done. [Putting more coals on is] not a clock thing. You really kind of go by when it goes to dying down, but you kind of gauge that—it's about every thirty minutes. It gets cooked, but there's a tremendous cost of the wood, the labor, and all. As I get older and I look at what may happen to the place—I don't know. I don't plan to [switch] as long as I'm able, but I don't know what will happen in the future. I don't know whether anybody [else] would be willing to put into it what it takes.

We do most of our cooking at night. We put them on and try to get them started by nine thirty or ten, and they're through the next morning about nine thirty or ten. We've got three different guys: one of them works four nights and one of them works two and one works one—seven days a week. And then we have other people come in the morning, take them over.

Start out every morning, we open the door at six. There's a crowd here that's got to go to work, but they come at six and they get out probably about seven. And then there's another crowd that starts drifting in of those that are retired or whatever, and they sit here and shoot the breeze from then until nine or nine thirty. Then it clears out, and then starts over again about eleven. It's a gathering place, I guess.

Of course over the years, we've added on some stuff. When I was at Griffin's, literally all we sold down there was barbecued chicken and barbecued pork. We have a lot of people that eat here several times a week, so we have a daily special, and we have seafood and hamburger steak and fried chicken and things like that. We have a barbecued chicken we cook one day a week on the pit, but the rest of the time it's the barbecued chicken that I brought the recipe [for] from Griffin's. It's cooked in the oven.

We cook beef on Wednesday night for Thursday. Cook briskets. A fellow came here and opened a barbecue beef thing down on the highway, and I decided I'd try [to cook] some of it, too. And everybody asks, "Is that Texas beef?" and I say, "I have no idea." I've never been to Texas, so I don't know what it's supposed to taste like. We chop ours; you're probably used to slicing. It didn't take long [to learn to cook beef]. I gave it away the first three or four times I cooked it. I tried it because it was entirely different than what people normally around here would think of. We've had good success with it. We'll cook about—raw beef—seven hundred or eight hundred pounds.

When you get started in something, I think there's a certain amount of challenge to it. But I can take the deed to this place and go down to the mall and I could ask one hundred people to take it if I give it to them, with the stipulation that they had to put the number of hours that I did, and I doubt if I would get one taker. [I work] seven days a week. [*Laughs*] Some weeks I come in eight days a week. It's not hard if you've been doing it for forty years.

The hardest part is the help, employees. With ninety employees, I've got ninety different opinions. [*Laughs*] I've got one waitress who has been here over thirty years, waitressing. I've got a cook in the kitchen that was here when I bought this place. (See, this place was built and another fellow bought it, and he got out after six months. He was used to making fast money. This is slow.) I've got one son-in-law that works [here]. He's not as committed as I am. [*Laughs*] Nobody is committed as I am. The boy behind the counter has been here almost twenty-five years, and there's another one that has been here like twenty years. He came in high school. As a matter of fact, my son-in-law came here in high school. He came to work here and then, you know, married my daughter. We still work high school students, but usually they come and go. That's been one of the biggest accomplishments I've had personally is just having high school students come and work, and we help them while they're in school, and they go on and lead successful lives.

We don't do a lot of advertising. It's mostly word of mouth, and we have become more involved in helping churches and schools.

Eating Stew at Wilber's

"There I was, raving blissfully over the thick, aromatic, luscious Brunswick stew and asking the busy waitress endless questions about types of chicken and potatoes, and cooking times, and why the stew was so reddish. Finally, in utter exasperation, she popped her order pad impatiently in the palm of her hand, looked down at me with a motherly smile, and uttered, 'Honey, why don't you just hush up and eat your stew?'"
—James Villas

Wilber's wall shows his devotion to N.C. State and FDR.

And the [air force] base—a couple times, they've come home and we'll have a pig-picking. I sponsored a softball team for twenty years. We played in New York; we played in Florida and Tennessee and South Carolina and various places, Detroit. It was Wilber's Barbecue Softball Team. So people would see the name. And then I've been involved in state politics, and I got known pretty much statewide. And I was involved in the [North Carolina State University] Wolfpack Club for twenty-five or twenty-six years, and that gave more exposure. So it's just been one thing or another. People see you here and there, at tournaments and ball games and stuff, and when they come by, they stop and eat.

A woman in here the other day said her grandson went to Disney World, and more people at Disney World saw that Wilber's shirt and stopped him—she said he was amazed. He'd be walking around in Disney World, and people were coming up to him. I had a similar thing happen several years ago. I went to Disney World and my wife wanted to check in her coat and all, so I walked up to the boy and I had on a Wilber's Barbecue cap and he said, "You know Wilber's Barbecue?" I said, "Well, I am Wilber." He said, "I used to eat there all the time." He was in the service and was stationed here, and he got out of the service and he'd gone to work at Disney World.

We've been written up in right many magazines over the years — *Southern Living* and what have you. This past weekend, there was a couple here from New Jersey, and they had seen it on the Food Network. There was a girl who interviewed me from a radio station from England. I said, "Who in England do you think is going to listen to you?" What she was going to do was take it back and use it on her radio show, you know — that she had been to the States and all. A girl from New York on ABC Talk Radio called up and asked [a Wilber's employee] to talk, and he said, "You don't need to talk to me; you need to talk to the man that's got forty-one years in his head and see if you can get it out of his head." And I guess that's the bad part about me because so much of this mess is in my head and nobody don't know where it is or what it is.

Depending on how my health holds out, I've got no plans to retire.

THE VISIONARY
ED MITCHELL, WILSON

"I like cooking barbecue this way because it's something to hold on to that hasn't been tarnished yet."

In 2003 Ed Mitchell set up his cookers on New York's East 27th Street for the first annual Big Apple Barbecue Block Party, and he was such a hit with the assembled Yankee foodies that his barbecue was featured in Food & Wine and Gourmet magazines and he has been going back for the festival more or less ever since. Mr. Mitchell uses an unusual (but traditional) "banking" technique to cook, and he had begun to source his hogs from former tobacco farmers who "pasture-raise" them when, in 2005, he ran into some legal troubles for not paying state taxes and had to close his restaurant in Wilson. (Maybe North Carolina should exempt pitmasters from taxes, the way Ireland does writers and artists.) In 2007 he teamed up with a Raleigh entrepreneur to open The Pit, a new place in the capital city that offers "an atmosphere somewhere between 'barbecue joint' and 'urban upscale casual.'"

Growing up, when we ate barbecue it was on special occasions, especially Thanksgiving. My uncles who had left the farm and gone up North, they would come back for Christmas-time. That was a time of celebration, and we would cook barbecue for them. During the course of those parties, we would kill about five pigs, cook them, then chop them up and put some of the cracklin' in because we knew that is what people would want. We would cook the collards and candied yams and potato salad. I can remember when the person who owned the tobacco farm my family worked on would give a barbecue to celebrate getting the harvest in. We had worked hard, and then with the barbecue we got to play hard. I would help out, but I didn't really pay much attention because I just thought of it as work.

I have to be honest: I would have preferred not to make a living cooking barbecue. When I graduated high school in Wilson in 1964, I got a scholarship to play football at Fayetteville State University. I ended up getting called into the service in my junior year, spent a

few months in Vietnam, then came back to finish my degree. I went to work for Ford Motor Company in Massachusetts and worked there for a few years before I came back to Wilson at my mother's request. My parents ran a mom-and-pop grocery store where the restaurant now is. It was called Mitchell's Grocery and Grill. I worked for a bit with the North Carolina Department of Labor and got into doing some real estate as well. It wasn't until 1990, the year my father passed, that I really got into cooking barbecue.

I'll never forget the day. I had come back to the store to visit my mom. She was worried and didn't think she was making enough money at the store, and she was depressed about my father being gone. So I said, "What do you want me to do, Mama?" And she said, "I want some old-fashioned barbecue." Okay, I'm a mama's boy—I went to the store and got a pig, a little small guy, about as long as a kitchen table. There was a little barn where we stored everything, and in the building we had a grill, so I pulled it out and managed to put the pig on, and about four hours later we had a late lunch. And I'll never forget it: we had just chopped up and seasoned the meat, and somebody had come in the store with the intention of buying a hot dog. But when he went back to the meat counter he said, "Y'all got barbecue, too" (not like a question really, more like a statement), and my mom said, "Yeah, we got some."

See, I had never intended to sell barbecue. I was just trying to make Mama happy. But she had something else in mind; she was trying to figure out how to generate some cash. So that night when I came back to close up the store, her personality had changed. She had sold all that barbecue. Now it wasn't that much, but whoever had bought that sandwich had gone out and told everyone he knew about that barbecue. She was so jubilant because she was making some money that day. [Then] somebody [else] comes in. My first thought is that they're going to rob us, so I put a little bass into my voice and say, "Who is it?" And the person said, "Mrs. Mitchell, you got any more barbecue?" So I said, "No, but we'll have some more tomorrow." And that's how I started into the barbecue business.

By the time I got the third pig to serve at the store, I was just curious, so I got a larger one, about a seventy-five-pounder. I wanted to see how much we could sell. My mom pointed her finger at me and said, "You know what? You keep cooking this barbecue the old-fashioned way with greens and candied yams and you'll be surprised." And here I am. So I won't take the credit for having a business plan. It started from a total fluke and became a roller-coaster ride.

I began to not have enough time, coming to Wilson from my other job, and that's where Mr. James Kirby comes in. I got some of the old-timers around and said, "Listen, who's alive who really knows how to barbecue the way my grandfather did?" And people listed them in order of who was best: Bud Jenkins, Sam Morgan, and Mr. Kirby, who was about sixty-five at that time. And I went to each one of them and was turned down. They all said it was too hard to do, that I shouldn't bother with it.

So a day or two later I was going out to get a cooker, but before I left I got a call from Mr. Kirby. He wanted to come out to the store to see me. "You really want to cook barbecue?" he said. So we got into the car and went up the road to look at this cooker, but it turned out to be electric. I liked it, so I said I would take it, [but] each time I went to get the money out of my pocket, Mr. Kirby would pull at my arm. I thought he was seeing something was wrong with the cooker. Finally, he said, "Come here. Do you really want to get into it? I mean do you really want to get into the barbecue business? If you really want to get into it, I'll put you in the water. It's up to you

to swim." He went on and said, "Come on, let's go and don't mess with that business of an electric cooker." So I came up with some excuse about not having the money with me, and we went back to Wilson.

When we got back, Mr. Kirby said we should empty out the barn we had been using as a storage shed, and we would build us a barbecue pit. He got down on his knees, drew out the lines of the pit, and then filled it in with sand, just like the old-fashioned way. That was what you had to have to do it right. He believed you did it the old way or no way at all. We took a barrel and carved it out and made a pit. Boy, that gave you the best flavor you ever want to taste. It's really all in the technique of cooking the pig that gives you the flavor.

It was only when I went to cook that first pig with Mr. Kirby that I learned you didn't really have to stay up all night to cook the pig. Old Man Mr. Kirby really played me good that night. We had two cookers built, and we ordered the pigs to put on about six P.M. that evening, so I went home to make some coffee and a few sandwiches. The pigs were 150 pounds each. Mr. Kirby had started the fire and gotten the oak out, so we were at the right temperature. He spread the cinders and coals out in the cooker. We salted the pig, soaked him in the vinegar, and he closed the lid and shut off the drafts. I got settled in for the night, and Mr. Kirby walked over to the other side of the building, got his hat, and put his coat over his shoulder, and I said, "Where are you going?" "Well," he said, "You can sit here all night if you want to. I'm going home." I said, "Are you going to leave the pig?" "Yeah, I'm not staying here with him. You can stay here if you want. We can come check on them about four or four thirty in the morning."

And that night I couldn't sleep a wink because I just knew that pig was going to wind up burning down the store. I didn't wait until four thirty or five. But when I went in and opened the grill, man, I could not believe my eyes. It was the first time I had seen the technique called "banking." I always thought you had to stay there and cook the sucker, but you can bank them, as the saying goes. It's simple: you just put it on and shut off all the drafts. She'll sit right there and simmer all night. And when you come back in the morning, it's so succulent, the meat just falls off the bones. You really got to know to strategically place the wood and the coals in the pit. So Mr. Kirby's the gentleman who showed me the finer points, even the technique we use that crisps the skin into crackling.

We've never advertised or said a word to nobody. But word spread like wildfire, and it got so bad that I just had to give up my job to stay here and cook barbecue. Then it got so bad that I could not keep doing this by myself. It was just wearing me out. Mr. Kirby stayed with me about three or four years and helped get the barbecue business off the ground.

Let me make this clear: there is no secret to cooking good barbecue. The only thing you need to know is that you should go back to the basics. Here, that starts with our pits. My pit is as close to authentic as possible in a modern restaurant. You don't need to reinvent the wheel, because once you taste the original way, the rest is just a fake. But if you really want the true character of barbecue, you got to do it the original way.

When you cook in a banking style, the barrel is anchored down in the sand. It gives you some insulation. That's the way the technique was done in the old days. In what I'm doing now, to be in line with the health codes, I had to build mine a little more modern-style. Back in our kitchen it's not your standard-looking pit—not your greasy-spoon kind of thing. Everything has to be kept clean, but when you're trying to be as authentic as possible, it's about taking that effect of cooking the pig in the ground and building it

aboveground. We devised these pits based on how Mr. Kirby had been cooking in the old times. These pits are the Rolls Royce version. We put firebrick on the interior, then a second layer of regular brick forms the exterior. We have stainless steel tops and ventilation systems and fans to keep the air flow moving to avoid carbon monoxide settling in the kitchen. As long as you stay with the basics, [you can get] that pit effect.

It's getting harder every day to cook with wood, but you have to try to keep it as close to authenticity as possible to satisfy the taste. Now people want to pipe in gas or electricity, automatic stuff. But a few people try to hold on to the original ways, cooking with charcoal and wood. We're trying to preserve this art. If you walk into a place that cooks over gas or on a rotisserie and it has the name "Barbecue" on the front and you've never had it any other way, then it's pretty good, I guess. But how do you really know what's good if you've never had it cooked the right way?

My brother preps the pigs; he cuts the feet and the ears off. We take all the feet and ears and make a delicacy out of them: we pickle the pig's feet and all of that good stuff. Before putting the pig on the grill, he soaks the pig in a little vinegar and then wets the wood for the smoke effect. We cook our pigs skin-side up—never skin down, because it will stick. Moving the coals around comes instinctually; it's a dying art, but after a few sessions you will know it, too. It's just one of those things you got to do.

Finally, you adjust the air vents to check the draft. After a minute or so, you'll see a spiral of smoke drawing up. That's because of our ventilation system. I had to devise three systems to let me cook the way I want to cook. That's because I'm a diehard, man.

We also keep a firebox for when we have heavy days, when we need to do a lot of cooking. That way we can put the wood and charcoal in there and always have it ready. We start that fire in the firebox up with wood, and the [charcoal] coals and [wood] cinders fall through the grates we put in at the bottom of the firebox, and we can shovel on more coals to the pits directly. We use coals to keep the heat and cinders for the flavor; you need to have both. The only reason you use charcoal is that they provide heat longer than the wood does.

When we're cooking it, it's not easy to be the pitmaster. Pitmaster has to stand all that heat and all that smoke. Like Mr. Kirby said, it's a lot of work. You really got to love what you're doing to give people an authentic product. This day and time, it's very difficult because people just are not programmed for manual labor. I really do want more people to get interested in barbecuing the old-fashioned way. If that means folks know our little trade secrets—that we pitmasters don't really have to stay up all night with the pig—then that's fine. It's a beauty, man, it's a real beauty. It's like loving old cars: you got to have a passion for it.

Cooking barbecue is a craft handed down from generations to generations. I like cooking barbecue this way because it's something to hold on to that hasn't been tarnished yet. It allows all of us to interact. Barbecue was one of the things that held the tension down during the race movement in the 1960s. When there was a barbecue, it did not matter who you were, the only thing that could settle any issue would be having a pig picking. It's a feasting time, a festive time. Nobody's upset or mad, and there's no other dish that powerful. And don't ask me why because I don't know. Maybe there's a connection with the Bible—prodigal son went away, and when he came back, they said, "Surely kill us a calf," and roasted it barbecue-style.

THE YOUNGER GENERATION (EASTERN)
HIGH COTTON, KITTY HAWK

After attending culinary school in Asheville, Will Thorpe moved to the Outer Banks in 1984 and opened Caribbean restaurants in Nags Head and Kitty Hawk. But his Nash County childhood prevailed in 2003, and he opened High Cotton, serving Eastern-style barbecue to vacationing Tar Heels and bewildered Yankee tourists. Like most new establishments, his uses a hybrid gas-and-wood cooker, but we like his missionary attitude.

"We have what we call tourists and purists, and we have to educate one and hold our own with the other."

I grew up in Rocky Mount, born and raised. We'd go for barbecue to Josh Bullock's, Buck Overton's, Bob Melton's, and even Doug Saul's over in Nashville. One of my fondest memories growing up is going to Bob Melton's on Sunday after church and getting the barbecue sandwiches and there being nothing but men in the back looking very angry at you and scaring you as a child, picking up your barbecue sandwiches. I can't afford to give that scowl now. After I've been here thirty years, maybe I can give that scowl.

None of my family members were in the barbecue business. It was just something I grew up liking to do, and I always went early to the dove hunts and all the things where the pigs were being cooked and watched them. I don't think culinary school changed my ideas much about cooking. I just began cooking what I considered nicer things.

The majority of our diners are non–North Carolinians, primarily from Virginia, Pennsylvania, Ohio, New Jersey, and New York. People in the North, when they hear "barbecue," they think of ribs. So they will actually sit at the table and go, "Do you have barbecue?" and they'll do their fingers like this, and it's like, "Yeah, we have ribs. But we have barbecue, too."

So we have what we call tourists and purists, and we have to educate one and hold our own with the other. For instance, vinegar has a bad name with the folks from out of state. Many folks ask, "Is the sauce vinegar based?" Before they've even tasted it, they've decided

they don't like it. Now, with gas and electric cooking, most of the flavor comes from the sauce, but when you smoke the meat with the hickory wood it takes very little sauce. So once we give them a taste, they quickly sit down and order more.

You're here in eastern North Carolina. The folks coming from the North, they want North Carolina products. There were a couple of places serving what they called North Carolina barbecue, but it was a thicker, red, sweet sauce, catering to what these folks are used to. And nobody used wood down here. I'd been thinking about doing this for a long time, and I would not have done it if I couldn't have used wood. Our cooker is a Southern Pride cooker, a gas-fired, wood-smoked, rotisserie cooker. The wood we get is from a fellow that cuts firewood, and he pulls all the hickory to the side for us. And all our meat is fresh, not frozen. We'd rather pay the fluctuating market price and get a fresh product. I feel like there's a difference in quality.

The vinegar sauce that we use here, we didn't want to do anything that would separate it from a traditional eastern North Carolina experience at Melton's or Parker's or any of those folks. Our red sauce is my brother-in-law's creation; we use it on our chicken and our ribs. But the barbecue is the top seller. People have come to find out that it's so affordable. It's cheaper than they can do anything themselves—hamburgers on the grill, cook a roast, whatever. It's good, it's faster than you can get it in a fast-food restaurant, it's well balanced, and it's not fried and all that.

The cornbread is done in the convection oven. We don't do hushpuppies; we do so much catering and takeout and they deteriorate so bad once they leave the building. Also, I want [High Cotton] to smell like barbecue, because that's what we do. Every place that I go into that fries hushpuppies or chicken smells like a fry house. So we don't have a deep-fat fryer, and we don't do french fries. I don't know how you can eat a plate of barbecue and an order of french fries at the same time, anyway. It will be too much for your system.

You can't appeal to everyone. I don't have a salad and I don't have a soup, and if they're vegetarian, they're in trouble. We have Brunswick stew, but a lot of folks that come in here don't even know what Brunswick stew is.

I've always cooked things that I like, and I know how they're supposed to taste. And I've always enjoyed a pig-picking versus going to a barbecue place. I think it's the smell of the wood cooking, the crisp skin and all that, and very little sauce, and just reaching in and grabbing a chunk off that pig. And this is the flavor that we've recreated here.

It's a chemistry, it really is. I like the sweetness of the slaw going with the vinegar of the barbecue, the very rich flavor of the smoked meat, and the beans add a nice little kick—a little smoky flavor there on the beans—and then the cornbread comes into play, to bring in the earthy flavor that it has.

[It's rewarding] being able to do food that's been done the same way for so long that there's a tradition, being able to reproduce something and know that it's the same as it was in these pictures [on the wall] from 1944. They're eating the same thing as what you've got in front of you [today]. You've got your barbecue, your Brunswick stew, your slaw, your boiled potatoes, cornbread here on the table, soda crackers, white bread, and the sauces in the Coke bottles. I think they're RC Cola bottles actually.

Cover of menu

"Like a fine wine, good barbecue should pass the lips with tang, roll around in the mouth with flavorful finesse, disappear down the throat and leave behind only a light sensation of having been there." (Larry Cheek)

"Clear to the bone, barbecue is a savory slice of Southern history, a pulled chunk of the region itself, at its ever-loving best." (John Egerton)

Photo on the wall at High Cotton: the white folks' table at a barbecue for tenant farmers, Braswell Plantation near Rocky Mount, 1944

Barbecue is a common ground. It's like football. It's something that everybody enjoys, you know. As much as folks try to hurry up and run and rush, here they're on vacation, and I think the slow pace of the food goes along well with the slow pace of the lifestyle down here.

Keith Allen has served fine barbecue to a couple of generations of UNC students and locals at Allen & Son, on Highway 86 north of Chapel Hill. (There's another Allen & Son on 15-501 toward Pittsboro, but someone else runs it now who doesn't cook with wood.) The hunting and fishing trophies that decorate the walls are almost as memorable as the barbecue, smoked over hickory wood that Mr. Allen splits himself. Given his location right near the Eastern-Piedmont divide, it's fitting that Mr. Allen serves Piedmont-style shoulders with an Eastern-style sauce. In 2007 the Southern Foodways Alliance honored him with its Tabasco Guardian of the Tradition Award.

"I keep cooking with wood because I'm chasing that flavor."

I started cooking barbecue because I needed money. I was hungry and I needed work and I know how to do the job and somebody was going to pay me to do it. So in order to eat beans, I split wood. I'm hoping my daughter will be smarter and don't have to do that—do whatever you could do—in order to make a living. So many times in the late fifties and sixties, that was the major concern. Around here there were still one-horse farms and board houses—there was just not a lot of money around. Jobs were just jobs; you just did what you could do every day to make things work that week. And you usually had a garden and put food in the freezer and lived out of that freezer in the wintertime. A lady called me one time and asked me if I had a recycling program. I said I've had a program like that ever since I've been alive. We didn't throw anything away. My grandmother would take the wrapper out of a cornflake box and use it to line her cake pans with.

In the mid-fifties my family had a little hot dog joint and gas station with two tables, and the owner of the building introduced barbecue there. [They cooked] just a shoulder or two and had a block, and they'd pull that one shoulder out and they'd beat it up and make a sandwich—that's the way it was done at that time. And every sandwich was different because they'd chop up different por-

tions, and then somebody'd just ladle some sauce on it and throw it on a bun and throw some slaw on it and hand it to you and you're out the door.

I must have been twelve or thirteen, and that was the first time I'd ever seen barbecue actually done. My father went down to what

is now our [Pittsboro] location and bought the business out and went into work down there and I started cooking. I don't remember how, actually. Maybe I didn't learn; maybe I just started doing it and it just happened.

We started here [at the location north of Chapel Hill] in 1970 or '71. Before we were here, a fellow had a barbecue place here and I came out on my lunch hour (I was a butcher at the A&P) and I set down and we ordered something, and I made the comment to my friend, I said it looks like the guy could do better than this. And my friend told me, he said, well, if you think you're so smart, you buy it—you do it. Well, I did. The next Saturday, I bought it and I did it. And that's how I got started. My father was doing more [business] than I was, so I had a chance to watch and observe and learn everything. He passed away when he was fifty-one, fifty-two.

In a typical day, I start the fire around two thirty, three in the morning. Normally I put the wood in the firebox the day before. Then I just light it, and while that's getting started I put the shoulders on it, and I fire it every thirty minutes for nine hours. I turn [the meat] over one time. The pit is going to quit cooking about noon, and I'm going to put that fire out and then split wood and get it ready to go. On Saturdays we serve three meals and we open at seven, but every other day we just open at ten and work till nine. We'll burn about a cord of wood each day. This hickory wood we're using came from Chatham County. Women in town will call me and want me to pick it up. I get it out of the yard, and they don't have to pay anyone to haul it off. I get the wood, and it doesn't fill up the landfill. It works out good for everybody.

Hickory wood is a little stringy, and that's the reason nobody wants it. They make railroad ties out of it, but as far as a building wood, it's not good for anything. It splits up and cracks. What it does have is a unique smell and a quality of keeping its BTUs. It will make a chunk of coals that will stay there all day and may be there in the morning still burning if you don't put it out really good. So that's the reason we want it. White oak is lighter weight and doesn't snarl up quite as bad, [but it] doesn't hold that coal very good and it burns to ashes completely about twice as fast, so that's the reason we use hickory mostly. Hickory is just the wood that works, because it's more BTUs than probably anything else, not to mention that

it's got that flavor. I don't know how you're going to duplicate that. Everybody has changed to maple and oak and dogwood and apple wood and all that kind of thing—people are going to get real upset if you go out and cut their apple trees down and burn them, you know.

I keep cooking with wood because I'm chasing that flavor. I want it to be really good. If I'm going to do something—I don't care what it is, you know—if I want to park the car, I want to park it straight. Wood is the best flavor I've seen. [But] after a while, it gets where you can't stay in here. I don't think I've ever got accustomed to all of the smoke. I try to avoid it as much as possible. I try to avoid cigarettes, too.

We get our pigs from Nahunta Pork Center in Goldsboro, and that's all they do is pork. The guys down there really do a nice job. They've got good quality, and everything about it is consistent. It's all fresh and nothing frozen, and so I use them only. I can get a lot cheaper stuff, but I can't get better stuff. There's probably about four hundred pounds that goes to the kitchen every day. This morning we have thirty-two shoulders on the pit, and we try to put the coals under the pit pretty evenly, going from right to left and spreading them out evenly under the shoulders. Each shoulder weighs about sixteen pounds, and it will cook down to somewhere between nine and eleven.

(opposite) Keith Allen's tools

"Pride, more than anything else— more, even, than profit—is what keeps them standing watchfully over the fires. Pride and honesty and stubbornness compel them to do it right or quit doing it." (John Egerton)

Pit with an ingenious roll-out grill

We used to do ribs off and on, but we keep them on hand steady all the time now. Supply and demand. I usually place the ribs right on top of the meat there in the pit. They're just going to sit in there, and smoke is going to cook them, indirect heat. You want them to be tender. If you put direct heat to ribs, you're going to wind up with a burnt and tough product. One good secret about ribs: if you sit down and the guy next to you has got ribs and he's got the butcher knife out and he's trying to whack those into two, don't order ribs. There is nothing worse than a tough rib.

When we cook whole hogs [for pig-pickings], we usually cook about 150 pounds total weight. It's a big pig. If you've got an under-developed, a child pig, you've got a lot of gristle which is not ma-tured out, and you will wind up with that in your barbecue. A lot of people say, "I want a hundred-pound pig," and that's great, and it cooks a little quicker, but you've still got the chance of having all that gristle in there.

Our vinegar-based sauce is my dad's sauce, and it was working, and I don't change things that work. I got other things to worry about than something that's working out. The vinegar sauce is just like everybody else's vinegar sauce—hot and spicy. I tell everybody that, and they look at it and they say, "Oh, that's not hot." They don't know until they do, when it catches up to them. I did have one lady call who was looking for a ketchup-based sauce for barbecue, [and] we had to send her somewhere else. We don't have that.

We have everything from hot dogs to seafood to fresh french fries to pecan pie. We make the ice cream and the desserts every day. It's a homemade ice cream; it's not a creamy ice cream—it's like you would make in the backyard with one of those crank ma-chines. Usually my wife comes in and does the ice cream. It's a family recipe we use, like what you would have on Sunday afternoon at the farm.

The cobbler recipe is my grandmother's recipe. It's my mother's recipe for the pastry. I make the pastry up in big balls all at once. I have a recipe that makes a huge amount at a time, and it freezes really well, and it's got a lot of elasticity to it so you can work it really well.

My wife comes in at eight, and she's the first after me. The other employees actually show up about eleven and just in time for the

**Keith Allen Muses
on Cobblers**

A good Southern cobbler
    is a summer treat.
Making good pastry and
    some fresh fruit stands
    for the season.
Put that homemade butter
    and sugar to it
And feed all the working
    farmhands.
And on Sunday make
    the ice cream for a
    topping.

lunch. I do all the prep anyway, so I don't really need them to be here in my way and I don't need to be in their way. They do the french fry cooking and the deep-fat frying and all that kind of stuff. They don't let me on the line anymore. They tell me I'm too slow.

You got to work [at cleaning] every day, all the time, every minute. You got to wipe behind yourself, and then you got to have somebody wipe behind you. So I pretty much got somebody dedicated to cleaning up as you go along, and then you got to kind of be neat, and then at the same time, you've got to be aware of what you left behind and you got to make sure you get all the things that nobody looks at. You really do care what builds up in the corners and cracks; if you don't keep that clean, long-term you're going to have a mess.

"*If there were an agency that monitored endangered cuisines, barbecue would top the list.*" (Jim Shahin)

Once I get home, I go to bed as soon as I can. Normally it's about eight or nine. Sometimes I'll go sooner and sometimes I'll go later. I always try to work from sunup to sundown, and in June and July, I have to work a long day.

It takes time to build up a name, but I think it takes time to build anything that you do and try to do right. We've been out here thirty-two years and we've got a lot of publicity over the last ten or twenty years, but all those building years when you were starving to death and you had no money and you were just banging it out and trying to do whatever you could do to get by—you think, geez, I ain't never going to live long enough to make money. But I managed to eat all along.

Nobody really wants to put in the kind of day of work that we do here. You don't see everybody picking up hammers and wedges and going to work in the mornings. But the interest in quality food has changed over the past five years, so things may turn around in that aspect. Somebody may decide that, you know, the quality is worth keeping. I think people are going from fast foods to convenient foods to quality foods and good foods that will actually be good for them rather than just be quick for them. They tried to class barbecue as a fast food, but it's not a fast food. You can't rubber-stamp barbecue and have good quality. You can put it out there, but that don't mean it's good. The people that come here to eat, I know they're interested in the quality of what they're getting because they have to come out of their way to drive here. I'm not exactly the handiest guy in town as far as locations go. I'm not on the corner you walk by. You don't just happen by here.

I think people are comfortable here. I think a worker can get out of his pickup truck, he's been sweating all day, and he comes in here and gets a glass of tea and a sandwich, and he knows the food is going to be good and the prices are going to be fair. And he's going to get it relatively quick. And he can relax. That's how I think the majority of our business has always come about. The lunch-hour crowd are workers [who] can have a good break in the middle of the day that they can kick their shoes back and relax and they're not on carpet; they're not worried about whether or not they track up the floor. I mean, we've got red mud in here—we don't care. We clean it up and we go on for the afternoon crowd. We sweep and mop every day after lunch. Food has got to be good—ain't no question—but I think people need to enjoy themselves while they're eating rather than that collar snapped around you and the tie cramped up, you're having to choke everything because you're uncomfortable, and you're sitting there trying to pretend that you're something that you're really not. And I think it's important that those guys can get that pitcher of ice tea and get all they want, and we give

free refills on tea and coffee. You surely don't want a twelve-ounce cup sitting in front of you when you take one swallow and it's gone and you can't get the waitress's attention long enough to get something again and you've got to go back to work and you've got twelve ounces of fluid in you and you really needed forty-eight.

Lunch hour on Saturday, that's when everybody from everywhere comes. They may come from Wilson, they may come from Asheville, they may come from Virginia—just to eat lunch. It's amazing to think that somebody would drive that far to eat. I wouldn't walk around the corner to eat, but it's nice to know that people would think of that as being something interesting to do.

Then the dinner crowd—usually on Saturdays when college is in, it's a lot of college students and husbands and wives going out, and early afternoon you have families. So it's a diverse crowd on Saturday. During the week, it's usually the workers during the lunch hour and then families at night.

If you go to a lot of barbecue places, you'll see a little knit community—you'll see Sally in there eating every day, and she'll be eating it because Frank has been cooking barbecue all day and his wife has been making the banana pudding. The community here [in Chapel Hill] is a transient community, and every five years, half of our community leaves town and we have a brand new group. I think it takes them two or three years before they know about us.

As far as catering, we go all over. We go to Baltimore, we did a wedding at the Outer Banks. . . . We ship barbecue all over the country, too. We've got some going out to San Francisco today. We really don't know folks there. We knew them from here and they [went] there, so the transient community actually does help, long-term. I cook it today, freeze it tonight, and ship it tomorrow, UPS guaranteed by ten thirty the next day.

I think I'd be stupid to be trying to cook something other than Southern food—butter beans and corn and cornbread and pigs, the things I grew up on and know—trying to go out and be a chef and try to be something from France when I have not a clue what those guys would consider good and bad. Most chefs are taught to make things attractive, and attractive is great as long as there's substance there, underneath them leaves and all that kind of stuff. When you get all that junk off and you go to eating and it's really good, the chef has done his job. But there's a difference between really good and really pretty. Of course, that has a lot to do with women, too.

I never go eat barbecue anywhere. I cook every single day. I have for years. When I get through cooking and I get through chopping and I get through seasoning and I taste that barbecue—that's about all the barbecue I ever eat. People always ask, do you know [the barbecue at] so and so? Well, I don't. I don't go places and eat barbecue. I guess if you wash cars for a living, you wouldn't go wash a car on a weekend. I usually eat salads—anything that's cold, anything that I don't have to cook.

THE ENTREPRENEURS
STAMEY'S, GREENSBORO

Chip Stamey owns Stamey's Barbecue, across the street from the Greensboro Coliseum. His father, Charles, and uncle, Keith, owned it before him, and it was founded in 1930 by his grandfather, the great Piedmont-style innovator and entrepreneur Warner Stamey. When President Bush ate there in 2006 and Mr. Stamey told him about the restaurant's history, George W. replied, "Well, I know what it's like to be in a family business." The *New York Times* once published a laudatory review of Stamey's and a reporter offered the restaurant's manager a copy to post on the wall, but he declined, saying that Stamey's customers already knew its reputation.

"We talk a lot about being a 'barbecue man.' . . . You got to be able to man the pits but also work the grounds and wait tables, work the cash register—that's being a barbecue man."

My dad had to work his school lunches at the restaurant. He remembered that, and he didn't make me work when I was young. My dad was working all the time. I saw him rarely, except on Sunday, when we were closed. Every once in a while, my mom would bring us up here, but it was sort of an unwritten rule that when he was working—doing business—he wouldn't want us to be around.

He started to really bring me into the business when I was about twelve, just sweeping up the parking lot and mowing grass. Then when I got of legal age, I started in working in the restaurant, from the ground up—washing pots, making barbecue sandwiches, and running the register, just doing everything. You are always around when you're in this business. I just remember that it was a 24/7 job. Even if we weren't open, the talk was about barbecue, work.

Then I went to Wake Forest, started out thinking I had no intentions of going into the business. As I was growing up, my dad always told me, "You should find something better to do. Try to be smarter and better." Did my stint in the corporate world, and that was three years, four years. Then I had my own barbecue place for a few years, and that was at a time when my dad was really near to

Chip Stamey

When Keith Stamey died in 2000, he left his entire estate— $7 million— to Wake Forest University for scholarships for North Carolina students, to keep his alma mater from becoming (as he put it) "another Duke."

hanging it up. We had a manager about to leave in 1994, and [my dad] came to me and asked if I was interested in going back into the business. And so here I am.

My family's involvement with barbecue got started with my grandfather, Charles Warner Stamey. Everybody called him Warner. He came from this tiny town outside Shelby in Cleveland County. He came from a family of (I think it was) eleven children. He was born in 1911. By the time he got into high school, his parents had passed. What he did was go to Lexington and stay with one of his sisters for a year, and he went to work for a guy named Jess Swicegood, one of the first two guys out of Lexington who were working with barbecue: Sid Weaver and Jess Swicegood, the fathers of Lexington-style barbecue.

So he got his indoctrination just like everyone else does, working around it for a few years. When he graduated from high school and moved back to Shelby, it was the Depression when there were no jobs nowhere, and he's like, well, I'm going to be in the barbecue business, that's what I learned while I was in high school. So he actually opened up his first restaurant in Shelby. And it was just like the ones he had worked with in Lexington: it was a tent, somewhere near the courthouse. Because that is what he knew. He had a man he bought his bread from and he had a cooler that he would leave his meat in. They would go get what they needed for the day and sit out there and cook. He was a pioneer there, and that was his start. He stayed there for about seven years and made some money.

For whatever reason, he moved back to Lexington and bought Jess Swicegood's business. My grandfather said it cost $300. Swicegood was getting to about retirement age, and my grandfather, he was going to buy him out, but Swicegood was going to work there for a little while longer. But back then they just worked out of a cigar box and there wasn't a cash register, no tickets, no nothing, and my grandfather learned that Swicegood was taking too much money from the cigar box, like many people of that time did. So my grandfather figured out real quickly that he was going to do it on his own. What my grandfather ended up doing—he was a student of it; he was always working to make it better. He never changed the way of cooking it, but when he put in a system to have paper tickets or waiters to write it down on a sheet of paper, he made it impossible for the old way to happen. That's when Swicegood got thinking that this was too newfangled, with the paper, pencils, and record keeping. And he decided to get on out of the business.

[My grandfather] was never satisfied with what it was. He was an entrepreneur, truth be told, a businessman. He was always looking at making more things go faster. Certainly he was big on quality, but he wanted the price to be low. He also made a lot of improvements in preparation. For instance, everyone gives his slaw a lot of credit. I'm not going to say he invented slaw, because he didn't, but he had an employee, Miss Dell [Yarborough, Sid Weaver's sister-in-law], who worked for him. She ought to get credit for tweaking the red slaw thing, which is what we still do here at Stamey's.

Now, my father started out working for my grandfather as a kid and had the same idea I had [about doing something else], but when he came out of the navy, he came back into [the business]. He hadn't meant to, but the recurring theme is that our family came back into it. I think at that point my grandfather had a place in High Point, a place in Greensboro, and some in Lexington, but when my dad moved to Greensboro, they sold the restaurants down there. What you end up doing is selling the restaurant to the people that work for you. My grandfather opened a lot of businesses and he ended up putting people into business because they took over these businesses that he started.

The young Warner Stamey

One of those was Wayne Monk. He worked for my grandfather. The Copes, and the guy from the Barbecue Center [Sonny Conrad], and Jimmy Harvey, and more—I can think of four or five—plus, around here, James Shelton and Henry Rogers [of Henry James Barbecue], they both were people who worked for my father. [The Bridges families] in Shelby now—well, one set of them are my cousins, the other of them worked for my grandfather. That is why Shelby is so much like Lexington, because my grandfather was in both places. When he left, he was in the process of building a restaurant, and he sold that to his brother-in-law, Alston Bridges. Then Red Bridges—that's the other one, at Bridges Barbecue Lodge—he worked for my grandfather. All us barbecue guys are inbred.

We started out [in Greensboro] with a drive-in here on High Point Road—that was in 1953. It was very limited inside, had car-hop service, all that stuff. Then in 1970 we opened up the one on Battleground Avenue. Today, we're open Monday through Saturday, from ten till nine. We cook every day, which is not what a lot of barbecue places do. Some of the bigger ones will cook every other day. We get in here right around four, four thirty, get the fire going, put the meat on the pits. There were times where we cooked all night. The third shift, it was dangerous—they were on their own, there could be a fire. We got it pretty tight where we can [start at four]. We don't rush it, don't want to cook it in two hours, but we believe we can get a good product out in about five hours. We talk about "pushing the pits," that means working to keep the fire up and the coals running so that you can get some of the smaller shoulders out in time for lunch. We try not to have a lot of leftover. Just do it over and over and you get good at it.

The managers will come into the restaurant about six. Make the slaw, the dip, then all the other stuff, chili for the hot dogs—we're making [everything] from scratch every morning.

We cook with wood, which we consider to be one of the more important things about ourselves. You know, what makes barbecue is grease smoke—the drippings off the meat hitting the fire, making smoke, coming back up—mixed together with the [wood] smoke. There's okay barbecue done with electric because they can get the smoke coming up from the grease. But they're missing the last piece of the real smoke.

When my dad was running things, there was a wood man who had a pickup truck, and he would go out and bring in little loads of wood. But we didn't have as much business back then. When we ended up having to cook a whole lot of meat, we actually had flatbed trucks we'd leave at a sawmill that made ax handles, and they would deliver these big bundles of wood. But then that mill went out of business. People quit using axes, I guess. Then there was a place in Greensboro that had these scrap blocks, little six-inch-long pieces of wood that was a by-product of what they did, all hickory. These people would see the wood pile getting empty and drive by and just dump it off. Now their business has essentially evaporated. So we went back to some people we knew from when we did business in Lexington, and now they're bringing us wood up from Lexington. I won't tell you who they are because I don't want you to use them. Used to be that we wouldn't give out our recipes, but we're now more secretive about our wood than our recipes.

Those folks still deal in hickory. It's certainly a great wood to barbecue with. It's hard as a rock, there aren't many other uses for it, and it exists in the forests of North Carolina. When they go clear-cut some land, they're going to run into some hickory trees and they're not going to know what to do with them, so they'll come to us. We do get oak and cook with that, and there's nothing wrong

You can get it sliced at Stamey's.

"All barbecue is local. It's a performance art enacted by one pitmaster, with a specific combination of setting, ingredients, goals, customers. . . . Even a brick by brick transplant of the really great joints to, say, the Cours Napoléon of the Louvre, with the same pitmaster as curator and all the ingredients flown in on Air France, wouldn't, couldn't, be the same." (Raymond Sokolov)

with it. We prefer hickory because it makes more coals, but I don't know anyone who can pick up on different notes between them.

Most barbecue restaurants just get boxed meat [from the big suppliers], but we go to the slaughterhouse. We get a pallet of meat—that's two thousand pounds. They just cut the shoulders in the factory, and instead of boxing them up, you pick it up with a forklift. It's less money, cutting out the middle man. One of the neat things about barbecue is that pork is just very inexpensive. It allows us to keep these prices down.

The shoulders, we don't want them to get too big, because we're manually putting these things on the grill. My arms aren't strong enough to get that back line if it was a twenty-five-pound shoulder. That's the main reason we don't want big ones, but the other reason is it's hard to get them done; they don't cook right. Shoulders are a tough cut, just like a brisket. Can't use it for anything else. Maybe put some sauce on it, but it's none of this high science of chefdom. It [was just] the cheapest cut of meat. But people started liking it, and now it's, you know, just like ribs were that way. Why black folks like ribs is because [white] farmers would say, "This is junk, you take this; I don't want to mess with this." But I like ribs better than anything. That's all it is, is practicality. Like our slaw is red. We didn't stop and say, "Doing red slaw is a great thing." It's because we didn't have mayonnaise. Now there are a lot of other reasons why not using mayonnaise in slaw is a good thing.

The pits we have now, they always talk about them as the biggest, best pits in North Carolina. But they were built in 1969–70. Basically it was my grandfather's blueprint; him and his pit men were like engineers. We built a lot of them, more than we needed, just because they could serve us well, and we're still keeping them going today.

We talk a lot about being a "barbecue man." That means you have to be able to do everything around the restaurant: you got to be able to man the pits but also work the grounds and wait tables, work the cash register—that's being a barbecue man. [My grandfather] would always get in there and work the pits. It was only when I was in high school when we stopped using our manager-types to cook and got Asian immigrants to cook for us. We started out with Vietnamese refugees and now Montagnards and Cambo-

Stamey's menu

Plates
Served with slaw, and hushpuppies or rolls.

	Regular	Large
Chopped Pork Barbecue	4.25	4.99
Sliced Pork Barbecue	4.75	5.29
Chicken with barbecue sauce - *white meat*	4.25	6.25
Chopped Pork Barbecue & Chicken Combo		5.75
Sliced Pork Barbecue & Chicken Combo		6.75
Brunswick Stew - *pint Brunswick Stew and choice of two sides*		4.49

Sandwiches
Slaw is served on our sandwiches.

Chopped Pork Barbecue	2.50
Sliced Pork Barbecue	2.75
"Chicken-Q" - *with Stamey's sauce*	2.75
Hot Dog - *mustard, chili, slaw, onions*	1.50

Side Orders

Hushpuppies	.99
French Fries	.99
Slaw	.99
Baked Beans	.99
Brunswick Stew	cup 1.60 pint 2.50
Roll - *(sandwich bun)*	.20

Beverages

Iced Tea - *fresh brewed*	1.20
Soft Drinks - Coke, Cheerwine, *caffeine free* Diet Coke, Sprite, Lemonade, Mello Yello	1.20
Bottled Water	1.50
Coffee - *regular or decaf*, Milk - *whole, chocolate, or skim*	1.20

Desserts

Cobbler 'n' Ice Cream	2.40
Homemade Cobbler	1.40
Ice Cream - *premium vanilla*	1.20

Kid's Meals

dians. It's not been that many different individuals. We have two guys doing it full time, and they just do a great job. One has been cooking for twenty-seven years and the other has been doing it for ten years. When one is out, I get in there and cook. We don't have as many high-school kids working now because kids don't want to work; their parents don't want them to work. We worked a ton in high school, but now kids do something else, want to be paid. We would work for anything.

Barbecue is one of the original fast foods. It's the slowest to cook but the fastest thing [to serve] because it's not cooked to order. Where I think some barbecue restaurants make mistakes is when they do these things that are cooked to order, along with the barbecue, and then it gets sort of messed up. My dad was always trying to cut it back. He was known to try and take french fries and hushpuppies off the menu: he was just trying to sell meat. I don't know if you've ever been to Texas, but it's like a butcher shop. They shave it off and weigh it. My dad's favorite place would be run something like that. He was always trying to take stuff away, and I was always adding it back. My father was a student of keeping it simple.

We do things the "Stamey way," which is to be very focused and sell one or two things as best you can. And go fast, and do big volume, and do it in a way that people want to come back to. That's what we try to do.

There are many good places in Davidson County and a handful of great ones, but Lexington Barbecue is on everyone's list of the best. Since 1962 Wayne Monk has been cooking dozens of pork shoulders at a time and serving them with a thin, vinegary, and, yes, tomato-red sauce to thousands of satisfied customers at a place that John T. Edge describes as looking "like an oversize dairy barn with a six-chimney nuclear reactor tacked onto the backside." His devotion to his craft won him an America's Classic Award from the James Beard Foundation in 2003. (Ayden's Eastern-style Skylight Inn won the same award the same year. Someone at the Beard Foundation understands diplomacy.) When Mr. Monk was asked to cook for the Economic Summit hosted by President Reagan in 1992, he sent some beef tenderloin as well as his famous pork shoulder and some chicken. He knows how to cook beef; he just doesn't.

"My way of advertising is work hard and let your clients do the talking."

hen we first started out, Mr. [Warner] Stamey was downtown. Mr. Stamey came here from Shelby. Just about everybody in this area was trained by Stamey or had a connection to him. I worked for Stamey two different times. We're all related, we're all tied in, like a can of worms.

Mr. Stamey cooked the same way Sid Weaver did, but he took it indoors and had more seating. I've been in it for fifty years now and it hasn't really changed a whole lot. Stamey cooked the same way we do today. The pits, the cut of meat, Miss Dell [Yarborough]'s slaw recipe—everything was the same then as it is today.

I was introduced to barbecue when I was fifteen years old and moved here to Lexington. [I was born in] Pearisburg, Virginia. My dad used to move every two years, and when I got to Lexington about 1950 I quit moving. He kept moving and I stayed here. At that time, you had a welcome wagon come around and they'd give you a little certificate good for barbecue. And the first one I tried, I didn't care for. So I have improved it since.

I got into barbecue work by accident. I was in a car with two other guys and we stopped at a local barbecue stand for curb service and someone came out and offered the driver a job and he turned it down. The second guy turned it down. I was the third choice; I took the job. This was back in 1952. My first job was a curbhop, which we still have today here.

[My father's] advice to me was to get out of the restaurant and go to the textile mill and make something out of myself. So I tried that for eight months for a dollar an hour, and I said that's enough of that. It didn't even have windows in the building. I tried other types of work, but I always drifted back into barbecue.

When I first started, every place I worked we cooked about three shoulders a day. [I worked at] Tussey's Drive-in Barbecue. It's now called Speedy's Barbecue—the place is still there, under different ownership. They let me take [the meat] out of the cooler and put it on the pit. They might even let you fire it, but you didn't really cook. I didn't actually start cooking until probably five years later. That was such a hard job I had to get out of cooking barbecue. I had to hire somebody.

In 1962 I purchased this place with a partner. When I got here, it had one little barbecue pit and no air-conditioning but a nice big paved lot. It was called Knob Hill Drive-in, and we thought Knob

Hill was a terrible name. We were horsing around one night and we got silly and we come up with the name Honey Monk, which is a combination of Honeycutt and Monk, our last names. He changed the name, not I—I'm more conservative. But I came in and they were outside changing the sign, so it had to be Honey Monk. Well, it went so good for so long I kept the name. But if you want to advertise or talk about your place out of town, Honey Monk's not serious enough to suit me. I legally changed it to Lexington Barbecue about 1980, somewhere along there, but we still have checks made out to Honey Monk and we're still cashing them.

We really were a teenage hangout the first two years—a grill or a short-order drive-in restaurant. [My partner] lasted about ninety days, and after that I decided that I was going to specialize in barbecue. It's been going good ever since. We added on, and we've had five or six additions since then, until we ran out of room.

The first ten years I worked in this, I wanted out of it. You had the long hours, the Sundays, the holidays, the late nights, and, see, I've been able to change all that. I've been able to tailor things the way I want it, and now we've got it made. We have ideal hours now. It's the perfect situation. People told me I couldn't do this and couldn't do that, and the only thing that did was make me try harder.

Our normal day starts at six A.M. We open up and start putting shoulders on the pit and all. A man actually has a ten-hour day for

barbecuing, cooking seven or eight hours and [then] he's got to clean the pits up and restock and this and that. Normally what we cook today we're going to use for supper tonight and to start off tomorrow, so really you're like a half a day behind.

We don't open for breakfast, but we do have a little coffee club every morning. Lots of my family work here; six or eight of us get together and this is where we start our day. This is our social life, too. You've got to have a few friends that come by—you know, the guy that's going to do your plumbing work or the guy that's doing the welding for you, if he comes by for a cup of coffee, you keep in contact where if you need a plumber Friday evening at six you can get him.

When I first came in business a local grocery store gave me a hundred dollars' worth of credit, and they would supply my produce for me. They're still doing it—the local grocery store downtown, Conrad and Hinkle. It's an old store, looks like it did back in 1930, and the third generation is now running it.

We cook the same way today [as we always have]. Really, it's a very simple thing. We use the same size shoulder and nothing else. The pit might be a little larger, but the distance from the coals is twenty-four inches, same as always. We're cooking [at] about 280 degrees. The cardboard [used to cover the meat has] two purposes—one, to catch ashes that fall back on the barbecue, but also it catches the heat. That's the way it's always been done. We've tried metal and that didn't work as good.

I had two original pits that are still in the wall; they're covered up. We built bigger and more modern-type pits, the ones that smoke less. There's still a danger of fire all the time, but it's contained. As long as you know what you're doing, you can put it out. Barbecue pits will catch on fire and it's a flash fire—the whole walls, everything will catch on fire—so we're always careful about that. Once a week, we'll actually set the [pit] on fire on purpose and burn it clean. Of course the doors we have to clean with oven cleaner.

Most of [the wood]'s oak. A little bit of hickory is tossed in with it. We'll use all the hickory we can get, [but] if you had a solid load of hickory out there—it's a very hot wood—you'd actually have to be careful or you'll burn the barbecue. So if I get a solid load of

"If the world is to have automated barbecue, it might as well want computerized opera. The whole thing is an affront to the natural order. We're agin it." (Charlotte Observer)

hickory I have to tell my cooks. We'll burn a pickup truck and a half a day.

In the pit room we'll have one or two men at all times. Their only real job is to cook barbecue and work it up, pulling the shoulder apart and getting it in pieces where we can use it. [In the kitchen] we'll chop it and slice it and all that. We serve any cut you want. Once you get to know our product you can order ground, coarse chopped or fine, sliced—however you want it—and that's what the locals do. If you want it brown, white, big, little, fat, lean—whatever you ask for, we'll do, but most of it is chopped or sliced. There's a price difference: we encourage you to eat chopped because if everybody ordered sliced I'd have a mountain of scrap left over. In my opinion, the chopped is better [anyway] because it's got a little bit of fat in it, which actually adds some flavor.

The company I'm buying from now is Lundy Packing Company from Clinton, North Carolina, and we've been using their product probably for ten or twenty years. We get one company and stay with them until they change. [I don't know the breed of hog.] I just know the size. I do know they're leaner now than they used to be. That has changed the cooking some, not in a large way, just a minute

thing, and we can adapt to that. People want leaner barbecue than they did years ago.

Our shoulders weigh about sixteen pounds when we start cooking them, and when we get through they weigh about nine and a half or ten pounds, which will yield five and a half pounds of lean meat. So you'll lose two-thirds of it altogether. That's the secret to all of it. There is nothing on it but salt. Nowadays, the volume we do, we do not marinate or baste it or anything like that. It's all put on after the meat is worked up. Actually, the barbecue is on a plate or a bun or tray before we put the sauce on it nowadays.

[For side dishes,] back in the old days, you was trying to have something you could handle in the hot weather but didn't cost an arm and a leg—what locally is available and what's cheap. You've got to remember, slaw is cheap. They grow cabbage here, especially the mountain cabbage. Used to, in the fall of the year, here comes the mountain cabbage. That was the big thing, when the mountain cabbage came in—like country tomatoes. And back [then], if you kept something out in the room you didn't want mayonnaise in it. And Miss Dell came up with the original form of the slaw. In Lexington I think everyone uses the same recipe, with just a little bit of variation—sugar, vinegar might vary, but [it has] tomato ketchup. All the slaw is made right here, in the big old food chopper. We make slaw every day, three or four hours a day, and mix it up by hand.

When we first started out, we didn't have hushpuppies. Stamey introduced those. The first restaurant I worked at, everything was on a bun and you didn't have a plate because you didn't have french fries. And when I first started, you didn't have ice tea in the winter, [but now] ice tea—sweet, sweet, sweet—well, that's what they want. We make so much tea that never even gets into the cooler. We go through one hundred gallons a day.

My daughter makes all of [the cobblers]. Peach and cherry and the berry, berry, berry—blueberry, strawberry, raspberry—sells real good, too. But you can't beat the peach cobbler. That's the old standby in barbecue.

Different family members have different jobs. My son is the manager and my son-in-law is one of my assistant managers. My son right now works more than I do, and he makes quite a few of the major decisions now. His son is working here too now, so we've got three generations working here. Each one has their own individual jobs, and in fact we have a little sounding board. Like if there is going to be a menu change, we've got two or three that work on that and play around it.

Nowadays we're trying to do something that's not fried and has not got meat in it. Now we got the barbecue beans, which are very similar to baked beans. While locally they don't sell good, during a holiday period or something they sell like heck. We don't actually barbecue them, so I'm not going to lie [and say] that's why we call them barbecue beans. They're cooked in a big steam kettle, and they've got onions and some mustard in them and some kind of a smoky barbecue sauce and this and that. My wife and son-in-law developed that recipe, and we kept giving them away until we found something some people liked. In fact, that's still a work in progress, but they are starting to sell. We're [also] trying to work with the new potato, and we're thinking about trying to do something with pinto beans. We're trying to get something that's not fried, but it's hard to do and sell.

Down the road, [Latinos] will be a factor in our business and might even be a labor supply for us because they are good hard workers. I'm sure we'll have to adapt to that. Like my grandchildren in school, I would encourage them to take Spanish because, you know, that would be nice. Just like sign language—we had a girl that worked here one time that could do sign language, and we were so proud of her because if someone come in and they couldn't speak, she could help them and that was great. I would love to be able to do that with Spanish-speaking, too, because if we know what they want, we can please them, we can serve them.

Every day you have a little crisis. You come in every morning expecting some little problem, but that just keeps things interesting. You know, it's not a real problem. I don't think we have any real problems. Our system is very simple, but it's been developed over a period of time. And it works so good now, we don't change much.

August is one of my best months because there's no holidays in August. We'll probably use five hundred shoulders a week. Monday is the slowest day and Saturdays are the busiest. We build up every week. We're closed on Sundays now, but in the old days it was seven days a week, six A.M. in the morning until two A.M. the next morning. When we started out, we had to do what you had to do.

Lexington has got about eight or ten good barbecue restaurants and we sort of draw from each other. The pride that we take in the product—we have to compete against one another and still be friends, so it works to our advantage to have all the locations. The town was trying to find some way to help downtown Lexington and they seized upon the thing that we're known for the most, which is barbecue. There's at least a hundred thousand people that shows up for the Barbecue Festival, and we'll have a line out the door from opening time to closing—just slave labor that day. But we enjoy it. It's a real competition, you know. You've got to handle it.

In 2007 New York's Institute of Culinary Education ran a four-day "Camp BBQ" field trip, with stops from Goldsboro to Lexington. It cost $3,750, airfare not included.

Several governors have been in, and [Senator] Elizabeth Dole comes in occasionally. Any time there's anything political going on, they seem to want to gyrate over this way. Barbecue is like apple pie and baseball. They like to be tied into that.

I don't know why we got so popular. We've been like this for years and years and years, and it seemed like one thing builds on the other, sort of like a snowball, you know. I think being on an interstate highway [helped]. The businessmen and women who can stop off the road are the kind that sort of spread the word for you. They're like ambassadors out there. If a guy that's working at the radio station, say, in Charlotte comes by here and gets a sandwich, we don't recognize him, but we get some publicity. I have never

Lunchtime at Lexington
Barbecue

advertised much at all. We had a couple of billboards when we first started out. We ran a few newspaper ads, [but] really we don't need that. My way of advertising is work hard and let your clients do the talking.

I think that Lexington barbecue now is sort of an anchor [for the community]. We take a lot of pride in that. We've seen a lot of things change, and we're the anchor now instead of the furniture [industry]. When the kids go off to school or to a new job and they come home, we're still here. This is like home cooking for them now.

This is my life right here, and I enjoy what I'm doing. No plans to really retire. You know it really is my life. My job could be my hobby.

THE LEXINGTON DIASPORA
BRIDGES' BARBECUE LODGE, SHELBY

"I've been blessed with workers. . . . It's kind of like a family out here—not black and not white."

Debbie Bridges is a woman in what is usually a man's business. She owns and operates Bridges Barbecue Lodge in Shelby, a restaurant founded by her father Red Bridges and her mother Lyttle "Mama B" Bridges. Her father learned his craft from Warner Stamey, and Bridges is about as pure as Piedmont-style barbecue gets: pork shoulders cooked without salt, pepper, mops, secret sauces, marinades, or anything else but wood. For many years it was cooked by pitmaster John Henry Williams, now retired. Employees like Williams are often what make these places such memorable institutions. When owners refer to their restaurants as "like a family," that's what they're talking about.

DEBBIE BRIDGES

My dad was in the war and he was a cook. And when he came out of the war, he went to work for Warner Stamey in a covered wagon uptown. They talk about how you could get a sandwich and drink for, like, thirty-five cents. And now you get a sandwich and drink, it's four dollars.

[After the restaurant started,] we had a catering business and Father did a lot of the catering. Mom is the one that was in here at eight in the morning until closing. She's retired, but she comes in. She's still the boss.

I've never changed the menu. I had a customer that came in and said, "I haven't been in here for twenty-some years, and it's the same as it was when I was in here." And that's something my mother says: if it's not broke, don't fix it. We have sliced, we have sliced brown, we have chopped brown (that's the outside crunchy part), and the mince is just ground up real fine with a lot of sauce put in it. I've thought about bringing beef in or barbecued chicken, but we just never have.

[The pit man] comes in about eight thirty or nine P.M. Usually he's got it rolling by ten. If you ride by here at nine thirty at night, you smell the aroma. He burns the pits off first, which gets a lot of people's attention going down the highway, and they call the fire

Debbie Bridges

department because they think we're on fire. But they've learned to send a car ahead because they get so many calls. I'd say it's at least once a week. It's not quite as bad as it used to be because people now know, but when you get people from out of town driving by. . . . Twice we *have* burned down.

We try to get all hickory wood, but it's just about impossible to do that now, so we throw some oak in there. But we burn the wood, get the ashes hot, and put them under. And that's the way it cooks. We had [gas grill representatives] come out here years ago and bring gas cookers and cook a full day for us. And it was awful. The taste was awful, the smell was awful, and Mom told them to pack that thing up. If [wood burning] doesn't survive I don't guess we'll survive because, you know, I'm not going to gas. So far I've been lucky. I've been very blessed with my employees. That's not an easy job. It's a hot job. I have had to do it. There was a night or two when [the pit man] had a wreck and had to go to the hospital and I had to come out here, and somebody said, "Did I see you pushing a wheelbarrow three o'clock in the morning through the parking lot?" And I said, "Yes, you did." But I had people calling and helping me, and you do what you have to do.

During the weekdays I would say we go through anywhere from forty to forty-five shoulders [a day]. Friday, Saturday, Sunday, anywhere from sixty to seventy shoulders. I cooked eighty one day, and I said, "When the meat is gone, we close the doors." And there have been some days we've cooked seventy shoulders and closed that door at six. I hate doing it, but if you have fresh meat every day it's a lot better.

[The pimento cheese] was something that my mom used to have on the menu and then she took it off the menu. I noticed a lot of people started asking for it, so I made her come out here. I said, "Show us what we're doing so we can put it back on the menu." It's good.

[One thing] we invented: the barbecue salad. It's where you've got lettuce and tomato and then we put barbecue all the way around

it and we put barbecue sauce on it. You have an option of more
sauce or a house dressing—it's like a Thousand Island dressing.
The salad is not on the menu, but you can get it. Fifteen years ago,
Charles, my ex-husband, invented that.

The tables are original, but I put new booths and new chairs in.
I busted a window out so we could get them in. We needed them.
The walls are still the same, and—as *Gourmet* magazine called it—
the "chandeliers" are still the same. That blew my mind when they
called them chandeliers.

My mother left me twenty-some children [employees]. They've
all been with me for years. I've been blessed with workers. Mom
paid them good and they'd get two bonuses a year and two vaca-
tions a year. We used to give them full insurance, but with the way
insurance has shot up, [now] I pay 75 percent of each. So we've
been good to them. It's kind of like a family out here—not black
and not white.

We cook our sauce. They start it the first thing in the mornings
when they come in. They mix it all up, bring it to a boil, and they let
it simmer for three, three and a half hours. When it sits [a while],
it's better; it thickens on its own. A lot of people think that sauce
goes bad in a month, but it's got so much vinegar in it I've had
some at home for a year and it's still fine. As long as I know, we have

*Before country music star Patty
Loveless was making gold records,
she made sandwiches and waited
tables at Bridges Barbecue Lodge.*

used White House [vinegar], and then that way, we can use the jugs for the sauce.

We've been here for fifty-something years. We still have people that come every other day, every week. I've got two ladies that go in the door at eleven every single day; they are here faithfully every day. They've got to have a certain table. They were late one day and two other people got their table and they was really upset. We've got a group called the Friday Boys that have been coming in here every Friday. They're kind of dwindling down now. A couple of them are still coming. And I've got my Sunday group that comes in after church. There's people that come in once a week, and if we miss them, we wonder what's wrong, what's happened, you know? We'll call and check on them occasionally. And then we have some that say, "Okay, we're going on vacation next week and we won't be here." When a new restaurant opened up, it would slow us down for a little bit because [our customers]'d want to try it out. But they always came back.

I have people calling me all the time and wanting me to ship barbecue for them, and if they want to pay for it I will do it. I really don't want to be responsible, but I will do it if somebody begs me, I guess you could say, or really, really wants it for a special occasion. I just package it in ice packs and I put it in a Styrofoam cooler and I put it in a box. [But] I have one man that comes and buys a whole shoulder—now, it's hot—he wraps it up and takes it, ships it, and it's there the next day and it's still warm. And that's the way he does it. But shipping barbecue is expensive. It costs more to ship it than the barbecue costs itself. I had somebody from Florida, the order was going to be, like, forty-some dollars, but the shipping was going to be sixty-something dollars.

I've never worked anywhere else. I've got a twenty-two-year-old daughter and an eighteen-year-old son and they're involved in the business now, so hopefully the third generation will not fail. My daughter is mainly a waitress now and my son has started making all the slaw. Ours is a barbecue slaw—a ketchup slaw, a red slaw. I don't see how anybody could eat mayonnaise slaw with barbecue. I know people like it, and the two little ladies that eat here every day bring their little container of white slaw with them in a little bag. And it stinks.

JOHN HENRY WILLIAMS

I retired seven or eight years ago now, but it don't look like it. And I just eat barbecue three times a week.

Red [Bridges] taught me. We had barbecued in the oven for a year until we got the pit built, and I was the first one to cook in it. We stunk up the whole town when we used to cook down yonder at the downtown rail track in the thirties.

You know, years ago they put out the word, don't eat too much pork. Now they say don't eat too much beef. But this pork, I've talked to a couple doctors that said you could eat this pork all the time because all the grease is gone. [A shoulder] starts out about

A photo of the young Williams hangs on the wall at Bridges.

When the staff at crosstown rival Alston Bridges Barbecue heard that Mickey Rooney had eaten at Bridges Barbecue Lodge, they found out where he was staying in Charlotte and sent him some of theirs.

seventeen pounds and all that grease and fat cooks down. Pigs change the flavor certain parts of the year and in certain parts of the country. Pigs will vary in their taste. But see, when they're in heat—[(*Debbie Bridges interjects*): That runs you out and they have a strong smell. (*Laughs*) Well, it's true.]

We use strictly wood. A lot of people used to use wood, but they don't no more because of the cost. They use heat; we use wood. You can't beat wood to cook pork.

[The slaw dressing has] vinegar and ketchup. Either you like it or you don't like it. Started out in '46, and still just made the same.

Lots of mornings we open that door at eleven and they're standing out there in line. We fill the place up within fifteen minutes. [Customers] may go try something new, but they'll always come back. "Yeah, where were you last week? We missed you last week."

Now when we was up on 18th Street, the place there, we had Roy Rogers. And we used to have a theater here in town that brought the cowboys in: Gabby Hayes, Gene Autry—he was in here. And Alan Ladd. Mickey Rooney, he went to every table. He was here when we opened up. We let him in, and the waitress come up there and said, "Guess who I waited on?" Nobody bothered him. We let him eat till about twelve and then he got up and he went around the tables and he was just as friendly as he could be.

Brandon Cook is the owner and cook at Cook's Barbecue in Cotton Grove, a wide spot in the road in Davidson County, near High Rock Lake. He's a young man, but he cooks the old way—with splendid results. Barbecuing is a Cook family tradition: his father worked for Wayne Monk and still runs his own place just up the road in Lexington.

"It's good when you see your health inspectors and your food suppliers in here eating."

Cooking barbecue is as simple as falling off a horse to me. I learned the cooking from my dad. His name is Doug Cook; he now owns Backcountry Barbecue in Lexington. My father was a welder and a blacksmith prior to getting into barbecue, but he was looking to do something else. He learned the business at Lexington Barbecue. He used to hop curb out there part time.

I grew up in this place with my brother, running around this place. I started working here as soon as I could see over top of the tables. I must have been about seven years old. So I always sort of knew this is what I wanted to do. This is my hobby.

Our location is a very nice spot. Nobody drops in accidentally; if you're coming here, this is your destination. Once they finish road construction on Highway 8 near the restaurant, we'll have a nice sign up there letting people know where we are.

We're real close to High Rock Lake, so we get a lot of lake traffic in the summer, though when the water's down less people come out here. Lake's down, between lunch and dinner gives me a break to enjoy the air-conditioning and a barbecue sandwich.

It's definitely an old-style place. The exterior is rough; my dad built a sawmill up the road and this whole place is built with timber he cut and processed. The saw blades out in the dining room came from the mill, and my brother killed the elk out on the wall when he was in Colorado.

The pits need some lining and firebrick put back in them, but they've held up good. We've upgraded and tried some new meth-

Brandon Cook

"There is no seasoning as pungent as authenticity." (Jane and Michael Stern)

ods, but you really can't beat the old ways. Gets a little hot in the summertime and a little smoky, can get your eyes running.

Some people stand by them newfangled electric cookers. Dad builds his himself and has it patented. It's in operation over at Backcountry. He upgrades his every year; he's constantly in the shop welding and working it. But this is the best way here, cooking over coals. It's not that hard if you stay ahead of yourself and know what you've got to have, and I grew up in it anyway. It's second nature for us.

We cook on hickory but use a little red oak and white oak too. Sometimes you can't help a piece of poplar falling in there also. Oak makes good small coals, but hickory is the best flavor. That is what we like to get. We go through about two truckloads of wood a week. Get our wood from a gal who comes up here—you can always hear them coming because the muffler on the truck is dragging, going blup, blup, blup, blup, blup. She brings up slabs from the sawmill her husband runs.

When my dad first started here, he worked alone. You would pull up to this window and you would tell him what you wanted and then take the food out in the yard. Then after a year, he built the first dining room; business picked up and he added on the second dining room maybe a year later.

We have barbecued shoulder, ribs, beef brisket, and chicken.

And I cook it all myself: I cook all the meat, make all the slaw, tea, and dip. My wife works in the front of the restaurant—we're about it. But I like to hustle and can do all this stuff myself. I probably didn't realize I was doing it all comfortably until it had already happened. I usually get here right around six A.M. to start things up. I try to get as much done in the morning [as I can] because it's cooler and you can get more things done. I really do stop cooking, though, once I leave the restaurant.

Usually we use Lundy's for our meat. We go through about fifteen cases of pork a week; it's all vacuum-sealed. We start with the

"[Barbecue]'s the antithesis of standardized, processed fast food served in the cookie-cutter buildings that, if not already in your neighborhood, soon will be." (Steve Storey)

meat out on the grill and lay the coals in there to get hot. Some
people like to put the coals in the pit with a wiggle, but I'm a slinger.
Folks are either wigglers or slingers. We put cardboard on top of
the shoulders because it keeps the ashes off of the meat. Keeps the
heat down, too. My father did it as well.

When there's no electricity it does generate a lot of ash. We'll
clean out the pits about once a month—we take out about three
wheelbarrows full of ashes.

If you can pull the skin off the shoulder when you flip it and that
skin is flexible and flimsy, you done a good job—you've never fired
it or got it too hot. If you get it too hot, then the skin will stick to
the meat and the grill and the pit. At the end of the week, I'll fry
all those skins up and then people will come and buy those by the
boxes.

We got a new chopping block put in in 2002. There's no telling
how many we've had—this is the third one I can remember. About
every equipment company in Lexington will carry them, custom
made. The dip recipe is what I learned from my dad fifteen years
ago. We make it daily. It's good with the pork rinds we make as
well.

We have flounder on Fridays and Saturdays and hope to add
some equipment so we can cook more stuff. I hope to have a place
to cook some steaks. We started cooking brisket because—well,

my dad built this place about 1970 [and] he had gone to Texas and studied how they done it. I don't put any coals directly under [the briskets] for about two-thirds of the time they're cooking; I just let them accumulate smoke. And the longer you can let it linger on the pit, the better off it will be. We do a dry rub on the brisket, start them meat-side down and flip it once while it's cooking, then flip it once it's done to get some of the extra fat out. We use Cattlemen's beef dip as the mop. No matter how good a concoction you put together, nothing is as good as Cattlemen's, no matter how hard you try. Some folks are wary of trying brisket the first time, but once they try it they all come back for more. You do got to know what you're doing with it and how to slice it.

There's really not many people willing to come in here to work, brave the smoke, get hot, sweat your rear end off, and come clean up afterwards. That's the hardest part about cooking, is cleaning up. There's more cleaning than there is cooking. Got a 97 1/2 rating from the health inspector, and that was because the bathroom door was dragging so I had to get my saw out and trim that thing. But it's good when you see your health inspectors and your food suppliers in here eating.

We've catered a few jobs here and there—weddings and some of the race-car industry folks in the area—and I like to put a lot of pride into it and do things well. We got some folks come in every day, some twice a day. They always sit here and eat; seems like a lot of business gets taken care of out there. We close between lunch and dinner, and we're open until eight thirty P.M.

Man, I tell you what: I'm a sandwich-a-day guy. I'm used to waking up in the mornings and smelling barbecue smell. I grew up doing this, running around the parking lot here. I see myself doing this for a long while. I feel like I'm loving it.

THE FREELANCER
GLEN WHITE, CABARRUS COUNTY

"We didn't really care about the money: it was just an excuse to get together and drink something a little stronger than Coca-Cola."

Glen White doesn't own a restaurant or even cook for one. He lives in rural Cabarrus County, north of Charlotte, and continues the old North Carolina tradition of itinerant barbecue men who cook for community occasions. (We first met him at a fund-raiser for Pillowtex employees laid off when the mill closed in 2003; he had been cooking all day in the rain.) Although he has cooked whole hogs—and, as he says, many other critters—he's primarily a shoulder cook, in the Piedmont tradition.

I've been around barbecue at least sixty years. I grew up attending at Flow Harris Presbyterian Church, just a mile or two from where I live. We had a log cabin church and were trying to build a new brick church, so they had these annual barbecues. Back when I was coming up, we were a pretty poor state. People worked in tobacco fields and textile mills and people didn't make a lot of money, but everyone could throw a hog in for a big event for cheap.

My dad was involved with them, and all the men of the church were involved, too. I was just a tag-along, but I was paying attention to what they were doing, I guess more than I thought I was. I learned a lot from the older guys who were barbecuing. I went to the woods with them when they took the axes and saws [and] cut down the hickory trees, took the axes and limbed the trees, took sledgehammers and wedges and split that wood, and then I remember we would generally cook about three thousand pounds of meat for the barbecue.

As time went on, I started working in the sandwich stand, helping make sandwiches. I was always going around the pit. The last year they had the event, my father was in charge of the whole thing, and he had been working all day. You always had a lot of help around until late at night when everybody disappeared and went home, [so] I agreed to stay and watch the pits. I looked around and there was my brother-in-law and myself and that three thousand

"Sometimes you see women helping their men as a team, but I don't think most women have much interest in it. Cooking barbecue started as more of a stag party." (John Thomas Walker)

Glen White

pounds of meat in the pit. It was a little bit scary, to be honest with you. Back in those days, you wouldn't have but a shallow pit between the meat and the fire, and when you're that close you got to be really careful—the most little fire can spread [*snaps fingers*] just like that. Fortunately we got it cooked, and we didn't burn any of the meat.

I grew up and was gone from the Carolinas from '64 to '79. I was [working for an insurance company] down in Florida for a while. One day there I was in a coffee shop talking about barbecue, and I said, "Well, I know how to barbecue." One of those guys at the shop had a nice country place near St. Petersburg and we went out there, built the pits, and bought a pig from a guy who swapped pigs. The pig was a little greasy, but we got it done. And we did that for a few years.

So I got back to Cabarrus County, and a guy from my Charlotte office got in touch with me. The insurance company I worked for had been feeding steaks to all their agents in the Carolinas as a treat. So this guy from Florida comes up one day and said, "Why don't you do a barbecue? Glen here can do it." My manager asked me if I could, and I said yes. It turned out to be quite an undertaking. Started out with maybe a hundred people, and by the time we quit, the year after Hurricane Hugo, we had three or four hundred people attending. My company's home office was in Detroit,

Shallow-pit barbecuing,
Bladen County, 1939

and it got to be where people were fighting for those invites to come down to Charlotte and eat barbecue.

I've cooked up to three thousand pounds of pork at one time and I've done as little as one or two shoulders. I'll cook barbecue for the local Democratic Party, and I've cooked for old commissioner of agriculture Jim Graham, former governor Jim Hunt, Attorney General Roy Cooper, and Lieutenant Governor Bev Perdue, too. We've had lots of fun. We don't do it to make money, just to have fun. I don't ever charge the Democrat Party since I'm an old Yellow Dog myself. I've enjoyed the fact that people like my barbecue. We make it juicy and smoky.

Now, why do you use a shoulder over a ham? You get the best meat out of the shoulder; that's why I cook them. Now, some people cook with the hams or the whole hog. I never really like to cook the whole hog. It's too hard to handle because you got the shoulder over here and a ham over there and ribs in between. You got to be real careful how you fire in there, or you'll burn the ribs.

I cannot stress enough to people, when you get barbecue, get the top-of-the-line pig that's been raised on a concrete floor and grain-fed instead of just fed out of a slop barrel. If it's the latter, the meat will be greasy and stringy. North and South Carolina are some of the only places I know of where you can get whole hams and shoulders at the store. They're just harder to find elsewhere.

Pork shoulder is pretty generic, but the two companies I use for pigs in North Carolina are Smithfield and Lundy, because you know you're going to get good meat. It's going to be lean, too. Used to be, in the old days, the North Carolina Pork Producers would say get a pound of pork per person—I'm talking raw meat. Today, three-quarters of a pound per person is what I use, and you could actually do a little less than that, probably a half pound per person. But you want enough to go around. If you happen to get a bunch of people coming over, you don't want to run out, right?

I want the shoulders to be the same size so they can cook up at the same time, so I'll get ones that all weigh fifteen to seventeen pounds. I've had some weigh up to twenty pounds; they end up cooking like a ham.

When the day comes I can't cook over wood, I'll quit. There's two types of wood we use around North Carolina: it's either hickory or oak. Hickory lasts longer, makes nice coals, but you want it at least one year old. Anything less aged than that is a little too green. You can use it for a couple of years after that as well. Oak wood will burn up a little faster, yields just a little sweeter taste to the meat than hickory does.

When using steel drum cookers, normally I keep the doors wide open to see how well the wood is making coals. That is extremely important. We use fifty-five-gallon drums; you don't get a lot of wood in there—if you ain't careful, people put too much wood in there. You got to have that wood small enough to burn up fast and make coals for you. When you're firing those cookers, the doors on the end I'll leave open and the two smoke stacks on top I'll leave completely open, so the smoke's billowing out. That's where you get that barbecue taste. I like the temperature where I can just lay my hand on the grill—lay your hand up there and you can't keep it there, then you're at just the right temperature.

The old-timers used to say, if it's dripping, it's too hot. I say, if

"I had seen pigs eat and the process did not seem to me pretty. It took praise of peanut[-fed] pig and the succulence in the wind of whole pigs being barbecued over pits in the back yard for some big party to still my young prejudice and stir my young greed. I am grateful for escape." (Jonathan Daniels)

it ain't dripping, it ain't hot enough. A fifteen- or seventeen-pound pork shoulder, if you've got good wood and things are clicking, you can cook it in about seven hours. You'll hear that meat dripping. That don't hurt, because that's what's getting the fat out of it. I've had people come up and say to me that they like my barbecue because there's so little fat in it, and some of us don't need that.

You can tell when the pork is done because there's a knuckle bone in the hams and shoulders. If it's hard to turn loose, it's done but not as much as it should be. But if you grab it, twist it, and it falls right out, that shoulder is good and done. I don't ever stick a thermometer in a piece of barbecue; I always prefer to twist it.

We'll also barbecue a lot of chickens. I've cooked about a thousand chicken halves for the Cooperative Christian Ministries as a fund-raiser over behind the local Catholic church. Most people either overcook or undercook chickens on the grill, and there's a knack to knowing when to take them up. If you pick that chicken up in your hand and twist that leg bone and pull that bone loose, man, take it up right then. Anything past that is downhill.

We baste the pigs and chickens a little bit while they're cooking. I used to baste them more than I do now, but I will always do it at the end. When I take them up, I swab them. I have these two sauces I make. One's a little hotter and it's called the Oh-My-God sauce, and we have a milder sauce called the wimp sauce. The wimp sauce was developed for Cornerstone Presbyterian Church. I use it because a lot of people today can't handle that other sauce. Matter of fact, I am not too thrilled with it myself. That Oh-My-God sauce isn't going to take you out, but when you taste it you say, "Dang, that's good," but in about five or ten minutes, see, you begin to wake up to it. A lot of people talk about how it clears their sinuses.

My barbecue sauce is vinegar based, and this recipe was around when I came along. What we do is we take two gallons of vinegar, a pound of red pepper, and a pound of black pepper, stir it up. Put in a pound of horseradish, and I usually put in a gallon of ketchup and one of the larger bottles of yellow mustard. You stir it up and boil it for five minutes. I've never had but one person in all my years of cooking identify that horseradish taste by name.

I've barbecued a shoulder, then put it in the refrigerator, and it will keep for a week. If you want to freeze it, you've got to chop it up into big chunks and not leave it whole. It'll reheat much better. [But] one thing [to] remember about cooking pork barbecue is, the best it's ever going to be is when you cook it, take it off the pit, chop it, and serve it. Once you refrigerate it, it's downhill from there. Not to say it won't be good, but it will never be *as* good. One of the big events here is Poplar Tent Presbyterian Church in the late fall of each year. They cook about fifteen hundred pounds of barbecue for the event. When I was a kid, my dad and two other men taught them how to barbecue, some fifty-plus years ago. Problem with cooking that much is, they start cooking ahead of time.

I used to set my cookers up in front of my garage. Anything you wanted cooked, we would do for a price. We didn't really care about the money: it was just an excuse to get together and drink something a little stronger than Coca-Cola. One year we had the Cokes freeze out there while we were cooking, it was so cold.

"In North Carolina, barbecue starts around midnight when the men get the hickory logs going. . . . There are always two sauces, one for the meat and one for the cook." (Merle Ellis)

My neighbor asked if I know how to barbecue deer meat. I said I'd always wanted to try it but knew that deer meat is so lean. He said, "Well, I got a deer shoulder." So we got that on the grill and laid some fatback on top of it and under it, we kept saucing it, and in the end, you could cut it with a fork. [Another time,] one of the local Highway Patrol men showed up here with a deer and it was so tiny when we cooked it up, hardly anything was left. He accused me of swapping it out with another deer, it shrank so much on the grill. It just tore him up that there was nothing left. For the longest time, we'd kid him for cooking Bambi.

A lot of people who've written books about barbecue and lots of people who've become so-called experts — it's not brain surgery that we're doing. It's just having the knack and knowing when to do the work. It don't take long to learn it. I taught the guys out at my church, and after a few years they're better than I am. It's one of those things I've learned over the years — it comes natural to me. But if you want to learn to barbecue, get with somebody who knows how and do a few of them, and then you can do it.

I've enjoyed the camaraderie. Biggest problem I have is too many people get gathered around the grill and I just end up running my mouth. I have to make sure I keep my mind on what I'm doing.

The Chevaliers du Tastevin are an exclusive fraternity of burgundy lovers. We think lovers of barbecue should have something similar, and here are our nominees. Only one actually runs a restaurant (and that's in Kentucky), but they've all demonstrated their knowledge of North Carolina barbecue and devotion to the cause.

BOB GARNER started doing features about barbecue on WUNC-TV's *North Carolina Now* in 1994. Two years later, he published his pioneering book, *North Carolina Barbecue: Flavored by Time* and produced a television documentary based on the book. *Bob Garner's Guide to North Carolina Barbecue* followed in 2002. Garner has done as much as anyone to publicize North Carolina's state dish and to establish and uphold standards for evaluating it.

JIM EARLY went to all 100 counties and to 228 barbecue places to write his invaluable guide, *The Best Tar Heel Barbecue, Manteo to Murphy*. Now he has founded the North Carolina Barbecue Society (NCBS) to celebrate and promote "the cradle of 'cue." He has established a Historic Barbecue Trail and a North Carolina barbecue "Wall of Fame" (both on the society's website). He hopes to videotape pitmasters at work and is working now to set up classes, sponsor festivals, and much, much more.

DENNIS ROGERS "grew up within smelling distance of Parker's in Wilson" and claims, "I have dined on the swine in every barbecue joint worthy of the name and have the clogged arteries to prove it." Yeah, well, a lot of us can say that. What puts Rogers in this elite group is not that, or even that he once had Parker's air-freight frozen 'cue to him in El Paso, but that for years he has used his column in the *Raleigh News and Observer* to champion the cause of real North Carolina barbecue (Eastern-style). His title "Oracle of the Holy Grub" is self-bestowed, but he's earned it.

Best-selling true-crime writer **JERRY BLEDSOE** grew up in Thomasville and now lives in Asheboro. He is a champion of North Carolina literature through his Down Home Press and has also championed the cause of real North Carolina barbecue (Piedmont-style) since his days working for papers in Kannapolis, Charlotte, and Greensboro. Bledsoe and Dennis Rogers have long been sparring partners, and have taken their Eastern versus Piedmont debate to venues as far afield as the *Washington Post* and the ABC *Evening News*.

Although he's from Tennessee and worked for many years in Kentucky, we nominate **VINCE STATEN** here because in 1988 (before barbecue was cool) he and Greg Johnson wrote *Real Barbecue*, the first appreciation of our slow-cooked heritage and still one of the best. The book showed that it knew what it was talking about by rating both Wilber's and Lexington #1 "as good as we've ever had." Staten has also put it on the line by opening a (great) wood-cooking barbecue place in Louisville. Not only running his mouth but actually running a restaurant makes this *éminence grease* almost unique among barbecue writers.

DOUG MARLETTE was a Pulitzer Prize–winning editorial cartoonist and a best-selling novelist, but he joins this list because of his down-home comic strip, *Kudzu*, from which he created, with Jack Herrick and Bland Simpson of the Red Clay Ramblers, what is surely the only musical comedy ever to deal with (as Marlette put it) "the eternal strivings for love, power and the perfect barbecue sauce." *Kudzu: A Southern Musical* debuted at Duke University in 1998, went on to a successful run at Ford's Theatre in D.C., and is still being performed here and there around the country. In the summer of 2007, it was well received at the Edinburgh Festival.

Clothing designer **ALEXANDER JULIAN** has found fame in New York City but hasn't turned his back on his North Carolina roots. The Chapel Hill native took payment in barbecue for designing the Charlotte Hornets' uniforms. (The uniforms, in teal, purple, and white, with baggy pleated shorts and V-neck tank tops in subtle vertical stripes of green, purple, and light blue, were not a hit with the players.) He gets frozen barbecue shipped regularly to his Con-

necticut home and has even written a book with 100 recipes for leftover barbecue (pasta, omelettes, etc.) but hasn't found a publisher for it.

Greensboro native **BARRY FARBER** also found success in New York, as a talk show host, but writes: "The poet loves the Arizona sunset. The art lover loves the correctly lit Rembrandt. The hair fetishist loves long, soft, fragrant hair. The North Carolina barbecue lover loves marinated pork shoulder in its twelfth hour of cooking over hickory wood." Like his runs for mayor and for Congress, his late-seventies experiment with a North Carolina barbecue joint in the Big Apple was a noble failure. He imported the genuine article flash-frozen from Fuzzy's in Madison but gave up when he found the Greeks who ran his place serving it on bagels.

When Raleigh's *Metro* magazine ran a poll for one of those "Best of" features in 2007, its readers gave the top three places in the barbecue category to a Memphis-style chain, a Texas-style chain, and an "Eastern-style" chain that cooks entirely with electricity. We've actually had decent meals at branches of all three, but to say that they have the best barbecue in *Metro*'s region—"From the Triangle to the Coast"—is simply an insult to the hardworking and dedicated men and women at a half-dozen traditional, locally owned, wood-cooking establishments in Wayne, Pitt, Wilson, and Johnston counties.

This story reveals epidemic ignorance among Triangle-area yuppies. It also illustrates several other distressing trends in the Tar Heel State's barbecue situation.

SMOKELESS BARBECUE

The Memphis-in-May World Championship Barbecue Cooking Contest and all its tributary contests define barbecue as "pork meat only (fresh or frozen and uncured) prepared on a *wood or charcoal fire*, basted or not, as the cook sees fit, with any non-poisonous substances and sauces as the cook believes necessary." The Kansas City Barbecue Society, the other major organizer of nationwide competitions, is more permissive about meats ("uncured meat/fowl, or other as allowed") but uses exactly the same language about how the cooking should be done: "on wood or charcoal fire." The Central Texas Barbecue Association appears ready to cook almost any mammal, bird, or reptile, but in its contests, too, "under no condition can gas or electricity be used for cooking." Similarly, in the U.S. Department of Agriculture's definition of barbecue, anything goes when it comes to meat, but even so, it must be "cooked by the direct action of heat resulting from the *burning of hardwood or the hot coals therefrom*."

In short, even Tennesseans, Midwesterners, Texans, and federal bureaucrats understand that cooking with hardwood makes

When Davidson County was cited for violating federal air-pollution standards in 2006, county officials pointed out that the monitoring station was located 200 feet from Smokey Joe's Barbecue.

They're not kidding.

the difference between pork barbecue and roast pork. No wood, no good. If you're not smoking, you're joking.

So what's gradually happening in the Old North State is really cause for concern. Jim Early's *Best Tar Heel Barbecue, Manteo to Murphy*, published in 2002, reports on how the alleged barbecue was prepared at 126 North Carolina establishments. Only a third (forty-three) even *claimed* to cook entirely with hardwood or charcoal in the old-fashioned way. The most common approach, found at about 40 percent (and an even higher percentage of the newer places), employed some sort of hybrid cooker that uses gas or electricity as well as wood. Nearly half of those used the cooker invented and marketed by the folks at Nunnery-Freeman Barbecue in Henderson; the next most common was the ironically named Southern Pride cooker, manufactured in Marion, Illinois.

We're inclined to agree with Jeff and Robin Clifton, who run Asheboro's Blue Mist Barbeque. Their menu generously acknowledges that "some places say they 'Pit Cook' their BBQ, and if you consider using gas and a piece of wood 'Pit Cooking', well . . . OK." But it goes on to say that the nineteen-hour wood-cooking process they've been using since 1948 "produces a taste that you will not find anywhere else," and they're right about that.

To be fair, these cookers are better than nothing. If gas or electricity is used primarily for ignition and to regulate the temperature, little is lost other than soul. Even if your cooker's heat comes from the utility company rather than the woodpile, at least those wood pellets or chips give the pork a little smoke flavor, if you re-member to add them.

And that's *much* better than what Early found at the full quar-ter (thirty-one) of the places in his book that shamelessly admitted cooking their "barbecue" entirely without wood. Bear in mind that Early was listing the *best* places, recommended to him by locals, so wood-burners were overrepresented. In 2006 Dave Lineback's bar-becue website listed nearly five hundred North Carolina establish-ments that served something called barbecue, of which only thirty-nine — one in twelve — were known not to use gas or electricity at all (and at least two of those have closed).

Sure, it's hard to run a wood-cooking establishment these days. As Early observes, "By the time you buy wood, pay a pit master, pay the higher insurance rates caused by chimney fires, operating a real pit is like pushing a Cadillac uphill with a rope. I'm not saying it's not doable, but it's getting tough." Air-quality concerns have led some municipalities, including Lexington of all places, to ban new wood-burning pits within city limits. (Why the wood-fired pizza ovens beloved of yuppies get a pass isn't clear to us.) It's also true, as we've mentioned, that county health departments don't cotton to ash and soot swimming around where food is prepared, and they aren't fond of cooking food at temperatures that hover around the 220° mark like a shy seventh-grader at a middle-school dance. Add fuel and labor costs, and there are powerful reasons to switch on the gas. But taste isn't one of them.

LAPSED FAITH DOWN EAST

For some reason, this distressing trend has advanced farther and faster in eastern North Carolina than in the Piedmont. To be sure, the correlation isn't perfect: Wilber's in Goldsboro, for example, arguably the most famous Eastern-style place, cooks its barbecue over hardwood coals, day after day after day. So do the Skylight Inn and Bum's in Ayden. Same for B's in Greenville and Stephenson's in Willow Spring (although admittedly the last two cook with char-coal from the bag, not from the burn-barrel). And some of the big names west of Raleigh are cooking without wood now, even a few places in Lexington itself.

"*The health inspector is trying to make me go to a stainless-steel cooker. He says they're more sanitary.... There's only a handful of us wood-cookers left.*" (Pete Jones, Skylight Inn, Ayden)

On Modern Technology

"One can't help but rue the commonplace of adequate 'cue, which is what electric cookers and automatic temperature control have wrought. Smoke is mysterious, fire is uncertain, and pit men are expensive. So the mystery, uncertainty, and expense of taking the chance to make great bar-becue is being replaced by the quantifiable methods of always making pretty good 'cue. The consis-tency of barbecue . . . has produced a terrible same-ness."
—Jim Shahin

"*The government is getting to be a real problem in the barbecue industry. Next thing you know real barbecue will be outlawed, and folks is gonna have to go out in the woods with the moonshiners to make it!*" (The Legendary Smokey Pitts)

Wood versus Fossil Fuels (You Decide)

The arguments in favor of cooking barbecue with gas or electricity come from cooks. (The first two below don't do it, but they see why some folks do.)

Pete Jones, Skylight Inn, Ayden: "Pit cooking is the hard way. The easiest way is gas or electricity; you put the pig on, turn a knob, and that's it."

Keith Allen, Allen & Son, Chapel Hill: "You have to be pretty stupid to make barbecue this way [with wood]. It's hot and miserable in the summer and freezing in the winter. It's greasy and dirty all the time, and you've got ashes and soot all over you."

John Thomas Walker, Hillsborough Hog Day Cook-off winner: "It may not be as romantic as wood, but I can't tell the difference in the taste. And gas has took all the hard work out of it."

Kent Bridges, Alston Bridges Barbecue, Shelby: "If I had to do it the old way, I'd quit."

Jimmy Harvey, Jimmy's, Lexington: "I used to do it the hard way. But after you've been doing it so long, you know how to do it, and if you put my barbecue up against any of these others I guarantee you I'll beat 'em."

Ralph "Bubba" Miller, Bubba's, Charlotte: "You can't make barbecue the old-fashioned way and still meet health codes."

The most eloquent arguments for cooking with wood come not from cooks but from eaters:

Charles Kuralt: "Something has been lost in such famous barbecue outposts as Rocky Mount and Kinston, where they now do their cooking with a gas flame."

Tom Wicker: "To anyone deeply into barbecue, the idea of cooking it any way other than over live coals is as repugnant as, say, artificial potato chips or 'whipped cream' that never saw the inside of a cow."

Jim Shahin: "With wood, sometimes you get an inferior plate. But then (and more often) you also get that unbelievable plate of meat so rich, so succulent, so deeply flavorful with whatever magic the pitman could command that you were connected with the ancient longings of the species itself."

Alan Richman: "Barbecue without wood is like French food without butter, inappropriate and insulting."

Calvin Trillin: "Not having [barbecue] cooked slowly over a wood fire by a sullen man with a squint is like saying that a symphony orchestra would be cheaper without the violins."

Still, three out of every five Piedmont places in Early's book relied entirely on wood, and only one in twelve tried to get away without it altogether. In the East, in what Early calls "the Flatlands," fewer than one place in five was a classic wood-burner in 2002, and nearly half—including some of the oldest and best known—used no wood at all.

Things have reached the point that most contestants at the country's biggest whole-hog barbecue competition, the annual Newport Pig Cookin', use propane. When the contest began in

1978, competitors burned oak, but, the contest's website explains, "the problem with using wood, you had to stay up all night to replenish the coals." It's not just Newport, either: in most Eastern cook-offs these days, judges no longer give points for smoke flavor and "gassers" usually win. As Mike "Big Moe" Moore of Bladen County observed after losing a contest in Elizabethtown, "They had all these fancy gas cookers. You cook one on those things and they do look pretty, like something out of a magazine, like they molded it." But he added, "I still prefer wood." We do, too—and so should you.

A good compromise at Bum's: First-class hardwood charcoal supplements real wood.

Eastern North Carolina used to be a bastion of barbecue tradition. When it comes to sauce, it still is. So what's happening down yonder? Bob Garner speculates that "eastern North Carolinians, with their large-scale farming mentality, tend to be immensely practical people, always ready to find a quicker, more efficient way to do anything," while in the industrialized Piedmont, barbecue "is more widely regarded as a way of paying homage to a simpler past and staying in touch with the state's heritage." He thinks that many Easterners, in other words, aspire to do for barbecue what Smithfield has done for hog farming—rationalize it, standardize it, amp up the volume, cut the cost, and make it pay. In the Piedmont, perhaps cooking barbecue more often remains a craft, increasingly (like other crafts) the object of nostalgia.

King's Bar-B-Que in Kinston, which opened in 1937 as a country store, now seats more than 800 customers and has pioneered overnight deliveries (1-800-322-OINK). It's hard to wood-cook tons of pork a week, so they don't anymore, alas.

Could be, but there are a couple of other factors as well. For starters, there's just more hardwood in the uplands. That's why the furniture industry is found there. (Stamey's, in Greensboro, has used surplus and scrap from a local furniture factory to cook its shoulders.) It's harder and more expensive to get a steady supply of hickory and oak in the East. In addition, while it's somewhat easier to cook shoulders with gas or electricity than with wood, it's a *whole* lot easier to cook whole hogs that way. You get more precise control over the temperature, so there's less danger of overcooking some parts or undercooking others. Finally, compared to shoulders, whole-hog barbecue has a smaller component of intensely smoky "outside brown," so not using wood may make less difference in the taste.

So, yes, we understand why some folks might want to turn their backs on their heritage. But however tasty a gas-cooked, machine-

"The next ten or twenty years, I'm not concerned about. But I think eventually it will die out. I don't think we'll be able to keep making barbecue the way we do. It's so old-fashioned." (Wayne Monk, Lexington Barbecue)

minced processed barbecue product may be, we stand with Pete Jones: "If it's not cooked with wood, it's not barbecue." That's easy for us to say since we're not trying to make a living at it and *we* don't have to get up before dawn to split wood, but the truth is that what many places serve these days is to real pit barbecue what Velveeta is to cheese. Sadly, as Bob Garner observes, some have been so successful at it that their customers no longer know what the genuine article tastes like or, worse, don't care. In some circles, "barbecue" has come to mean slow-roasted pork served with a tangy vinegar-and-pepper sauce: Barbecue Lite. We say it's faux 'cue, and we say to hell with it.

CHAINS

Perhaps chain barbecue restaurants were inevitable. As Jean-Jacques Rousseau memorably observed, "Man is born free, and he is everywhere in chains." We have no real quarrel with chain restaurants as a business model, and we've eaten in some that delivered what tasted to us like pretty good specimens of Texas-, Memphis-, and Alabama-style barbecue. But at least when it comes to North Carolina barbecue, writer Michael Lee West seems to be correct when she claims that "one thing is certain: Good joints are never franchised." For whatever reason, it seems to be next to impossible to run a good Tar Heel barbecue place without the proprietor around to keep an eye on things and to put his reputation on the line day after day.

Again and again, enthusiastic investors have thought a North Carolina barbecue chain would be a great idea. Again and again, if they tried to do it more or less right, they have lost their shirts. In the early 1970s, for example, a group of investors that included former governor Terry Sanford bankrolled Andy Griffith's Barbecue. At its peak, the chain had seven branches; despite Andy's imprimatur, however, it went out of business after two years. On the other side of the aisle, Republican lieutenant governor Jim Gardner tried to start a chain based on Parker's in Wilson—and also failed. More recently, Boddie-Noell Enterprises of Rocky Mount— the folks who brought you Hardee's—came a cropper with their BBQ & Ribs chain, which opened its first place in Siler City in 2002, won a string of national awards for its hickory-smoked Eastern-style barbecue, won our hearts with its motto ("Y'all Down South Now") and its shagging pigs logo, and grew to four branches before shutting its doors after four years.

At least so far, the only commercially successful chain operations are lowest-common-denominator enterprises like a couple we could name that advertise fried chicken and Eastern-style barbecue: their chicken's pretty good, but their pork has never been touched by wood smoke. For now, it's probably a good idea to follow the policy of Keith Allen of Allen & Son in Chapel Hill, who says, "I look for the mom-and-pop shops when I travel. That's where the pride is. There ain't no pride in no franchise outlet."

ALiEN 'CUE

Say this for the Memphis- and Texas-style operations in the Metro survey, though: at least they expose their ribs and brisket to some

"Many of the newer barbecue places are yuppified theme restaurants; their walls decorated with framed photos of old cars and rusted farm implements[, while they're] changing the food itself almost beyond definition." (Jim Shahin)

savory hardwood smoke. Many other newcomers also understand the need for smoke and manage to use it—in Charlotte, for example, where the (French-trained) chef at Gone Hog Wild BBQ has produced a reasonable facsimile of the famous hickory-smoked ribs from Dreamland in Tuscaloosa, Alabama.

These outfits are proud of their barbecue, and sometimes justifiably so. The trouble is that, although they may be cooking barbecue in North Carolina, they don't even claim to be cooking *North Carolina barbecue*. Some even see themselves as missionaries, bringing the true gospel to those who have lived in darkness. Texan Dan Ferguson, pit boss at Durham's Q Shack, for example, candidly admits, "We're trying to put in the Texas style versus the North Carolina–style barbecue. I don't crave North Carolina barbecue."

Aside from the fact that it's based on a serious lack of judgment, there's nothing wrong with this attitude. In fact, we applaud it. Generally speaking, folks ought to evangelize for their native cuisines. But that goes for North Carolinians, too. If Tar Heels just enjoyed brisket and ribs the way they do sushi or Ethiopian food—as something different, when they want a change of pace from their normal, everyday diet of *real* barbecue—we'd welcome these purveyors of out-of-state 'cue. We're *happy* to encounter the outlandish barbecuing traditions brought by recent Latino and Asian immigrants, but there's no danger that North Carolinians will confuse these exotic newcomers with actual barbecue anytime soon. As the *Metro* poll reveals, however, that's already happening with the Texas and Memphis products—and that should fire the Tar Heel patriot's breast.

A word about those foreign imports: Remember *barbacòa?* After a long strange trip through Mexico, it's now being cooked all over North Carolina by recent immigrants. (Originally a word for an apparatus to raise meat above an open cooking fire, now it means meat buried in a pit and cooked by steam from hot rocks.) Meanwhile, Chosun Ok Korean BBQ cooks traditional *kalbi* (marinated ribs) in Durham, while in Charlotte Van Loi Chinese Barbecue Restaurant offers Eastern-style barbecue—*Far* Eastern-style (talk about whole-hog, how about heads and stomachs, too?). Add our state's new outposts of South Asian tandoor cooking, Southeast Asian satays, Jamaican jerk dishes, and other food more or less recogniz-

Kansas City Blues

"Critics [of competition barbecue] decry the one-world–one-barbecue effect, arguing that when national organizations set standards for great barbecue—when excellence is defined by trained judges measuring smoke rings instead of veteran eaters conjuring memories of past feeds—individual expression and local tradition lose out."
—John T. Edge

Each summer since 1994, scores of competitors and thousands of observers have followed the fragrant smoke to the banks of the Pacolet River in Polk County for what has become one of the most successful barbecue festivals in the United States. The Blue Ridge BBQ Festival was listed among the top ten barbecue festivals in the world by the Travel Channel and has won the "Spirit of Barbecue" award from the *National Barbecue News*.

Funny thing, though: Very little North Carolina barbecue is cooked at this event. Like Shelby's annual Hog Happnin', Rockingham's new Smoke at the Rock cook-off, and a growing number of other competitions around the state, this one is "sanctioned" by the Kansas City Barbecue Society empire, which endorses over 200 contests nationwide, trains and certifies the judges, establishes the competition categories and the rules for judging, and in general does its best to impose some Midwestern tidiness on the unruly world of barbecue.

Running a North Carolina competition by Kansas City rules is like admitting Boston College to the ACC: You may understand why they did it, but you sort of wish they hadn't. With thousands of dollars in prize money at stake, maybe it's not a bad idea, but it does mean that teams have to compete in the KCBS's four required categories. (In deference to its location, the festival has added a whole-hog category, but it's optional.)

Pork shoulder's no problem, of course, and most pitmasters know how to cook chicken, too. But ribs per se and beef brisket—well, like ice hockey in Raleigh, they can be undeniably good, but they're not From Here. So it's not surprising that most of the competitors and nearly all the winners are from out of state. In fact, precisely two North Carolina teams accounted for precisely three of the twenty-four overall champions and runners-up in the contest's first twelve years—and one of those won on its ribs and the other on its brisket.

We're sure there's mighty good eating to be had at the BRBBQF, and we look forward to checking it out someday, but it does strike us as odd that governors Hunt and Easley have both designated this the North Carolina State Barbecue Championship. Notice, however, that they didn't call it the *North Carolina Barbecue* State Championship. Possibly our 'cue-sodden elected officials understand the difference.

able as the result of something like barbecuing, and it's clear that we're looking at a brave new world indeed. And a tasty one.

LIPSTICK ON A PIG

And then there are new forms of barbecue that are even more alien—as in extraterrestrial. These can be so innovative that they have almost no discernible relation to any known barbecue tradition; other times the connection is more obvious, but the departure from tradition is what it's all about. Consider the "Redneck Reuben" served at the Barbecue Joint in Chapel Hill: cedar-smoked pastrami on grilled Jewish rye. The BJ also offers smoked duck hash, smoked wild boar sausage, a fried eggplant muffuletta with smoked mozzarella and house-made kalamata olive salad—you get the idea. It's all *really* good eating, but when it comes to barbecue, we don't quite trust people who get playful and postmodern.

Another disturbing development was revealed by a *Charlotte Observer* report in 2006 that a local lawyer, restaurateur, and nightclub owner was implementing a "new dining concept" (the word "concept" is generally a bad sign) offering "pit-smoked, all-natural Neiman [sic] Ranch free-range, hormone-free pork in a choice of Eastern, Western and S.C. style sauces," as well as "Memphis style barbecue ribs" specially cut for the restaurant. It's probably only a matter of time before we see more posh urban eateries with posh urban prices and what Vince Staten calls a "Rand McNally" menu of offerings from Texas, Memphis, Kansas City, and occasionally even North Carolina.

Rule of thumb: Be suspicious of barbecue places with valet parking. As Jim Shahin puts it, "Doing this to barbecue is like taking a t-shirted, barefoot, dirty-faced boy to the opera. Barbecue was not meant to be all dressed up. It is a proletarian food, and its upscaling will be its undoing." Shahin is a Texan, but he knows what he's talking about.

A TRADITION WORTH DEFENDING

Where will it end? "Vegetarian barbecue"? Don't laugh: Your local grocery store may already stock it. Ours does.

Look, North Carolina barbecue is an edible embodiment of Tradition. For many of us, barbecue symbolizes Home and People. It's linked to what oenophiles call *terroir*—roughly, "place": a fancy way of saying that when you drive a hundred miles, the barbecue changes. Calvin Trillin jokes about this. He tried to find "real North Carolina barbecue," he says, but every time he returned to New York, expatriate Tar Heels told him he went to the wrong place. "If I was west of Rocky Mount, they'd say I should have been on the

Martha Stewart has a recipe for "North Carolina Barbecue" that Publishers Weekly says looks "as precious as watercress when piled on soft buns."

"They'll give you a little bit of 'Texas barbecue' or 'North Carolina barbecue' or any kind of barbecue you want. . . . You end up with kind of a mishmash, which is sort of what the country is right now. That's what's happening to a lot of our food, our music, our art—it no longer springs from the culture that gave it birth." (Lolis Eric Elie)

PETA recently named Asheville the top vegetarian small city in America.

east side, and vice versa. As someone from Kansas City, it's hard to get on the right side of Rocky Mount."

Different places have different traditions, but the fact that these are *traditions* and not just *tastes* means that in each place there is a right way to cook and serve barbecue. It may or may not be the best way (most locals think it is), but it is the *right* way for that place. As Miles Efron has observed, "Barbecue purists are concerned with the authenticity of their product. This authenticity derives in large part from issues of place." And this is a good thing. Efron again: "Much of eating's appeal stems from its ability to remind us where we live, or least where we happen to find ourselves at a given moment." Television barbecue personality Steven Raichlen may be part of the problem (not him personally, but the fact that there is such a thing as a television barbecue personality), but he's right on the money when he remarks that "barbecue is a window into the soul of its practitioners. . . . I love barbecue that people eat within a 25-mile radius of its birthplace."

Established traditions resist change, and this is true for both Eastern and Piedmont styles. Dennis Rogers, speaking for the East, correctly observes that "we barbecue lovers are, to say the least, rarely experimental and never forgiving when it comes to pig cook-

In 2003 the Animal Liberation Front struck the Little Pigs Bar-B-Que in Asheville, spray-painting "Murderer" and "Stop Killing Us—3 Pigs" on two of the restaurant's catering vans.

ing," but devotées of Piedmont-style barbecue have become every bit as conservative as the most hidebound Easterner—maybe even more conservative. When local boosters proposed to build a barbecue museum in Lexington, Wayne Monk was skeptical. "I don't know what you could put in a museum," he said. "We're doing the same thing we were doing fifty years ago." When Lexington barbecue man Johnny Stogner listed the "many innovations [that] were made" when Warner Stamey bought the Swicegood place—"The steam table was moved; a new counter was put in, new booths and a new front window"—Peter Batke suggested as a law that "successful and visible innovation in stable food cultures involves primarily carpentry."

Deano Allen of Deano's in Mocksville says, "People ask me why I do things this way and I say it's because everybody else always did it." That's how traditions work, and folks who have inherited good ones shouldn't mess with them.

THE CHARACTER OF NORTH CAROLINA 'CUE

Whether Eastern- or Piedmont-style, North Carolina barbecue has a distinctive character that should be respected. When cooking or eating it, you should eschew two extremes.

First, avoid the easy way. Save that gas for burgers and steaks. David Lauderdale suggests that "for all the flavor you get from [gas], you might as well buy a Magic Marker and draw grill marks on your food." In fact, why not forget the grill marks and just put some pork in the oven at 220° until the meat thermometer reads 180°? Chop it and sauce it, and you'll have the same thing that's served these days at all too many "barbecue" restaurants. As John Egerton says, "You can't reach the highest pinnacle of true barbecue without hardwood smoke, a slow fire, and time, precious time"—those things, and honest hard work. Patronize places that take the trouble to do it right.

On the other hand, don't let folks tart it up, and don't do it yourself. If you get the bug, eventually you might want to go the "competition barbecue" route, with a fancy smoker, complex rubs and mops, fruity sauces, and endless, picky discussion of woods, times, and temperatures. We're not knocking that. But real North Caro-

"We're still in the past but I like that. That's the way I want to live my life. I'm still back in the 50s and 60s and I really don't want to change." (Wayne Monk, Lexington Barbecue)

"Honest barbecue will survive all the assaults of women's magazine food editors, asinine judges at frivolous competitions, instant experts, smoke blowers, media frenzy and pop culture." (Smoky Hale)

lina barbecue is simple—open-pit cooking, salt rubs, vinegar-and-pepper sauces. It's a workingman's food: no cheating, but nothing fancy. There's a lot of mystique but not much mystery.

In other words, North Carolina's barbecue at its best is like its people at their best: good, honest, unpretentious—in the words of the state song, "plain and artless." Though the scorner may sneer at and witlings defame it, it doesn't avoid hard work and it doesn't get above its raising.

But it's not just for farmers, millhands, and factory workers, or even just for those of us—most of us—who are only a generation or two removed from the farms and mills. Barbecue is for anyone who wants a tasty, tangible connection to the Old North State and its heritage.

M&K, Granite Quarry

Smokey Joe's, Lexington

Wilber's, Goldsboro

Allen & Son, Chapel Hill

Stamey's, Greensboro

Barbecue Center, Lexington

Blue Mist, Asheboro

Bridges Barbecue Lodge, Shelby

Carolina Barbecue, Statesville

Fuzzy's, Madison

Grady's, Dudley

Hursey's, Burlington

Stamey's, Tyro

Backyard BBQ Pit, Durham

Skylight Inn, Ayden

Troutman's, Denton

"Barbecue men" at Stamey's, Greensboro

The Bagley family at Turnage's, Durham

TO LEARN MORE . . .

Here are all the books we know about North Carolina barbecue:

Peter Batke, *Lexington Barbecue: An Autobiographical Reverie about Life, Food, and Death* (Philadelphia: Xlibris, 2003). An Austrian-born Chapel Hill Ph.D. in German literature offers a quirky account of his love affair with Lexington-style, with some important things to say about traditions.

Jim Early, *The Best Tar Heel Barbecue, Manteo to Murphy* (Winston-Salem: Privately printed, 2002). A valuable guide to 140 barbecue places from one end of the state to the other, by the founder of the North Carolina Barbecue Society.

Bob Garner, *North Carolina Barbecue: Flavored by Time* (Winston-Salem: John F. Blair, 1996). This pioneering book-length examination of the Tar Heel tradition and current scene by the WUNC-TV food maven offers some serious history and some very well-informed opinions. Essential reading for students and eaters of the subject.

Bob Garner, *Bob Garner's Guide to North Carolina Barbecue* (Winston-Salem: John F. Blair, 2002). More explicitly a guidebook than Garner's first volume. We keep this book in our glove compartment.

D. G. Martin, *Interstate Eateries: A Guide to Down Home Cooking along North Carolina's Highways* (2004; revised edition, Greensboro: Our State magazine, 2008). Includes nearly all the great barbecue places near interstates, as well as some wonderful meat-and-threes and country buffets should you tire of 'cue (unlikely as it may seem). Another glove-compartment book.

Johnny Stogner, *Barbecue, Lexington Style* (Lexington, N.C.: Stogner Publishing Co., 1996). A charming memoir by an old-time barbecue man, with lots of great detail about the Lexington barbecue scene in the years after World War II.

And a few treatises that ought to be consulted by anyone seriously interested in the subject of barbecue:

Wilber W. Caldwell, *Searching for the Dixie Barbecue: Journeys into the Southern Psyche* (Sarasota: Pineapple Press, 2005). A wise and amusing essay on barbecue and the Southern soul, with particular attention to the funkier side of each.

Lolis Eric Elie, photographs by Frank Stewart, *Smokestack Lightning: Adventures in the Heart of Barbecue Country* (1996; reprint, Berkeley: Ten Speed Press, 2005). New Orleans journalist Elie and photographer Stewart examine the history of barbecue and the forms it takes in South Carolina, Texas, Kansas City, and Memphis, as well as North Carolina.

Lolis Eric Elie, ed., *Cornbread Nation 2: The United States of Barbecue* (Chapel Hill: University of North Carolina Press, 2004).

A collection of essays on the sociology, politics, and culture of barbecue from the Southern Foodways Alliance.

Vince Staten and Greg Johnson, *Real Barbecue: The Classic Barbecue Guide to the Best Joints across the U.S.A.* (Guilford, Conn.: Globe Pequot, 2007). This revised reissue of the 1988 book (the first we know of that took barbecue seriously) has history, restaurant reviews, cooking tips, and more.

It's hard to come by the histories of down-home dishes—the kind children learn to cook from their parents and grandparents, everyday dishes made without recipes or (in the case of barbecue and Brunswick stew) foods learned in ritual settings, bearing the weight of tradition. Here are some books we found useful. (We haven't listed modern cookbooks, except for those with a serious historical focus.)

Marion Brown, *Marion Brown's Southern Cook Book* (1951; reprint, Chapel Hill: University of North Carolina Press, 1968). An encyclopedic compilation of Southern recipes built on a solid North Carolina base.

Mrs. Lettice Bryan, *The Kentucky Housewife* (1839; facsimile, Bedford, Mass.: Applewood Books, 2000). Mrs. Bryan was a Kentuckian, born about 1805, whose family came from Virginia. Hers is the first use we've found of the word "cobbler," hers is the first mention we've found of barbecue and slaw together on a menu, and she has recipes for sliced sweet potato pie and fried pies.

Mrs. Helen Bullock, *The Williamsburg Art of Cookery; or, Accomplish'd Gentlewoman's Companion: Being a Collection of upwards of Five Hundred of the most Ancient & Approv'd Recipes in Virginia Cookery* (1938; reprint, Williamsburg: Colonial Williamsburg, 1966). Some of these recipes are modern, but many are from old Virginia cookbooks and some are from nineteenth-century Virginia manuscripts.

Joseph Earl Dabney, *Smokehouse Ham, Spoon Bread, and Scuppernong Wine: The Folklore and Art of Southern Appalachian Cooking* (Nashville: Cumberland House, 1998). Encyclopedic, readable, quotable—this book is a treasure.

Mrs. S. R. Dull, *Southern Cooking* (1928; reprint, Athens: University of Georgia Press, 2006). Mrs. Dull edited the Home Economics page of the *Atlanta Journal Sunday Magazine* and was extremely influential. We're sure every Southern bride in the 1930s got a copy of this one.

John Egerton, *Southern Food: At Home, on the Road, in History* (Chapel Hill: University of North Carolina Press, 1993). The subtitle almost says it all, but cannot show how generously conceived and masterfully executed this book is. A splendid wedding present for any Southern couple.

Damon Lee Fowler, *Classical Southern Cooking: A Celebration of the Cuisine of the Old South* (New York: Crown, 1995). An important book, both scholarly and practical. It introduced us to Lettice Bryan and Annabella Hill, two of our favorite sources.

Mrs. A. P. Hill, *Mrs. Hill's New Cook Book* (1867; facsimile, Bedford, Mass.: Applewood

Books, 2001). Annabella Hill's parents moved from Virginia to Georgia before she was born in 1811.

Martha McCulloch-Williams, *Dishes and Beverages of the Old South* (1913; facsimile, with an introduction by John Egerton, Knoxville: University of Tennessee Press, 1988). Mrs. McCulloch-Williams was a Kentuckian, born in 1848, but her father was from Granville County and she grew up next door to her Tar Heel grandparents. The recipes are old-fashioned, based on the foods of her childhood, but the narrative style is modern and highly entertaining.

Bill Neal, *Bill Neal's Southern Cooking* (Chapel Hill: University of North Carolina Press, 1985). Neal was a serious food historian and went out of his way to make it easy to replicate old recipes.

The Picayune's Creole Cookbook, 2d ed. (1901; reprint, Mineola, N.Y.: Dover, 1971). Mostly Louisiana food—and there's nothing wrong with that—but also useful for reconstructing Southern cooking more generally at the turn of the twentieth century.

Mary Randolph, *The Virginia Housewife* (1824; facsimile, Columbia: University of South Carolina Press, 1984). Thomas Jefferson's cousin (reputedly the best cook in Richmond) described and subsequently shaped the cooking of the Upper South with her 1824 book.

There are thousands of articles on aspects of barbecue and at least hundreds on North

Carolina's version. Here are four scholarly ones we found especially interesting:

S. Jonathan Bass, "'How 'bout a Hand for the Hog': The Enduring Nature of the Swine as a Cultural Symbol in the South," *Southern Cultures* 1, no. 3 (Spring 1995): 301–20.

Clarissa Dillon, "*A Hog Drest Whole*: Early Barbecue References," *Food History News* 7, no. 2 (Fall 1995): 1, 6.

Steven Smith, "The Rhetoric of Barbecue: A Southern Rite and Ritual," *Studies in Popular Culture* 8, no. 1 (1985): 17–25.

Michael D. Thompson, "'Everything but the Squeal': Pork as Culture in Eastern North Carolina," *North Carolina Historical Review* 82, no. 4 (2005): 464–98.

Until they perfect smell-o-vision, no film is going to do justice to North Carolina barbecue, but these documentaries do a good job of showing what it's all about:

Barbecue Is a Noun (2005). North Carolinians Hawes Bostic and Austin McKenna interview a great many North and South Carolina pitmasters, celebrated and obscure, although they concentrate on a few who are so odd that their film sometimes feels like a freak show.

North Carolina Barbecue: Flavored by Time (1996). This affectionate survey began its life as a television special produced by Bob Garner and based on his book of the same title.

Slow Food: Fast Times (1995). Appalachian State professor Joe Murphy's fascinating log of a two-year, seven-state journey, examining the social, economic, and culinary significance of barbecue in the South.

Smokestack Lightning (2002). Lolis Eric Elie directed this documentary, based on his 1996 book of the same title.

Barbecue websites come and go almost as fast as barbecue joints, so we offer this list hesitantly, knowing that, sadly, it will soon be out of date. But a number of devotees of North Carolina barbecue have taken to the internet to post comments, reviews, and (usually strong) opinions, and if these guys—they're all guys—are still around when you log on, they're definitely worth reading:

"Carolina BBQ Joints," <www .carolinabbqjoints.com>. Tar Heel Jim Morgan, exiled to Myrtle Beach, maintains a site devoted open-mindedly to the barbecue of both Carolinas. The moderated forums are first rate.

"Kent's North Carolina–Style BBQ Page," <hkentcraig.com/BBQ.html>. H. Kent Craig of Cary has been running this site since 1998, offering recipes, a discussion group, reviews of restaurants (some, sadly, in a section titled "Reviews of NC-BBQ Establishments No Longer with Us"), and links to other sites with thumbnail restaurant reviews.

"The Lexington Collection," <www.ibiblio .org/lineback/lex.htm>. Dave Lineback started this site in 1996. It may have gone inactive, but it still includes everything from philosophy to bibliography, menus to barbecue-pit construction tips, restaurant

reviews to "ten uses for a gas grill" (none involving cooking). This is the home of the Society for the Preservation of Traditional Southern Barbecue and the legendary barbecue philosopher, Smokey Pitts.

"NC Barbecue Musings," <ncbbq.blogspot .com>. Chapel Hill's Dave Filpus pulls no punches in his ratings of barbecue places. Even when you disagree with him, you have to admit that he's got his reasons.

"NCBBQ.com," <www.ncbbq.com>. Donald Williamson runs this site, which features a calendar of barbecue competitions in the state, a restaurant list (not reviews), recipes, a discussion forum, informative articles, and an online shop.

"North Carolina Barbecue Society" <www .ncbbqsociety.com>. The tireless Jim Early, president and CEO of the NCBS, has established this site to promote the cause of real North Carolina barbecue and to educate the public about its rich history and the wonderful diversity of cooking styles that make North Carolina the "Barbecue Capital of the World." It also offers calendars of events, news of the society's doings, recipes, and much more. While you're there, think about joining—or at least buy an apron.

"North Carolina Pork Council," <www .ncpork.org>. The official site, with recipes, news releases, and calendars of festivals and cooking contests.

"Varmint Bites," <varmintbites.wordpress .com>. This isn't exactly a barbecue website—it's much more general than that—but Raleigh's Dean McCord (a/k/a

"Varmint") blogs on food and restaurants in the Triangle and central North Carolina more generally, so naturally Tar Heel 'cue is very much a presence. Check it out.

And speaking of websites, if you're unlucky enough not to be able to find stuff like stoneground cornmeal and Duke's mayonnaise in your local grocery store, these days you can order Southern staples online. Try these two first:

"The Lee Bros. Boiled Peanuts Catalogue," <www.boiledpeanuts.com>. Don't be fooled by the name. Charleston food writers Matt and Ted Lee started this website to bring all sorts of down-home delights to homesick expatriates.

"A Southern Season," <www.southernseason .com>. This famous Chapel Hill food emporium (Zabar's is New York City's version) offers a great assortment of Southern food and much, much else.

This book would have been impossible without the help of scores of friends and kind strangers who generously contributed illustrations, interviews, recipes, anecdotes, cartoons, poems, song lyrics, and opinions.

The wealth of photographs we turned up was astonishing. You may think there are a lot of illustrations in this book, but you should see the ones we *didn't* use. Those who gave us permission for the ones we did are acknowledged in the list of credits, but we *thank* them here. We're especially obliged to Amy Evans, documentarian for the Southern Foodways Alliance; Kim Cumber at the North Carolina State Archives; Eric Blevins at the North Carolina Museum of History; and especially Bob Anthony, Nicholas Graham, and the rest of the helpful staff of the North Carolina Collection at the University of North Carolina, Chapel Hill. Oh, and to Professor Elizabeth Minchin of the Australian National University for the lead on the Boeotian vase.

Speaking of libraries, in Chapel Hill, Davis Library at UNC was essential, as always. John and Dale also used the services and resources of the libraries at Louisiana State University and The Citadel and thank those folks. Librarians and archivists are Krispy Kremes in a world of academic doughnuts.

As for our recipes, some are from friends who shared their family secrets; others are from friends who've written splendid cookbooks. Obviously, we're blessed when it comes to friends. We're particularly indebted to Jim Auchmutey, Corbette Capps, Al Carson, Sonny Conrad, Mildred Council, H. Kent Craig, Shirley Dennis, Duke's Mayonnaise, John Egerton, Lydia Gill, Damon Lapas, Carroll Leggett, Susan Metts, the North Carolina Pork Council, Nancy King Quaintance, Dennis Rogers, Dori Sanders, Bland Simpson, Bill Smith, Vince Staten, Robert Stehling, Shifra Stein, John Stogner, Fred Thompson, and Jim Villas.

William and his buddies from the Carolina Bar-B-Q Society did the interviews in this book and took many of the accompanying photographs. The CBS doesn't go in for titles like producer, director, gaffer, grip, and best boy, but the crew included Christopher Sellers, Charles Epstein, Aaron Smithers, Mark Slagle, and Russ Jones. Thanks, obviously, to the men and women who shared their time and thoughts and to John T. Edge and the Southern Foodways Alliance, who gave William the opportunity to do the interviews in the first place and then gave us permission to use them here. William would also like to thank Dr. Eric Mlyn, the Carolina Bar-B-Q Society's original faculty sponsor.

We talked with a great many other barbecue folk. Without exception they were gracious and hospitable and eager to talk about their craft. We must mention and thank Bob Burleson, Jonathan Childress, Sonny Conrad, Joe Cope, Billy Cotter, Bum and Shirley Dennis, Daniel Ferguson, Helen Gibson, Keith Hendrix, Gene Hill, Chris Hursey, LeRoy McCarn, Richard Monroe, and Jim Warren.

Special thanks also to Wilber W. "Pete" Caldwell for the references to Homer and the Harleian manuscript and his wisdom in general; Sam Farthing for access to his remarkable database of barbecue restaurants and menus; Ken Myers at <mapanything.net> for answering some vital statistical questions; Dan Schultz, keeper of <Porkopolis.org>, an amazing repository of piglore; and Robert F. Moss of Charleston and the *Al Forno* blog for sharing his great historical material. We owe debts too varied to list in detail to many others, including Alex Albright, Jim Applewhite, Jack Betts, Roy Blount Jr., Corbette and Joyce Capps, H. Kent Craig, Clarissa F. Dillon, Jim Early, Walter Edgar, Clyde Edgerton, Tommy Edwards, John Egerton, Barbara Ensrud, Barry Farber, Damon Lee Fowler, Gary Freeze, Bob Garner, Tom Hanchette, Bill Harmon, Bill Keesler, Susie MacNelly (and Jeff), Doug Marlette, D. G. Martin, Jake Mills, Allan Parnell and Ann Joyner, Dennis Rogers, Bland and Ann Simpson, Vince Staten, John Stogner, Ted Teague, Mira Waller, and Annette Wright. Thanks to you all.

We're also obliged to the many people who helped us just by writing good stuff that we read with pleasure and borrowed without compunction. By academic standards we've been grossly lax in the matter of citations — bad scholarship and, worse, bad manners — but this isn't a scholarly book and it was too cluttered already. (Any reader who wants a source for anything here should first try online, which is where we got a lot of it; if that fails, drop us a line and we'll try to track it down.) We thank those whose articles, books, and websites we've mined and hope y'all will understand. Feel free to help yourselves from our book.

Finally, we thank the staff at the University of North Carolina Press, especially our editor, Paula Wald, and book designer, Rich Hendel, who together brought order and even a measure of elegance to our sow's ear of a manuscript while retaining its porcine auricular character, and David Perry, editor-in-chief, for his personal interest in this project from the beginning.

CREDITS

"Holy Smoke," courtesy of Tommy Edwards
(© 2007, Hidden Gem Publishing)

"Barbecue Service" and "How to Fix a Pig,"
courtesy of James Applewhite, originally
published in *Ode to the Chinaberry Tree and
Other Poems* (Baton Rouge: Louisiana State
University Press, 1986)

"Ode to Pork," courtesy of John Egerton,
originally published in *Southern Food: At
Home, on the Road, in History* (Chapel Hill:
University of North Carolina Press, 1993)

"True 'Cue," courtesy of Bruce Tindall,
originally published in *Now & Then* 11, no. 2
(Summer 1994)

"Real Pit!" courtesy of Doug Marlette, from
Kudzu: A Southern Musical

"Barbeque," courtesy of Jack Herrick and
Bland Simpson (© ABD Music, ASCAP/
Southern Melody Pub. Co/BMI)

"A Quiche Woman in a Barbeque Town,"
courtesy of Clyde Edgerton

We tried—really, we did—to track down the
owners of the rights to our illustrations,
but eventually we used a few whose owners
we don't know. If you're one of them, get
in touch and we'll do what we can to make
things right. Here are the sources we can
acknowledge, with the pages on which
their illustrations appear.

Andover-Harvard Theological Library,
Unitarian Universalist Congregational
Resource Files (bMS 902): 47

Jerry Bledsoe: 277 (1st)

Braswell Memorial Library, Rocky Mount: 61
(top)

Bridges Barbecue Lodge, Shelby: 264

British Library: 12 (© British Library Board;
all rights reserved)

Childress Vineyards: 198 (bottom)

Collection of the authors: 102

Mark C. Connor, graphic artist for LIB
Screenprinting & Embroidery of Kinston,
N.C.: i, ix, 59

Corbette Capps: 103

Davidson County Historical Museum: 66
(top), 92

DixiePix: 9 (bottom), 15, 19, 34 (bottom
right), 39, 42, 55, 62, 63 (top), 64, 70,
72, 74, 76, 79, 87 (bottom), 89, 93, 99
(bottom), 108, 109, 110, 112, 113, 115, 117,
119, 122, 123, 127, 128, 132 (top), 133, 135,
137, 139, 140, 143, 152, 154, 157, 162, 164,
167, 172, 179, 183, 185, 189, 195, 196, 197,
200–201, 203, 205, 212, 226, 238, 239,
247, 251, 260, 267, 277 (4th), 280, 283,
284, 285 (bottom), 289, 292, 293

Duke Medical Center Archives: 65

Jim Early: 276 (2nd)

Amy Evans, Southern Foodways Alliance: 187,
218, 234, 235, 254, 257

Barry Farber: 278

Sam Farthing: 158

Bob Garner: 276 (1st)

Glenmary Research Center: 34 (top)

Johnston County Heritage Center: 23

Charles F. Kovacik: 32

Library of Congress: 16, 22 (top)

Susie MacNelly: 151

Doug Marlette: 116

McIntyre Photography: 277 (3rd) (© Will & Deni McIntyre)

William McKinney: 87 (top), 90 (top), 99 (top), 124, 168, 204, 210, 214, 221, 223, 225, 228, 229, 232, 242, 250, 253, 259, 261, 263, 266, 268, 271

North Carolina Collection, University of North Carolina Libraries: ii–iii, vii, 7, 9 (top), 13, 22 (bottom), 32, 53, 54, 61 (bottom), 63 (bottom), 66 (middle), 66 (bottom left), 67, 75, 85, 90 (left), 91, 111, 129, 132 (left), 142, 145, 147, 148, 149, 191, 198 (top), 215, 216, 262, 285 (top)

North Carolina Museum of History: 57 (bottom)

Office of Archives and History, North Carolina Department of Cultural Resources: v, 2, 4–5, 17, 26, 49, 51, 52, 57 (top), 82, 88, 106, 130, 131, 150, 230, 272

Mike Page: 58 (bottom)

Raleigh News and Observer: 276 (3rd)

Saint Louis Art Museum: 30

Skylight Inn, Ayden: 207

Southern Historical Collection, University of North Carolina at Chapel Hill: 29 (right)

Chip Stamey: 34 (bottom left), 36, 243, 245, 246, 295 (top)

Vince Staten: 277 (2nd)

Jim Warren: 295 (bottom)

Note: References to illustrations are in italics. County names are in parentheses after listings for towns and cities. When known, place names are given after names of establishments and public events. Unless otherwise indicated, places are in North Carolina.